$10

CORE
ENERGETICS

LifeRhythm
PUBLICATION

Illustrations by Reina Rubel and Ciemen Drimer
Cover: Alois Hanslian and Siegmar Gerken

Printed in U.S.A.

ISBN: 0-940795-00-0 Hardcover edition
ISBN: 0-940795-08-6 Paperback edition

Copyright © 1990 LIFERHYTHM, Paperback edition
P.O. Box 806, Mendocino, CA 95460 USA (707)937-1825

Library of Congress Cataloging in Publication Data

Pierrakos, John C.
    Core energetics; developing the capacity to love and heal
by John C. Pierrakos.
300 p.
Bibliography $18.95
ISBN 0-94975-08-6
1. Psychotherapy. 2. Mind and body therapies
I Title
RC489.B5P54 1989   88-38809
615.8'56--dc19

CORE ENERGETICS

Developing the Capacity to Love and Heal

by

John C. Pierrakos, M. D.

LifeRhythm
Publication

Table of Contents

Page

Part I.   *The Essential Unity: The Basis of Core Energetics* 11
Chapter 1. The Foundation of Core Energetics 12
Chapter 2. The Innermost Reality: The Core 21

Part II.   *The Energetic Foundations* 29
Chapter 3. Eastern Theories of Human Energy 30
Chapter 4. Western Human Energy Theory 37
Chapter 5. Modern Human Energy Theory 47
Chapter 6. Observations of the Energy Field 55
Chapter 7. The Phenomenon of the Aura 69

Part III.   *The Dynamics of Dysfunction* 83
Chapter 8. The Sources of Dysfunction 84
Chapter 9. Patterns of Denial 93
Chapter 10. The Origins of Dysfunction 102

Part IV.   *The Results of Dysfunction* 111
Chapter 11. Creative Aspects of the Ego 112
Chapter 12. The Dynamics of Pain I:
Its Nature and Origin 125
Chapter 13. The Dynamics of Pain II:
The Attachment to Pain 136
Chapter 14. The Anatomy of Evil 146

Part V.   *Dysfunction in Everyday Life* 157
Chapter 15. Aggression in Men and Women 158
Chapter 16. Aggression in the Upper Body 175
Chapter 17. The Case of the Broken Heart 189

Part VI.   *The Work of Integration* 199
Chapter 18. From Distortion to Self-Truth 200
Chapter 19. The Four Stages of the Work 210
Chapter 20. Core to Core: Group Therapy 227
Chapter 21. The Forces of Love, Eros, and Sexuality 249

Part VII. *Synthesis and Unity* 263
Chapter 22. The Birth of a New Age 264
Chapter 23. Toward a Holistic Synthesis: The Fusion
of Energy and Consciousness 275

List of Figures

Page

Figure 1. Levels of Inner Reality 22
Figure 2. Graphic Energy Field in Air 62
Figure 3. Energy Field at Sunset 62
Figure 4. General Appearance of the Inward Energy
Movement of the Field of Air 64
Figure 5. Comparisons of the Frequencies of Pulsations
in Air and Over Land and Water 64
Figure 18. Functional Diagram of Pain and Wellness 127

Colorplate

Figure 6. The Human Aura, Front View ....
Figure 7. The Human Aura, Side View ....
Figure 8. The Energy Bodies ....
Figure 9. The Principal Energy Centers in Profile ....
Figure 10. The Principal Energy Centers at the Front of the Body .....
Figure 11. The Principal Energy Centers at the Back of the Body ......
Figure 12. The Aura and Principal Energy Centers
of the Normal Person ....
Figure 13. The Aura and Principal Energy Centers
of the Oral Character ....
Figure 14. The Aura and Principal Energy Centers
of the Masochistic Character ....
Figure 15. The Aura and Principal Energy Centers
of the Schizoid Character ....
Figure 16. The Aura and Principal Energy Centers
of the Psychopathic / Aggressive Character ....
Figure 17. The Aura and Principal Energy Centers
of the Rigid Character ....
Figure 19. Aura of a Typical Coronary Case ....
Figure 20. Aura of a Person Who Had a Recent Coronary Attack ......
Figure 21. Aura of Angina Patient ....
Figure 22. Four Successive Stages of the Energy Field of a Rose ....

I wish to acknowledge my indebtedness to Wilhelm Reich who was my teacher and who inspired me to take the direction which led to Core Energetics. I owe the deepening of my knowledge to the inspirational lectures from the Guide delivered through Eva Pierrakos and which are the foundation for the unity of this work on the levels of body, mind and spirit. To Dora Gomez for her support I want to express my gratitude. My special thanks to editors Sally Gran and Ian McNett. To Siegmar Gerken, my student, colleague and publisher, goes my appreciation for his constant support while writing this book and his inestimable and continuing help in shaping it as well as his supervision of the German translation. I want, too, to acknowledge the wonderful illustrations of the aura done by Reina Rubel and Ciemen Drimer. I would also wish to express my gratitude to Dr. Serge Silby for his study of flowers.

Our language is still limited in the use of the masculine pronoun for both sexes. Although I tried to avoid an overuse of it, I still hope, that the reader does not assume that I am referring to men, male developement or masculine principles.

Preface

This is the work of many years during which time I experienced a multitude of changes in my life. The roots of this work began to grow with my knowledge of Wilhelm Reich's work which brought the concept of the psychosomatic identity into the psychoanalytic process and his later development of the energetic dimension. This led to my association with Dr. Alexander Lowen with whom I created the Bioenergetic approach.

I went on to found the Institute of the New Age incorporating the spiritual dimension into my work through the influence of the Guide Lectures given through Eva Pierrakos. With the help of many of our colleagues, Eva Pierrakos and I established a community called the *Pathwork*.

At present I am director of the Institute of Core Energetics which is devoted to the development of the human capacity to love and to heal. This work is rooted in the rich legacies transmitted through the ages by philosophers, scientists and physicians who taught about the existence within us of a "creative essence" as a source of healing.

Core Energetics is a new integrated approach for the growth and evolution of the entire person. The common denominator is the way in which energy and consciousness manifests in the human entity and in the universe. A more specific inquiry relates to the stream of life energy which emanates from the core and flows in health but is blocked in dis-ease thus creating illness or dysfunction — a process where disharmony counters the real needs of the organism.

In ancient hippocratic medicine the patient was called "asthenis" meaning a person who lacked strength or vital energy; the doctor was "iatros" which means the healer who re-establishes the "sthenos" or vital energy in the person. The field of medicine has moved away from this model toward the pathology of life omitting the source of health which is the vital energy of the Core manifesting as pleasure, joy and love.

This book focuses on the importance of the Core and because of this is of an intuitive nature while based on facts arrived at through scientific and psychologic inquiries. This is not a how-to book. Nor is the material based on statistics. Is is based on my perception of how life manifests as it flows or is blocked from flowing — in effect, the human struggle. Work in the laboratory must be done to substantiate our insights of the nature of the phenomenon of energy and consciousness in life.

July 18, 1986

Part I:
The Essential Unity
The Basis of Core Energetics

Chapter 1
THE FOUNDATIONS
OF CORE ENERGETICS

Three main theses are woven together in the therapeutic approach that I am developing, which I call core energetics. The first is that the human person is a psychosomatic unity. The second is that the source of healing lies within the self, not with an outside agency, whether a physician, God, or the powers of the cosmos. The third is that all of existence forms a unity that moves toward creative evolution, both of the whole and of the countless components. In a sense, I am just saying the same thing in three different ways, but I will speak of them separately in order to build toward a central conviction in core energetics. As Chapters 23 and 24 will elaborate, I believe that humankind stands on the threshold of a new age, an era when we can propel ourselves beyond the tragic wastes of destructive conflicts, beyond even the constructive endeavors to correct harm, and can focus our lives on creativity.

We have reached this threshold after millions of years of learning who and what we are, where our place is in the realm of being, and how we can fulfill our destiny: Our understanding of the direction of our potential. At various points in this long history, observation and experimentation have made us aware that we could allay some portion of the fragmentation in our existence. Therapies were born and systematized. Care of the body, the physically visible aspect of the person, developed into the discipline of medicine. What medicine could not puzzle out — the causes of sicknesses and death — joined other mystifying phenomena as the proper domain of religion, the therapy of the spirit of man. Each field of activity recognized mental disturbances as a distinct category of illness and each made efforts to treat them, but no more than glimpses of how to relieve them came from these bodies of thought. Only with Sigmund Freud's monumental discovery of the unconscious could the healing arts extend to the mental-emotional intersection of the human personality.

Yet even early colleagues of Freud saw that the unconscious, despite its wealth of information about the life and state of the personality, was not the sole key to psychic illness. Freud's emphasis lay in the ideational content of the individual's mental substrata. Carl Jung included the soul in psychiatric treatment. He recognized that "the God image in the human psyche" constitutes a powerful and, in itself, a healthful component of the collective human unconscious. Wilhelm Reich merged physiology with psychology in perceiving the psychosomatic unity of the person, and launched a massive scientific synthesis based on his theories of orgonomy. Bioenergetic analysis, founded by Alexander Lowen and myself, established the volitional element in psychiatric disorders and the necessity of engaging the will of the suffering person in the treatment along with the body, the emotions, and the analytic mind.

Each of these expansions of healing theory came closer and closer to envisioning the whole person, rather than one or several areas, as the proper domain for therapy. At the same time, all schools of treatment continued to center on the patient's wounds, in effect excluding the essential being of the sufferer — the life force afflicted by the wounds. Worthy as well as unworthy reasons account for the persistent persuasion that a given healing art should restrict itself to its own field of expertise. The worthy ones relate to the conscientious practitioner's realization that any defined profession embraces only a part of human learning. The unworthy ones, which bear analogies to societal imbalances that I will touch on later, express an attitude of superiority about the practitioner's particular knowledge and gifts.

Over my first twenty years of psychiatric work, developing through the bioenergetics approach, I found myself more and more concerned with the nature and innate functioning of the life force itself. I wondered: What is this energy? Is it both substance and attribute, as yogic theory and the early Greeks saw it? Is it universal spirit, individualized somehow in matter, as viewed by the sixteenth-century physician Paracelsus and the nineteenth-century poet Walt Whitman? Is it essentially material, either a self-contained electrodynamic system, as the Yale biologist Harold Burr and his colleagues defined it in the 1930s, or else a variation of what Reich called the common functioning principle? Is it essentially spiritual, as religious thinkers and healers from Buddha through Jesus to Pierre Teilhard de Chardin have conceived of it?

The question preoccupied me professionally because of its relevance to psychiatric practice. Two aspects of the human life force seemed especially important, both of which express its creativity.

First, the work with patients demonstrated that every part of the human person, from the structure of the body to the clarity of the perception, is molded by internal energy. Genetic inheritance, family background, societal conditions, and many other influences affect us. But we create our lives ourselves through what we do with our energy: where we decide to go with it and how we direct it. A person is vulnerable to circumstances only so long as survival depends on them, as during infancy. In maturing, we have the choice of whether to fuse our energy internally or block it, and whether to move into or withdraw from the outside world.

Second, I found that almost all patients increasingly sensed a lack of deep fulfillment as they progressed toward the freeing of their functioning and improving their life situations. They showed this invariably as a yearning for greater unification with external reality. The French philosopher Henri Bergson wrote of this as the vital leap or impulse *l'élan vital*, made by creative energy, *énergie créatrice* (the title of a 1906 book). People carry out the impulse in many ways: they give themselves to philanthropic activity, to the healing professions, to the practice of a religious ethic, or to social, political, or economic reform. They call the source of the movement by many names: the soul or spirit, the creative ego, the social conscience, the higher self.

I agreed very much with unifying and comprehensive perspectives such as these, which were germinating spontaneously not only in those I was caring for but also in larger societal contexts. Other therapists as well as the people who sought help were becoming aware that the mending of wounds is not enough to generate fulfillment. More extensively, beyond the healing community, many healthy people were questioning the fragmentation of their person among their various operating arenas. They were sensing the isolation of human living from its ecological habitat. They were struggling with the disconnection between life at home and at work. They were recognizing the negative impact of cold and hot wars, the "war between the sexes," overspecialized jobs, unequal rights of some groups, generation gaps, and a plethora of other divisions that were impoverishing the quality of life. And very importantly, they were exploring positive, expansive alternatives to the patterns that constrained their creative capacities.

Through the 1950s and into the 1960s, the search for deeper meaning in life gathered momentum, emerging in the last decade and a half as a widespread tide named the human potential movement. Many currents contribute to this groundswell, whose impetus is carrying us toward the new age I hope to see humankind enter. Fundamentally, they encompass a single proposition: that the person is a unity, within the self and in interaction with his or her surroundings. I would say that unity and interaction connect every thing that is in the totality of existence. For while the individuality of each being is quite real, the interchange of energies among all beings is con tinuous and coextensive with the universe. Let me expand on this statement, because it summarizes my understanding of the nature of the human person and therefore the purpose of core energetics.

Energy and Consciousness

Centrifugal (outward) and centripetal (inward) movement is observable throughout the physical universe. The most popular explanation in astronomy for the creation of the universe, the Big Bang theory, hypothesizes that a vast explosion of a central core dispersed material substance into space. Swirling masses of this substance then accumulated to form the celestial bodies that make up the galaxies, which cohere because of gravitational pull even as they continue to move away from the center of explosion at immense speeds. The dual movement, toward as well as away from the originating center, is replicated in every phenomenon mankind has observed. In the human anatomy, for example, cells expand and contract. So do individual organs, such as the heart, and systems, such as the gut and the lungs. And so does the total human organism. The basic substance of the person is energy. The movement of that energy is life. The freer the energy movement within each component, in keeping with its own integrity and cohesion, as well as that of the whole organism, the more intense the life.

Imagine the human person as a microcosm. To our eyes, tissues and organs are "solid" and make up "solid" systems that in turn compose our "solid" body. But like the billions of celestial entities in the macrocosm, the billions of cells in the total organism form clusters of varying densities in space. Under a magnification of, say, 500,000 times, skin tissue would look like stars spread far apart; bone would look like a thickly populated galaxy; the heart would resemble a celestial sphere, and the whole of the body might model the whole of the macrocosm. Again as in the whole universe, the energy of each part of the body moves both internally and externally, contracting and expanding, pulsating inward to the nucleus of the part and outward to other parts and into the whole. I will come back to this pulsatory process in a moment.

So energy, whether in the cosmos of all existence or the cosmos of the human organism, moves like streams from a watershed. The streams form brooks, the brooks form rivers, and the rivers run to the sea. Each drop of water joins with other drops in larger and larger watercourses that unify ultimately in the ocean. In the same way, each "drop" of human energy melds with other "drops" to unify ultimately in the organism. I use quotation marks because actually energy flows undivided.

This living energy is not just quantity or mass. Its qualitative aspect, its capacity of direction, has consciousness, or actually is consciousness. The intelligence and harmony of creation point to a consciousness that is both wholly comprehensive and minutely specific. The organization of all existence is manifest in the energetic functioning of each entity, including the *homeostasis* of the human individual as well as of human society when its collective ego is not unbalancing its movements. The seeming chaos of certain natural phenomena does not argue against a unified and unifying consciousness. Again and again, humankind has discovered elegant design in an operation of nature that a previous generation saw as random or capricious.

The proposition that energy is consciousness both affirms and contradicts the classical discrimination between substance and form. Every entity has form, yes. But more than that, each is its own form. The fact of taking "shape", of being an identifiable individual, entails being what it is, being its attributes. Shape, mass, density, and all other characteristics are definitions derived at bottom from the entity's motion in time and space. Energy is that motion. Its cohesion in its spacetime direction is its consciousness.

Everything, therefore, is consciousness. Conventionally, we distinguish between inorganic and organic orders of being, then between nonsentient and sentient, and then between unconscious and conscious. These classifications reflect the hierarchy of increasing complexity found in the universe. But consciousness invests every specific unit, from the smallest subatomic particle yet to be discovered up to the totality of being, the macrocosm. Each unit has a special function, a plan for fulfilling its potential, inherent in its fact of being.

Since every minute particle of life knows exactly what it is doing, it is not whimsical to say that it has a mind: a reason, which understands its inner plan, and a will, which directs its actions to that plan. If you plant a little apple seed, for instance, it grows in a few years into a beautiful tree, which blossoms and bears fruit in fulfillment of its inner plan. As energy flows undivided, so this inner consciousness flows undivided. The difference between the apple tree and the person, in very simplified terms, is that the human being knows that it knows. Its outer mind, the waking reason and the will combined with the unconscious mental processes, can direct both the organism and its environment, which the apple tree cannot. From this hierarchy of consciousness in nature, the French phenomenologist Teilhard de Chardin concluded that ". . . universal energy must be a thinking energy."

The Energy Body

The outer mind of the human being is, in a sense, a crystallization of the inner mind possessed by every living thing, just as the physical body that we can see and touch is a crystallization of our quantitative energetic entity. The material and the nonmaterial functions differ in vibratory frequency, not in substance. This is why the whole of a life, even to the length of the bones and the degree of fine-motor coordination, is literally sculpted by its internal energy. The "sculptor" is the energy's consciousness: the integral awareness from the gene to the spirit. This is why, too, the state of our life depends on how we move to meet external events, although outside reality has a part in shaping our perceptions and actions.

The qualitative differentiation of internal energy movements entails the whole consciousness, our inner as well as our outer awareness. We think of ourselves as having independent domains of powers. Our perceptions are defined as sensory, emotional, rational, or intuitive, and our actions as instinctive or directed, responsive or initiated. These are very useful distinctions because of the immense diversity of perceptions and actions that even a single experience generates. But I see the various powers as operations of consciousness that surface according to the scope and specific purpose of the internal energy movement. Emotion is a whole-organism pulsation. The feeling of wellbeing, for example, is the outer mind's recognition that energy is streaming freely.

The outer mind in the healthy person can "attend", attune or align itself, to the energy flow, or it can withdraw. We know that yogis can direct some of their autonomic nervous functions, and healers (I have seen some of them working) can intentionally channel their life force into a sick person. Such people have exceptional integration of their consciousness, but the capacity for holistic self-awareness and self-direction is innate in everyone.

To speak of the integration of consciousness implies that an energetic entity can disintegrate while living. This can happen, not in the sense that the being's life force severs into parts, but in the sense that the movement among the vibratory frequencies can be hampered by illness. The different frequencies, which are also called vibratory planes or energy bodies, compose distinguishable particulate forms with distinguishable powers. The material form, our physical organism, has the slowest-moving energy. The forms are categorized sometimes according to their kinds of operations, from the physical or sensory to the spiritual or intuitive, and sometimes according to whether they coincide with earthly life or continue to exist beyond it. Such questions, long studies by metaphysicians and observers of occult phenomena, are beginning to find their way back into the mainstream of scientific research, as we will see in Part III. For present purposes, let me define them basically as functional aspects of a unitary energy body.

The planes of energy can be compared to a block of ice floating in water in a pan. The ice represents the physical organism. The crystallized form, of course, is made of the water, and the solid and the liquid give off vapors that we usually can't see or feel but that mingle with the surrounding atmosphere. The energy body is like all these forms taken together, except that the higher vibratory frequencies totally permeate the lower.

Under ordinary circumstances, we can only perceive the energy plane of the physical body with our senses. However, some effects of the higher frequencies can be registered experimentally by technical devices, for example, the *electroencephalograph* and the recently invented *Kirlian* photography equipment. These energetic activities generally are defined as electrical or electromagnetic. But the energy body does not consist of only such recognized types of charges. Its substance is a living energy that carries these as components, as Chapters 6 and 7 will discuss further.

Vital force spills beyond the perimeters of the skin into the atmosphere to create an energy field, or aura, which provides a great deal of information about the nature and functioning of human beings. For instance, the so-called etheric double, which is the next higher vibratory form to the physical body, shows in the aura as an exact duplicate of our physiology. It has a heart, a thyroid gland, tonsils, feet, hands, a torso. Moreover, if a person has an organ or limb removed surgically, its double remains in the energy body for some time afterward. Thus, any medical intervention, no matter how seemingly minor, must be undertaken only if it is necessary. It provokes a systemic trauma because it invades not just the physical part being treated but the integral energy entity as well. The penetration of the higher vibratory frequency explains how nonmaterial events — experiences of the emotions, the mind, and the spirit — can shape our very physiology. The quality of the energy movement in the event makes an imprint on the energy body. If the experience is intense or repeated, the imprint becomes visible in the flesh as well as the aura.

There is more than speculation and analogy behind these phenomena of human energy. While only in our own century has much progress been made in investigating them scientifically, they have been a subject of concentrated study throughout recorded history, as Chapters 3, 4, and 5 will survey. My own introduction to them came at the beginning of my professional life, when I worked with Wilhelm Reich. I will always be grateful to him for opening my mind to this subject. I used equipment he invented as well as adaptations I made of Dr. Walter J. Kilner's screens for some years before I discovered that my eyes could see auras without visual aids. Chapters 6 and 7 will describe some of my observations in detail. This faculty needs training to develop, just as does the ability to discern quartertones in music. But I am convinced that many people have the capacity as part of their normal perceptual system. By extrapolating from the characteristics of the energy movements in the aura I have reached the conviction expressed at the end of the previous section: that unity and interaction integrate all things that exist, the whole of creation. The unifying agency is the pulsatory process that, in infinite variety, is the basic pattern of movement in all energy entities.

The Pulsatory Process in the Universal Life Principle

The vibratory movement that pervades every known energy form expresses itself in a pulsatory rhythm, exchanging emanations of its substance with other entities and yet retaining its own integrity during its lifetime. The network of exchange demonstrates not only peripheral contact, or a domino effect, as technical research reveals, but actual unity of substance. Physics sustains this concept: If energy in the cosmos is never destroyed, but rather just transforms its qualitative aspect; if the source of the transformation is the consciousness of the energy entity itself, and if the new, discernibly independent consciousness participates, as it does, in the whole movement which is the whole of the universe, it seems there must be an essential identity of the whole with its myriad parts. Thus, while life force individualizes itself in billions and more types, each of the billions of individuals in each type not only shares but consists in the totality of energy / consciousness. I call this totality the universal life principle or universal life force.

The pulsatory rhythm in the human being, as in all individuated embodiments of the universal life principle, has three beats: the assertive phase, the receptive phase, and the rest phase. The pulsation occurs in every component and in the organism as a unit. I gave the example earlier of the heart, which contracts to send blood through the body and then relaxes to let blood into its chambers. The hand can reach out to take or lie open to receive. Sexual movement can thrust forward and then pull back to allow the pelvis to fill with energy. The totality of the pulsations in a relatively healthy person would have perfect harmony, due to the consciousness unifying the energy entity. Consciousness, then, is not only the operation of the integral power of knowing, from the cell's to the outer mind's. It includes the innate movement of the organism outward into external reality.

In both voluntary and involuntary movement, to assert means that we act: We set in motion, move toward, determine, and use purposefully the forces at our disposal. To receive means that we are acted upon, from within or without: we accept motion, wait for it, allow it to determine us, and incorporate the forces that pulsate within or into us.

Each phase can be constructively intensified, and each can be pathologically exaggerated. As the hand can either hit or lie limp, the sexual movement can thrust aggressively or withdraw coldly. We will see some effects of distortions of the rhythmic phases in Part III. Here, let me repeat that in the healthy organism the assertive and receptive phases are balanced in beautiful reciprocity.

Considered from the perspective of its basic pattern of movement, the universal life principle can therefore be termed the principle of reciprocity. The concept bears some analogy to the traditional Chinese definition of yin and yang, which incorporates the notion of the feminine and masculine principles in creation. But there is a fundamental difference. The yin-yang and the male-female distinction presume two irreducible forces, contrasting with although complementing each other. The principle of reciprocity presumes the identical life force operating with balanced movement in each of two phases. There is and there can be no intrinsic duality in this perpetual motion. No fundamental ground exists, then, for conflict between man and woman, between individual and group, between group and society, or between society and its setting on the earth and in the cosmos.

Yet there is conflict within and among these energy entities. There is illness and war, and there is isolation and ostracism, to name only a few categories that encumber creative human unification. It is my belief, and the basis of core energetics, that we ourselves cause these many diameters of affliction by unbalancing the flow of reciprocal energy through our particular center of universal life. This center is the human core.

Chapter 2
THE INNERMOST REALITY: THE CORE

The concept of the core as the nucleus of individuated universal life is quite literal. As I have said, every cell and every more complex entity, up to the whole of the organism, consists of pulsatory energy that is conscious. Each of these elements has a center and periphery, and each emits and receives vital force. The totality of the centers is the core of the human being.

To delineate the human core, let me use a graphic shape, a cone, as an illustration (see Figure 1). Bisected, the cone shows three areas, schematizing three levels of energy movement, which correspond with three levels of personal reality. I say "levels", and I will use terms such as "higher" and "lower", not as locations but as operations. In fact, each layer permeates each vibratory plane, from the physical body to the soul. And while "core" implies depth and therefore descent, it is closer to the truth to picture it as the summit of being, the level to which we should ascend. Most accurately, in terms of moving with vital energy, we neither descend nor ascend through these levels but rather transcend them. One other feature of the drawing represents an aspect of energy flow that Part III will describe in some detail. The movement from level 1 to level 3 and outward takes a spiral form, as does the movement of external energy into the organism.

In overview, the nature of the core can be described by an evocative acronym: center of right energy. "Right" does not imply a moral judgment; it means direct energy, undeviating, flowing as an unobstructed river of life from level 1 to the periphery. Two layers intervene between level 1 and outer reality, and both have the function of balancing the energy emanations from and into the core. The layer next to the core contains the capacity of the organism to counteract external force moving inward and to alter core force moving outward. The periphery, level 3, is the area of defense and mediation between forces moving in both directions. Level 1 and 2 constitute the true inner reality of the person, or the inner self. Level 3, which is the outer mask self, is a distorted reality, and therefore, though a necessary filter, a deceptive territory in which to live.

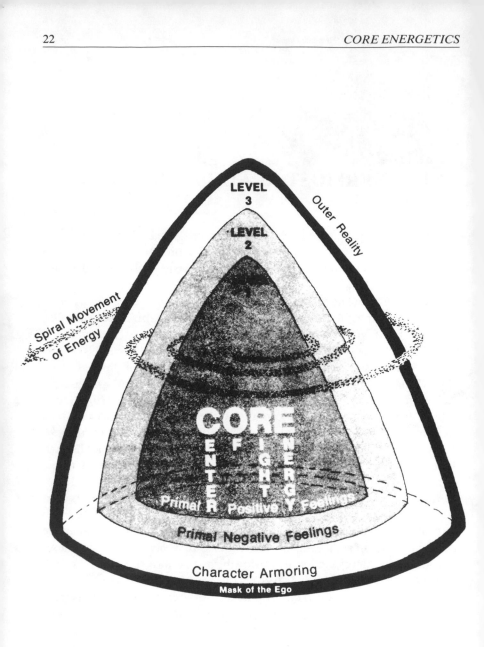

Levels of Reality

Fig. 1

The Protective Layers

Levels 2 and 1, however, are diametrically opposite in expression. The second level contains the negative primal emotions, the negative unconscious impulses described by Freud. In his view, the ego and superego had to control, organize, and unify the negative impulses. These destructive emotions are galvanized when positive impulses of life from level 1 are negated, whether from inside or outside the organism. This negation is the seat of the flight or fight reactions in their various forms and degrees: rage and hatred, panic and terror, cruelty, selfishness, destructiveness. These movements separate the self from the outer universe.

The core is entirely assertive and receptive. It has no faculties for dealing with excessive calls or attacks on its substance, or for answering frustrations or rejections of its pulsatory flow. The primal negativities and their distortions in layer 3 serve these purposes. The primal negativities do not deny life but rather protect and affirm it. They express life and respond to the dualities in existence. They are not death instincts as Freud saw them and not intrinsically pathological forces as Reich sometimes considered them. Our energy has to battle perceptual intrusions on its integrity just as it has to battle physical intrusions by germs.

As regards movement, however, the second layer incorporates energy that is altered, condensed, and slowed in its vibrations. But there is much more compression and deceleration in the energy of the defensive perimeter. From the standpoint of dynamics, the inner self, the core and the negative level, is a fluid form, whereas the outer self becomes a relatively fixed stratum.

Every order of being, inanimate or animate, has an outer self, which is the regulatory mechanism for maintaining equilibrium between the various forces working through the entity from within and without. In the human being, this peripheral layer encompasses the element of self-consciousness, the ego, which is the agency of self-aware thought and outer will. This third level has a protective function, too, like a rheostat or the skin of a tomato. Lodged in the outer self also is the corpus of unconscious material that influences the ego's conscious perceptions and decisions. Thus, the defensive perimeter is both the storehouse of the ego's self-aware powers, volitional thinking in core-energetic terms, and the area of what I call negation or denial.

In the totally healthy organism, energy flowing into and out of the person could move freely as circumstances permit, in something of the way that a rose gives off perfume and takes in sunlight through its petals. But at humankind's present state of evolution, we impose restrictions on our expressiveness, positive as well as negative, from childhood up. Psychoanalytic theory established that we begin to ingest these prohibitions at an early age and to impose them on ourselves internally. Freud and his followers saw the internalized negations as ideational, but Reich demonstrated their impact on the entire organism, the physiology as well as the psychology.

Fragmenting the Unity

Just how the patterns of denial develop and persist will be explored closely in Chapters 8, 9, and 10. Briefly, the child's ego learns to control expressiveness by knowingly and unnaturally constraining the flow of energy into and out of the organism. The acts of control disrupt the clear-running force from levels 1 and 2, the core and the negative layer, and compact it over time into energy blockages. This last term, which Reich formulated, is quite literal. Blocks are stagnated pools of vital substance that accumulate in the defensive perimeter and armor it in dysfunctional patterns that Reich named character structures. In our bioenergetics practice, Lowen und I traced five major constellations of armoring, and I am defining other relationships. I have further perceived that in all cases, there is an element of choosing to maintain the pain. Willfulness appears most strongly in the defensive perimeter, where it maintains the facade of manners and mores required by society. But volition penetrates through the entire organism because of the psychosomatic identity of the human person.

Core energetics is finding further crucial factors beyond the implication of the will, or, in our schematization, the outer will — the agency of conscious choice. As inner energy is increasingly trapped in the defensive perimeter, this layer swells into an instrument of denial that can mire the person's perceptions in the outer self. The effects are systemic, as I said, because the disruptions of energy distort the consciousness of the organism throughout its vibratory planes: not only the physical and the emotional, where Reich perceived them, but also the mental and the spiritual. As a result, the ego abandons its regulatory functions to maintain the mask. The more the blocks intensify, the more the outer mind concentrates on them, which in turn expands their energy quotient. The vicious cycle progressively confines the person's self-awareness to the periphery, and so closes the sufferer off both from outer reality and from the inner reality of the true emotions. This is why I call level 3 a state of distorted reality.

In the severely neurotic or psychotic person, the self is virtually bricked into a monumental wall of denial. But all of us carry some character armoring, and move according to the distorted perceptions and decisions that match the distorted energy. Whenever clean expressions of emotion are blocked, they issue deviously on level 3 as feelings of negation. Deviated fear, for instance, might prompt the mask to say, "I am better and you are worse", or "You are low and I am higher", or "I have to impress you".

A picture in my mind illustrates such an interaction between levels 3 and 2. Imagine a general sitting in the midst of government dignitaries and reviewing an army parade mounted in his honor. As the troops go by, the thought flashes through his head, "Boy, I bet Mom would be proud of me now." This is a man who stands on his accomplishments and thinks of himself as a powerful personage. Yet he is still a child, winning his mother's attention through feats of command. Level 2 has sent him a message that conflicts sharply with his mask.

The tragedy of identifying with the mask of the ego is that it necessarily diminishes us. It subverts our very substance, our core energy, and underlies the whole continuum of human afflictions from physical pathology to spiritual barrenness. Assessing others by only their personality traits likewise diminishes them, because it values them for their appearances rather than for their being. The uniqueness of each person comes from the fact and the form of his or her individuation from the universal life principle. The person's fundamental identity, therefore, is shaped by the purposeful movement of the energy of the core.

The Innermost Level

The core is the human being's whole capacity, a glowing, vital mass, both the source and the perceiver of life force. The core has complete unity. No duality exists at this first level of reality, no either-or, no good-bad. It is an indivisible vibratory operation, a process in which every person knows the truth instinctively by sensing the pulse of life. The qualitative characteristics of the core's movements are the primal positive emotions, or movements to make contact and unify with the outside world. These can be summed up as one supreme expression: love.

The core's energy flow, as I said at the beginning of the chapter, takes a spiral form. This can be likened to the formation of the fibers of the heart, which twist as it is created. Human wisdom throughout the ages has rightly pictured the heart as the wellspring of the positive emotions. Dante intuited the helical movement of core energy in *The Divine Comedy* with the image of man ascending in a spiral up a conical mountain. At the top is love. Dante also pictured man descending a spiral cone into hell. At the bottom, he meets the Devil, who is frozen in a lake. Others are imprisoned in the ice as well, some up to the knees, some up to the belly, some up to the neck. Translation: an outreaching life spirals upward to love; a frigid life spirals downward into hell.

Dante's metaphor highlights an aspect of the core that is strongly called on in my therapeutic approach, and this is its perceptive genius. The human center has the highest ability and intelligence. This intelligence functions beyond the strictly intellectual capacities of assimilation, analysis, and synthesis. It gives us intuitive solutions to the extrinsic problems and mysteries of life, because it can comprehend existential realities objectively and unify opposites, thus unveiling root truths.

The great innovations on earth have been made through intuition. Freud saw this. Walking with him one day, the playwright Thornton Wilder asked him, "If your discoveries are so important, how come nobody has thought them up before you?" Freud smiled sweetly and answered, "I didn't discover them. The poets have always known these things." Other giants in the history of human knowledge have had the same insight. The brilliant leaps of understanding, to use the term recorded by such disparate geniuses as the Christian mystic John of the Cross and the physicist Albert Einstein, originate in the core. But all of us can make these leaps, because all of us can have access to our core. We may not create new knowledge that the world has yet to receive from its peoples. But each of us has had what some call insights, or moments of truth, or flashes of perception, whose source we cannot trace but whose profound reality floods us with conviction. These come from our core. Here is the person's eternal uniqueness, and here is the interpenetration with the immeasurable universe: the whole of external existence, the being many perceive as God. The force that operates in the universe is the same as the force that operates in the core.

Because of these attributes, the core can heal. No matter what happens on the periphery of a person, the center of right energy strives again and again to reestablish the processes of life. The core has the capacity to create and re-create. It is able to unify opposites, and so can resolve the duality of the human person, the separation of the inner being from outer reality. The core also can disperse emotional conflicts. I mentioned in Chapter 1 that healers can direct their energy into another's physical sickness to cure it. This is energy from the core. Exceptionally integrated people can also marshal core energy to counteract ordeals that break others. There is the example of Lieutenant Hiroo Onoda, who returned to Japan after 30 years of jungle living in the Philippines in superlative physical and mental condition. There are the men and women who survived Nazi prison camps at body weights below those of all their fellow internees with similar physical structures who had died. They utilized the force from the core.

To tap this force, whether for meeting adversity or opportunity, the human being must transcend the outer self. People who report on psychic experiences or experiments with drugs often speak about a dark tunnel. As they enter the experience, they have a constricted or tortured feeling, as if they are going through a tunnel, transcending from one space to another, from an outer space to an inner space. Similarly, from core energetic work, I have arrived at a concept of inner space.

The inner space relates to the movement of life energy in the body. Energy pulsates not only out from the core but also into the organism from outside in a movement that charges the life center. This movement enters our inner space. Here is an example: when a person has an intense encounter, time, space, and motion fuse. In an ecstatic sexual relationship, for instance, a minute or two extends to centuries, to eternity. The core can merge these objectively separate dimensions. So it is that the cosmos, the out-there, coalesces with the individuated center of the universal life principle, our in-here.

These aspects of the human core represent a vision that is destined, I think, to evolve all the days of my earthly life. I say this for three reasons. One is that the people who seek my help continuously reveal new facets of the human center to me. Another is that people working in other fields of endeavor are broadening my understanding — and my awe — of how infinitely varied is the universal life principle. And the third is the testimony of inspired teachers who have investigated the phenomena of human energy throughout recorded history. Let me turn next to some of these thinkers of the past.

Part II:
THE ENERGETIC
FOUNDATIONS

Chapter 3
EASTERN THEORIES OF
HUMAN ENERGY

In the deep reaches of the past, even before the advent of the prehominids, the ancestors of our species were absorbed in the task of trying to understand their place in the universe. In common with every living thing in their era and with us, they used the instrument of consciousness inherent in their energy form.

Like all our families of progenitors, our race of *Homo Sapiens* initially concentrated on discovering who we were by experiencing our own inner pulsatory movements and becoming aware of the world within ourselves. Then we undertook to grasp the facts and meaning of the environment around us through our perceptions. Our inner pulsatory movements, our sensation, and our perceptions gave our ancestors and give us the experience of being and the consciousness of our persons both within the self and in the context of external reality.

As Chapter 2 described, those inner pulsatory movements are the sum total of the human life processes, of all the energies metabolized with the body that are generated both internally and externally. These energies also flow out of the body the way heat radiates from a furnace. They create an energy field made up of lines of force moving on the periphery of the organism as well as inside it. The body lives within this energy field, which extends as an aura several feet beyond the skin und which at times can be seen traveling several dozen feet outward.

After my introduction to these basic operations of human energy some twenty-five years ago, I discovered gradually that the phenomena of life force and energy field have been studied over thousand of years of human history. The concepts I am developing are based on my own direct observation and experimentation, which Chapters 6 and 7 will review. But as Michelangelo said, the horizons that each generation of painters can see are visible to them because they stand on the shoulders of their fathers. From this perspective, core energetics is supported by a lineage that dates from more than three millennia ago.

Chinese Energy Theory

The first systematic references known to us are inscribed in Chinese literature from perhaps as early as 1000 B. C.: the appendix to the *Book of Changes (I Ching)*, which introduces the yin-yang principle, and a chapter in the *Book of Scriptures (Shu Ching)*, which described the doctrine of the five elements — water, fire, wood, metal, and earth — on which all creation is based.

Yin and Yang are the two polar forces in which universal energy expresses itself. Yin originally signified the northern and yang the southern side of a mountain. Thus, the qualities of yin include cold, darkness, femaleness, and negation; and yang personifies warmth, maleness, light, and positiveness. These two forces are in constant conflict in the human organism, as in its environment, nature on earth, and in the universe. Yet at the same time, they form a whole, so that they symbolize harmony and equilibrium. Yin and yang represent the law of heaven and earth, master of all living things, mother of change, the origin of birth and death.

In nature, the yin-yang principle produces the changing of the seasons, the sequence of day and night, the ebb and flow of the tides. In the human body, the principle is expressed in the activities of inhalation and exhalation and in the conditions of waking and sleeping. It also accounts for parallels between the sympathetic and parasympathetic nervous system. Good or bad health is determined by the fluctuations of the two opposing forces.

When they are balanced, the organism is healthy. But if the basic energy, *ch'i* (the original meaning was breath), is displaced in any one direction, it denotes illness. Overly powerful yang results in excessive organic activity; conversely, predominant yin makes for insufficient functioning. Moreover, illness affects the whole body, not merely one part, since good health represents a condition of equilibrium in the whole organism. Tao, or the law of nature, encodes the proper balance of yin and yang in all things. It regulates development in all phenomena of life.

The harmony between man and his environment, according to the *Book of Scriptures*, traces back to the five elements, which compose the macrocosm of the universe and the microcosm, man. The sequence of the elements in the order of creation is water, fire, wood, metal, and earth. The number 5 refers to a great many groups: the five seasons (as the Chinese divided them), the five senses, the five possibilities of human happiness. Also among these groupings are five human structural components, with blood vessels being related to fire, the muscles to earth, and so on. Five yin organs, which have a passive, storage function (such as the kidneys, linked to water), and five yang organs, which are the active, working ones (such as the large intestine, corresponding with metal), are defined by the doctrine of the five elements. Thus, nature and the human body interrelate in numerous ways.

This theoretical formulation accompanied the practical medical development of acupuncture. Perhaps as early as the Stone Age, the Chinese discovered points on the human body which, if pressed or punctured, helped alleviate pain or produced other beneficial effects. The pressing and rubbing of painful and diseased parts of the body, together with attempts to revive dying newborn infants, may be regarded as the predecessor of systematic massage. Changes in breathing rhythms were observed to tighten and loosen the muscles and later to produce changes in the organism. Through these discoveries, it was found little by little that puncturing or pressing given points could also influence the functioning of certain internal organs.

These points were arranged in order of degree of connection with the vital organs, and the original number of the meridians along which they were located was twelve. In time, more points were discovered, and all known foci were classified into eight special meridians. *Ch'i,* the basic energy of the organism, flows along the meridians and interconnects the organs. Therefore, any abnormality in the flow produces an unhealthy excess or deficit of energy and upsets the harmony of the whole body. Acupuncture stimulates or reduces the circulation of *ch'i,* as the disorder requires, in order to reestablish systemic equilibrium according to Tao. The practitioner of this art, in fact, does not focus on the presenting complaint only, as does the conventional physician in the West. The acupuncturist endeavors to come to terms with the true nature of the universe itself. He utilizes the life energy in the patient's organism to give him a prolonged and satisfying balance of functions.

At present, acupuncture is gaining increasing attention outside its country of origin. The Chinese have expanded the classical number of points from 365 to 900 and have developed electroacupuncture, which sends a five-volt current through the implanted needle. Moxibustion, a process for raising a small blister over the relevant point or points, appears to work as well as the insertion of needles. Because the meridians do not correspond entirely with established nerve paths, non-Chinese investigators are seeking other fundamental explanations besides the yin-yang principle. Soviet Russian scientists, for example, hypothesize that bioplasma, a "fourth state of matter" — a new form of energy different from electrical, magnetic, or mechanical energy — explains the operation of acupuncture. But there is virtually total agreement that some form of bioenergetic flow underlies the proven efficacy of the techniques.

Indian Energy Theories

To return now to antiquity, the history of medicine in India has a venerable and seminal tradition equal to China's. Beginning in the early centuries of the first millennium B. C., observers and practitioners developed concepts that came to be called ayurveda, or the science of longevity. According to this system, the formative elements of the universe also make up the human body. The organism is the material expression of space or emptiness, wind or air, fire, water, and earth, along with the element of thought, which resides in the body. The elements form the seven substances of the living person: chyle (lymph), blood, flesh, fat, bones, marrow, and sperm. All of these elements are made alive by a radiant liquid known as ojas, or force. This is the material of vitality, the "vital juice". It stays in the heart and is the basic of prana, or breath. Ojas and prana are distributed in the body by the blood vessels.

Prana is divided into several categories that are related to the movements and various functions of breathing: respiration, air for the internal "cooking fire", and so forth. Fire similarly takes multiple forms, operating as five kinds of bile. And water in the body is phlegm, again in different forms and with various purposes. Illness is a result of hyper- or hypoactivity of one or more of these three chief elements. Treatments consist in exciting or sedating the acitivity, whichever is needed, through drugs, diet, and dwelling place.

Partly out of the ancient concepts of ayurveda, there developed a predominant system, yoga, as well as others that were formalized in the third and second centuries B. C. In common with them, yoga sought for an ultimate extrication of the individual soul from the bonds of mortal existence and freedom from the wounds of rebirth.

By this time, philosophic-religious thought in India had propounded a foundation of abstract ideas concerning the nature of experience that was widely accepted by the different schools of doctrine. In this body of concept, the universe is perceptually evolving. The process of evolution comes about by the interaction of three factors: (1) inertia, or heaviness, mass, gross matter; (2) intelligence, understood as lightness, luminosity, and comprehensibility in contrast to inertia; and (3) change, a balancing force. These three elements, called gunas, are both substances and attributes, and they combine in various dynamics to make up the substratum of the evolving universe.

The human mind is a material phenomenon, and though the guna of intelligence is predominant in it, the mind contains the elements of inertia and change as well. It is not the soul or part of the soul, which is the eternal and unchanging consciousness in a person, the true self. The gunas, intertwined so to speak in a single rope, bind the soul in the meshes of worldly experience.

Some schools of yoga that developed over time continued to believe in the cosmic soul, Brahma, proposed in classical Hinduism. Others came to see ultimate reality as an infinite number of individual souls. Correspondingly, yogis may regard their idealistic goal either as the resorption of the soul into Brahma or as the total realization of the soul's own freedom. But in both orientations, the approach to the goal is evolutionary, both within a given lifetime of a particular soul and through its reincarnation. From the earliest days, yoga has emphasized arduous physical and mental training to direct the path of the practitioner upward — from heaviness (matter) through lightness (mind) and to independence of the soul from the limitations of existence on earth.

Independence becomes permanent only when the soul is eternally freed from further rebirths, but it can be achieved repeatedly if temporarily in a wordly life by means of the yogic discipline. Beginning on the physiological level with the systematic control of reflexes, postures, and respiratory functions, yogic training progresses to the higher, mental processes, especially seeking the development of states of mental concentration. The combination of practical physical application with a mystical objective has served to attract worldwide attention to yoga. The coordination of a school of thought with a program of daily exercises has proved of great interest in physiological psychology as well as in religious philosophy.

Let me focus for a moment on Tantrism, a monistic yoga that has probably drawn more Western students in recent years than any other form. Tantrism introduces another set of concepts: the three envelopes, or bodies, of the human being. (Other schools count seven.) These are vibratory planes, coexisting but distinct. The highest is the causal body, containing the expression of the divine universal energy, Brahma. Here lives the human soul, the creative, masculine principle of individual being. The second envelope is actually composed of three bodies, which contain the so-called manifestations of the individual existence. Collectively they are in contact with the lowest envelope, the gross physical body. Therefore, they comprise the psychic essence of the five senses and the mind. They are formed of prana, the vital breath that also makes the fleshly body live. The subtle and physical bodies express the universal, plastic feminine principle of being: the evolving universe differentiated into its countless forms through the interaction of the gunas.

All schools of yoga consider prana a universal energy more basic than atomic energy. Whatever moves, works, or has life is an expression of prana. It is all around us: Currents are found in the north, south, east, and west. There are also currents of prana in the subtle and physical envelopes. On the physical plane, we inhale and exhale it and circulate it through the body in our breathing. Prana is present in every cell and molecule of living organisms. It has a special connection with the endocrine glands, and its flow is responsive to the individual's psychological state. The yogic discipline of pranayama (breathpause) is designed to teach one how to retain prana and send it through the body, particularly to the energy centers called chakras, so they can be vivified and expanded. There are many different methods of breath control, all aimed at regulating the inhalation, holding the breath, and exhaling it according to a certain rhythmical sequence. Pranayama is the foundation of the disciplines that train the person to identify with the creative principle, the soul.

The subtle envelope has seven chakras, through which energy is continously exchanged between the person and the cosmic sphere. Within the body, prana is diffused by way of thousands of nadis, or subtle arteries or tubes, articulated in a network. The principal channels, according to Tantrism, are three. Yogic tradition in general places the seven chakras at the coccyx, the base of the sexual organ, the solar plexus, the heart, the throat, the space between the eyebrows, and the crown of the head. Six of them correspond with six of the sympathetic nerve plexuses of the body.

A special kind of energy called kundalini is thought to flow through the body in a spiral fashion when activated. For that reason, it is called the serpentine fire. It does not derive from solar energy, which is the source of prana, but is related in some way to the magnetic core of the planet. According to theory, kundalini is located in the first Chakra, at the base of the spine, which is normally inactive. When it is aroused, it moves through the spinal nadi, which is the central canal. Kundalini is linked to both the sexual and creative energies. If it is not released in normal sexual or creative expressions, it produces a state of illness in the organism.

Various techniques are advocated for awakening kundalini. One method is to send prana flowing down the spine to strike violently the imaginary door leading to the dwelling place of kundalini. This assumes, of course, that the practitioner has mastered the preparatory positions and breathing that allow such a command of prana. Yoga breathing is very deep and directs a potent charge of prana toward the site of kundalini, while normal respiration is quite shallow and cannot reach it. Once kundalini is awakened, this energy can flow up the spine and in turn will animate the other chakras, causing them to grow and opening these reservoirs of power. An important American experimenter with kundalini yoga, Hereward Carrington, outlines the sequence of stages as (1) inhaling, holding, then forcing the breath downward; (2) concentrating on the heart chakra; (3) mentally projecting a flame to the coccyx chakra; (4) moving it up to pierce the door to the second chakra, the the next, and so on into and through the other centers.

Much mental concentration is involved in activating kundalini, since the energy aroused seems to want to return to its resting place, the center at the tip of the spine. Once the energy rises into the crown chakra on top of the head, it must be retained for three days before greater psychic gifts become available. Its presence there is taken as a sign that the person has attained a merging with the universal consciousness.

While kundalini yoga is based on the movement of energy in the body, there is an apparent contradiction in that kundalini in a sense opposes physical sex. That is, the sexual force is intended to be marshaled in its subtle form and directed upward rather than "descending" in the grosser physical liquids. However, Tantric yoga embraces the idea of the interpenetration of prana, kundalini, and the whole of the physical body, and makes a sacrament of copulation. All yogic systems hold that energy is constantly being exchanged between people, between the person and the planet earth, between planets in the cosmos. Tantrism teaches that the sexual union arouses and is intensified by kundalini. The sensations of the communion are deliberately prolonged through physical self-control and various ritual acts of intimacy so that the final physical joining floods the entire body. The purpose of this is to create greater love for the partner as well as participation in a divinely ordered experience. Orgasm is held to be life-restoring and life-enriching.

Indeed, sexual union is considered a fundamentally religious act by Tantrists, because it joins the static female and dynamic male energy principles. Many religions in both the East and the West developed a similar outlook. For instance, the devotees of Isis in Egypt, Aphrodite in Greece, and Diana in Rome recognized the importance of the union of male and female energy. Tantric philosophy assumes that the experience in the flesh leads to the divine. As a sentence in the literature states, "The man who realizes the truth of the body can then come to know the truth of the universe".

Chapter 4
WESTERN HUMAN ENERGY THEORY

The conviction of cosmic unity that continues to infuse Oriental investigations of reality is perhaps the main reason for their increasing acceptance beyond Asia. The history of the major thought systems in the West is marked by dichotomy, despite the efforts of philosophers and religious theorists to embrace all of creation in their systems. Over two millennia, the trend has been for one discipline or endeavor, or even one aspect of life, to develop at the expense of other proven good paths. Judeo-Christian spirituality articulated a brilliant theology, a society-supporting ethic, and deep philosophical compendia, but spent much effort on stifling innate human impulses and scientific inquiry. The Age of Reason, the Enlightenment, allied itself to the mind while downgrading emotion, intuition, and religious spirituality. Covering this period and flanking it, the two industrial revolutions and the age of empire building emphasized material progress and acquisition (bodily welfare) to the point of sacrificing basic human securities and freedoms. These imbalances were followed by the formalism of the Victorian era, destructive of emotional values and physical expression, and by the human stalemate and disintegration that erupted in World War I.

This criticism is not intended to imply that the East has not suffered crippling developmental deformities. Its traditional approaches emphasized animism and vitalism at the expense of material life and sociopolitical thought. Cyclical wars have rent the East; perennial floods, particularly in China, aggravated famines whose like the West experienced much more rarely. And in our century, reaction to these imbalances has driven parts of the Orient to equally disproportionate emphases on the material and sociopolitical.

The point here is that Eastern traditions have striven to reinforce the perception of the unity underlying all things, while the dominant Western schools have tended to reinforce the perception of the dualism (the disunity) of all things. As regards human energy systems, this Western tendency has fostered a cleavage between humanity and nature, between intuition and rational thought, and between the human person and the inner self.

Early Greek Thought

This schismatic tendency has not always been paramount in the Western world, nor does it characterize all patterns of thought. In a study of the migration of symbols by D'alvela, it was found that from 1300 B. C. to approximately 1000 A. D. there was a universal symbol expressing the sun's energy and movement. It originated with the Aryans and Greeks. This symbol is the Gammadion and it has been used in variations by several cultures. It originated as an expression, possibly, of the perception of the sun and its rays. But it is actually in the form of the swastika, a representation of the movements of the energetic processes of the energy field of the human being, as my own observations of the energy field have determined.

Early Greek thought also theorized about the unity of all things. In the era preceding the Age of Pericles, systematic explorations of reality came to presume identity between universal forces and the forces within individual entities. Pythagoras, born around 582 B. C., is known best for his work in mathematics and astronomy, but the articulation of his theories during his own and the next century speculated equally on what post-Platonic interpreters clarified as the concept of supreme unity.

Pythagoreans considered all phenomena to be composed of two oppositions, which they listed in ten categories: odd-even, male-female, rest-motion, and so forth. They realized that the union of these opposites is the universe (the "grand man"). There is a constant interplay between it and the human being (the "little universe"), and an understanding of the one predicates a knowledge of the other. Heavenly bodies encase souls, minds, and spirits in the same way that the visible human form serves as a vehicle for an individual spiritual organism, which is in fact the conscious individual. The famous Pythagorean letter Y signifies the part of choice. The young person, walking the path of life symbolized by the central stem of the Y, reaches the point where the path divides. The left fork represents his lower nature, and following it will lead to a span of folly and dissipation. The right branch is the road of industry, sincerity, and integrity, leading ultimately to union with the superior spheres.

Early Pythagoreanism did not expound on a coherent explanation of how the fulfilling and unifying process came about. Systematizations were undertaken later, notably by Plato and Aristotle, who conceptualized the fundamental distinction between form and substance and proposed comprehensive (though differing) theories for their interaction. But the Pythagoreans recorded one insight that would increasingly fade from prominent scientific and philosophic inquiry until revived by Paracelsus: the perception of a vital energy in a luminous body. They held that its light can produce various effects in people, including cures. Cabala, the Jewish mystical theosophy that arose in the seventh century A. D., refers to the same energies as the astral light.

Hippocrates, who followed Pythagoras by 120 years, inherited the still-dominant presumption of ultimate unity, and on this legacy he established a body of theory that bears some analogies to ayurvedic teachings. Four humors, he believed, make up the human organism — blood, bile, atrabile, and phlegm. These correspond with the properties of heat, dryness, cold, and moisture. But paralleling the developing concept in Greek philosophy of spira (spiral one) as an energy specific to life, Hippocrates subscribed to a special power of nature, which he called enormon (indwelling power), and to a spiritual restoring essence of principle, physis.

Hippocrates' therapeutic processes and materia medica derived from his unswerving thesis that nature, not the physician, heals the patient. Thus, while the aspect of his work that earned him the title "father of modern medicine" was his astute observation of diseases and his efforts to replace superstitious practices with empirical, the connecting thread in his system was the presence of an all-healing nature that directs the energies within the patient. The physician must ally himself with these internal energies to effect treatment. And he must also look to the relationship between the disease and cosmic circumstances such as the status of the constellations, the season, and atmospheric events.

It was perhaps the peculiar organizational genius of the Romans that drove the critical wedge of dualism into Western thought; the hypothesis is beyond our subject here. But the wedge was surely not formed by the founder of Christianity, even if very early expounders, such as Paul, oriented the creed toward dichotomy. There are many references in the Bible to curing through the transmission of energies. Not only did Jesus heal by using his hands, his eyes, or his words, but his followers succeeded in duplicating his work. One episode among many that suggest a healing force concerns a woman who had had a hemorrhage for twelve years. When she touched the hem of his garment in the crowd, Jesus said, "Who touched me? . . . Someone touched me, for I perceived that power had gone forth from me" (Luke 8:46). The orthodox Christian belief is that all such Biblical acts of healing were strictly of supernatural origin. But many contemporary healers maintain that the sacred act summons the natural healing energy in the body and in nature, as Christ did. They claim that Christ and the apostles exercised an art open to all persons who are capable of tapping these energies.

Later European Energy Theory

During the Reformation, the revolutionary Paracelsus (1493-1541) broke away from the medical tradition that had developed almost undisputed from its second-century roots in Galen. Paracelsus attempted a synthesis as closely linked to observation of natural phenomena as Hippocrates'. Combining his own work as a physician and chemist with Greek philosophic notions, tenets of Christian theology, and concepts from the East, he posited God as supreme cause and essence but not as the whole of primordial existence, which he called iliaster. Iliaster, he said, is both vital force and vital matter. Nature is one, an eternal unity, in which all beings harmonize and sympathize with each other. So the macrocosm of the universe and the microcosm of man are fundamentally one. There is a sympathy between certain individual things in each, for instance between particular human organs and particular plants or stars. The interaction is a function of a correspondence or "magnetism" between their vital principles, their life spirits.

Every corporeal form — whether a stone, a metal, a person, a vegetable — has a specific spirit. Each is a twofold being, with a material (visible) and a spiritual (invisible) aspect. In living things, these are linked together by a soul, a semimaterial form equatable with the entity's self-purpose or will to be. The material aspect of a being consists of invisible elements that have become visible, and the spiritual elements of movements (in humans, feelings and thoughts) originating in the macrocosm.

The human soul is, in effect, made up of three souls during the person's earthly lifetime. The lowest, like that of a lower animal or plant, regulates organic functions. The highest is a uniquely human phenomenon, reason and the noblest emotions. This faculty survives into immortality. Between the two is a medium soul that higher animals also have. It is this level that the person interacts with the universe. In its material aspect, this soul is called the sidereal or astral body; in its spiritual aspect, it is called the astral soul. Sidereal man is the ethereal counterpart of physical man, illuminated by the spirit.

The magnetism between the universe and the person as wholes and between certain of their parts works, so to speak, through subtle emanations of force, called archeus. This is the vital principle that contains the essence of life and character of everything. It is archeus, for instance, that uses food one eats to make hair, blood, and bone. Mumia, a similar concept, is the life power inherent in the flesh. Paracelsus liked to say that nature cures, the doctor only nurses. Mumia is nature's healing in the human being, and it is not enclosed within the skin but radiates both within and around the person like a luminous sphere. The mumia of a sidereal body can be made to act on another at a distance for good or ill, for restoring health or causing disease. This is especially true after earthly death, when the sidereal person separates from the corporeal body and remains intact for a time until its material aspects are absorbed into its natural surroundings.

Paracelsus' intuitions outreached the perimeters of demonstrable knowledge by centuries: His concept of iliaster foretells Einstein's energy-matter equation; archeus is very like what we call metabolism; mumia bears analogies to DNA and the body's immune responses. His emphasis on direct observation and careful experimentation offended orthodox physicians and chemists, and his efforts to create a new synthesis of learning fell on unwelcoming ground.

Yet his indisputable cures helped revive scientific research. And though he did not claim the ability to physically see the life-shaping and healing forces he described, he inspired others to continue on the roads of inquiry he had opened.

One such was Jan Baptista van Helmont (1579-1644), a Flemish physician who discovered gases and established some important principles of biochemistry. He defined magnetism as unseen influences that bodies often exert over each other at a distance, and he visualized a universal fluid pervading all nature. This fluid is not corporeal or condensable matter but pure, vital spirit that penetrates all bodies and acts on the mass of the universe. In humans, he said, its seat is in the blood, and it is called forth and directed by volition. He stressed that the healer must have more power than the patient and that the patient's openness to therapy is very important. In his lifetime, Van Helmont utilized his own healing powers through the laying on of hands to save victims of a seventeenth century plague.

Among other prominent doctors and scientists who followed Paracelsian investigations was Athanasius Kircher (1601-1680), a German Jesuit biologist and physicist, who was perhaps the first to understand that disease and putrefaction are caused by invisible living bodies. Valentine Greaterakes (*1628), an Irish healer practicing in England, worked striking cures attested to by men of such stature as Robert Boyle. Greaterakes called on the energy of the body — Paracelsus' mumia — to combat disease by stroking with his hands. About a century later, an Austrian priest named Johann

Joseph Gassner (1727-1779) blended Roman Catholic demonology with the notion that mumia can be used to cause harm. He inferred from this that most diseases arise from possession by devils. In the context of his faith, he set about curing the sick through exorcism, with notable success.

Three brilliant men whose lifetime spanned the seventeenth century undertook to create bodies of theory relating the particular to the universal: René Descartes (1596-1650), Baruch Spinoza (1632-1677), and Gottfried Wilhelm von Leibnitz (1646-1716). Descartes' contribution to the history of human energy concepts is more negative than positive, because his extreme rationalism led him to a mechanistic view of reality that served to reinforce the dualistic orientation in the West. But he acted as a stimulus and a foil to the two later thinkers, whose perspectives were both more balanced and more integrated.

Descartes, the French philosopher, mathematician, and scientist, worked from a hypothesis that two heterogeneous substances exist — thought and extension. Only in God are these to be found truly unified. In creation, all material beings are equatable with extension, including the human body. Animate as well as inanimate entities are set in motion by God, who, so to speak, winds up the universe like a countless array of clocks and lets them run their natural course. The substance of thought (intellect and will) makes up the soul, which humankind alone possesses. This soul has a unity of composition with the body but not a unity of nature. Nonetheless, Descartes conceived of all matter as being essentially a homogeneous substance with a unity of movement throughout creation. He asserted that motion propagates itself in vortices. Spinoza and Leibnitz would extend the first of these ideas into theories of unified substance; and a countryman of Descartes' three centuries later, Teilhard de Chardin, would incorporate the perception of vortices into a vast phenomenology.

Spinoza, born in Amsterdam as Descartes was reaching his prime, began his speculations on a solidly Cartesian base. But even his first known writings contained the premise that he would use to attempt to resolve Descartes' dualism. Spinoza said that while individual bodies and minds do exist, they are parts — "abstractions" — of the whole of a universal life. When viewed *sub species aeternitas*, under the form of eternity, they "disappear" into the infinite. There is only one substance, then, an infinite and universal substance, which Spinoza identified as God and as nature. Created things are expressions of it in modes (aspects) of thought or extension. They are not merely set and kept in motion by a clockmaker God but are "stirred by an inward energy", as the poet Goethe would put it a century later.

Leibnitz's impulse to synthesize and integrate emerged in a many-sided career. He was a historian, diplomat, and inventor as well as a mathematician, scientist, and philosopher. His travels brought him in contact with Spinoza, whose life work in optics and natural philosophy interested him equally. Like the older Dutchman, the German took off from a Cartesian base, and he too broke through the dualism of Descartes' system, but in another way. Leibnitz proposed that substance is force, and that the essential elements of the universe are centers of force, which he called monads. These units are not inert matter, activated by outside causes. They are metaphysical or spiritual microcosms that contain their own wellsprings of motion. They mirror the infinite number of other entities in the universe through their power of perception. Because they are innately active and perceptive, they move in harmony, though by nature they are distinct substances and do not interact. That is, they do not exchange the force that makes them up. But they can merge in dynamic aggregates, known to themselves as well as to external entities. The degree of their perfection and reality depends in the degree of their ability to surpass the resistance of corporeal limitation by means of perception. In this hierarchy of beings God is the supreme monad.

A fundamental question remains in Leibnitz's and Spinoza's system. It is the question of how, in pragmatic terms, a unitary substance such as a human being actually holds together and acts, how the parts or aspects relate to each other and the universe. Concrete observation and experimentation did not keep up with rational theorizing in the Enlightenment, despite the remarkable advances in science and technology that had been launched during the previous century. In the latter 1700s, thinkers would concentrate again on the physical phenomena in the universe.

Observation and Experimentation

In the modern era, the first known scientific attempt to understand living systems in their natural milieu was made by Sir Isaac Newton (1642-1727). In his second paper on light and colors, he speaks of an electromagnetic light, a "subtle, vibrating, electric, and elastic medium". This medium was excitable and exhibited phenomena such as repulsion and attraction, sensation and motion. Newtons concepts anticipated in many ways the electromagnetic field of Michael Faraday (1791-1867) and James Clerk Maxwell (1831-1879). In 1704, Richard Mead (1673-1754) made an attempt to place living systems under the laws of the Newtonian principles. His theory on atmospheric tides (which are caused by the gravitational effects of the sun and moon and cause periodic shifts in the atmospheric gravity, elasticity, and pressure) is that these tides act as an "external assistance" to the "inward causes" present in animal bodies. Mead spoke about "a nervous fluid with electricity." About this time Nollet and Fretke published related theories and experiments on the nervous fluid.

The theory of extracorporeal influence was taken up and given international impetus by Franz Anton Mesmer (1734-1815), a Viennese-trained physician who moved to Paris in 1778. Mesmer known, of course, for his use of hypnotism, had discovered that passing a magnet over diseased parts of the body often effected a cure. Further experiments and speculations led him to propose that all things in nature possess a particular power that manifests itself by special action on their bodies. This power, a fluid that he called animal magnetism, impregnates all entities, whether mineral, vegetable, or animal. It operates without chemical union. Animal magnetism can be communicated to animate and inanimate objects in different degrees, operate at a distance, and be accumulated and transported. It can be activated and invigorated in the human body not only by a pass of a magnet but by sound, and mirror light will reflect it.

A discordant rage surrounded Mesmer in France, and critics pronounced his findings and cures the result of overheated imaginations. Among his gainsayers, a royal commission of inquiry in 1784 (Benjamin Franklin was a member) declared all the principles of Mesmer's work invalid. Yet the work itself was replicable, and it continued to draw investigators. One who attempt to integrate Mesmer's theories into a synthesized explanation of reality was a nineteenth-century American mental healer, Phineas P. Quimby, who in turn was consulted by Mary Baker Eddy, the founder of the Christian Science Church.

The Italian physician and physicist Luigi Galvani (1737-1798) began experiments with the action of electricity on the muscles of dogs, probably after his appointment as a lecturer in anatomy at the University of Bologna in 1762, when he was 25. His first major work, published in 1791, reported an energy specific to the organic kingdom that he then called animal electricity but later termed life force. He had observed that when he placed one metal in contact with a nerve in a frog's leg and another with its muscle, the muscle jerked. He concluded that his movement is not exclusively provoked by the externally applied materials but the results from bioenergy-life force-circulation system.

Alessandro Volta (1745-1827) and other contempory researchers in electricity disputed Galvani's explanation and attributed the muscle movement solely to the effect of electricity passing between the two dissimilar metals. They regarded the nerve and muscle as simply conductors. But Galvani rejected this argument and continued his experiments. He came to see bioenergy as having an important and complex interconnection with atmospheric electricity, whether the body is in a normal or pathological state. Karl von Reichenbach (1788-1869) was similarly convinced that a universal energy, which he called od or odyl, pervaded natural bodies. He spent the last 30 years of his long life (he died at 81, in 1869) investigating it. The German biochemist undertook research into magnetism, electricity, heat, and light and their relationship with vital powers, and published a number of studies on his findings. A basic observation was that when a strong magnet was passed along a person's body, it produced unusual sensations. These generally were more intense in an emotionally disturbed subject than in a normal one. This response, he concluded, is due to od. A property of all matter that also interpenetrates and fills the structure of the universe, odylic force flows in concentrated form from special sources such as heat, sound, and electricity. It possesses polarity and has luminosity; it can radiate at a distance; and substances with it. The od in a human being makes the surface of the body glow — surrounds it with an aura — and follows a diurnal fluctuation, increasing and decreasing in the course of each 24-hour day.

Reichenbach's work spread. William Gregory (1803-1858), a professor of chemistry at the university of Edinburgh, verified his basic experiments and translated his major writings, rendering as "vital force." *Force vitale* was term also chosen by Dr. Hippolyte Baraduc (1850-1909), who published some initial findings under that title in a French medical journal two decades after Reichenbach's death. In this and later studies, Baraduc described an energy field that surrounds the body and penetrates it. He theorisized that the energy itself is a cosmic force that enters and leaves the human organism through respiration.

In the early twentieth century, Emile Boirac (1851-1917), an experimental psychologist and rector of the Acadamy at Dijon, reported investigations he had been making into psychic energies. From his work with sensitives — people susceptible to remote passes of the hands and to weather changes — he concluded that the human organism possesses an energy that can act on other bodies at a distance. He called it magnetic or nerve radioactivity, a polarized force as demonstrable as the "radioactivity" of light and heat. He found that this energy appears to be stored in the parts of the body where it has been directed. It can have healing effects, which Boirac termed curative magnetism.

Many other French scientists carried out experiments in vital phenomena. Boirac cited one whose observations may come as a surprise: the noted physician Ambrose-Auguste Liébeault (1823-1904), known to students of psychiatry for his work in hypnoses during the latter 1800s. Liébeault had concluded from research on young children that one person can have healthful or unhealthful effect on another simply by his presence, independently of any suggestion,

Yet suggestion, not transmission of energy from without, was the explanation that Liébeault offered for how hypnosis operates. In this he departed not only from Reichenbach and his followers but from equally renowned figure in the history of psychiatry, the neurologist Jean-Martin Charcot (1825-1893). In Charcot's view, hypnotizability had the same basis as hysteria: an organic weakness of the nervous system, compounded by malingering. Sigmund Freud's monumental discoveries would be grounded in both theories, but especially Liébeault's.

Chapter 5
MODERN HUMAN ENERGY THEORY

The discovery of the unconscious mind, upon which Freud's psychoanalysis is based, was revealed with hypnotic techniques. Freud was a pupil of Charcot and a co-worker of Bernhim. In his very earliest work, Freud, with Josef Breuer, noted the importance of the blockage or discharge of energy in the formation of hysteria. He extended this observation in his studies of anxiety neurosis and his development of the libido theory. Freud and his colleagues later abandoned this thread of inquiry, but Wilhelm Reich called it the "living nerve" of psychoanalysis. Therefore, neither Freud nor other Western thinkers contributed significantly to human knowledge of other systems in living beings. This field of inquiry would progress apart from psychiatry until the articulation of orgonomy by Reich, beginning in the 1920s.

Almost simultaneously with Boirac, Walter J. Kilner (1847-1920), of London, was revealing the results of his experiments in making the physical emanations from the body visible. *The Human Atmosphere*, issued in 1911 and revised and republished in 1920, described the aura as it appeared through colored screens or filters he devised using the chemical dicyanine. Viewing patients through these, he could perceive a slightly glowing oval "mist" around the whole body. The envelope had three zones: a dark edging, the densest part, closest to the skin; then a thinner layer streaked perpendicularly to the body; and finally a delicate exterior luminosity with indefinite contours.

Kilner and associates found that the appearance of the aura differed considerably from subject to subject, depending on age, sex, mental ability, and health. The color was often bluish, and when the pole of a magnet was brought close to the subject, a ray formed in the emanation between the pole and the nearest of most angular part of the body. Certain diseases showed as patches or irregularities, which led Kilner to develop a system of diagnosis on the basis of the color, texture, volume, and general look of an envelope. In my own work with auras, described in Chapter 7, I have used some of Kilner's techniques and chemical screens until I was able to observe the phenomena without visual aids.

Toward the end of World War I, L. E. Eeman began a lifetime of investigations into healing through life energies by performing a remarkable cure on himself. A nonmedical experimenter who was long a prominent member of the British Society of Dowsers, Eeman developed methods of "cooperative healing" that demonstrate the movement of life energy from person to person. The process is activated when two or more people form a closed circuit, whether by holding conductors such as copper wires or cotton threads that run between them or by touching each other directly. In the laying on of hands, Eeman discovered, the best results are obtained if the healer lightly joins opposite hands — right to left and vice versa — with the ill person, or places the healer's hands so that they rest on the patent's opposite sides.

An American contemporary of Eeman's, Edgar Cayce, discovered as a very young man that he was often able to "read" the nature of an illness and prescribe effectively without seeing the sick person. In these readings as well as direct consultations, he relied on the appearance of the aura, which he described in great detail in his file notes over his lifetime. The energy field, he observed, emanates from the whole body and is usually heaviest and most visible around the shoulders and the head. Different colors and shades indicate different characteristics and states. Red, for example, denotes force and vigor, while dark red signals high temper and emotional turmoil. The fundamental color changes as the person "develops or retards."

It would take many pages to follow in detail the work done by the many other investigators in this field. However many people in England and the United States have been working on the fringes of the scientific world and experimenting with the vital energies in different fields, such as radiaesthesia, mediumship, and the phenomena of parapsychological investigations. The work of Edgar Cayce and the studies of the chakras and energy movements by the yogis, and later the theosophists in the work of Leadbeater, have described in detail the vital energies of man from a metaphysical point of view. It can be said that all of these experiments and studies are based on some specific expressions of the vital processes of the organism and the energetic processes of life. Recently, such work as that conducted by Bernard Grad of McGill University on the growth of plants has shown the great effect that a healer's hand could have on the growth processes of experimental seedlings of barley. In the United States, a group of well-known scientists, at the institute for the Study of Life Energies (now disbanded), conducted serious work and attempted to define the energy field of human beings, under the late Robert Laidlaw of New York.

Another American, George Starr White, spent the better part of his life in experimental investigations and applications of auric effects. Like Kilner, White developed techniques for seeing the energy emanation, which he also called by such names as psychomagnetic radiation, life atmosphere, and vital force.

Every living thing, White stated, has its own characteristic magnetic atmosphere, which is acted upon by both natural and artificial components of its environment. Thus, metals like tin and iron enhance the growth of plants when placed near them or when fertilizer for them is first stored in a metal container. Animal and human auras are influenced by metals too, as well as by other living organism, various colors, orientation to the earth's meridians, and a host of other agents. White found that the psychomagnetic radiation of a body is disturbed in distinctive ways by certain diseases, and again like Kilner, he used these observations for some succesful diagnoses and treatments.

Evidence of auric energy continued to emerge, both from naturally gifted laypeople and from practitioners of various disciplines. Besides Cayce, many others versed in paranormal phenomena, such as the medium Eileen Garrett and the healers Olga and Ambrose Worrall, have described auras in terms similar to Kilner's. Among trained specialists, George de la Warr, an English civil engineer and talented inventor, began technical research into human force fields early in World War II that he and his colleagues developed as the system of Radionics.

De La Warr was deeply interested by the efforts of the California pathologist Albert Abrams to detect radiations from living tissue with the help of calibrated instruments. De la Warr set out to pursue this branch of inquiry. Radionics comprises methods for analyzing and treating disease through the use of machines designed with dials in a resonator arrangement. The machine operator's energetic responses to the energy of the specimen being tested with the equipment, usually a blood sample from the patient, provide the diagnostic information or indicate the appropriate radionic therapy. Delawarr Laboratories (as the name is spelled) report that their instruments and techniques have been used to trace sources of environmental pollution and to restore soil balance as well. A camera functioning on the same principles as the medical instruments has been developed that will photograph an animal or human organism at a remote distance. While radionics is a disputed science, its assumptions have been lent support by research in the United States since the 1960s through the use of biological transducers and biofeedback mechanisms, through the work of William Teller, professor of physics at Stanford University.

Highly technical explorations of the innate physical properties of energetic phenomena were begun in the early 1930s by a group of American investigators spearheaded by Harold S. Burr, a professor of biology at Yale university, and Leonard J. Ravitz, of the College of William and Mary. Working over the next three decades with their own discoveries and with contributions from the philosopher F. S. C. Northrop, the physicist Henry Margenau, and others, they evolved what Ravitz named the electrodynamic theory of life.

Burr and Northorp have conducted a detailed study, in the biological domain, of the vital energies of organisms. They felt there must be some force behind the living organisms' ability to organize, direct, and hold together the complex chemical interchanges which accompany biological processes. They have published a great number of articles dealing with fields in primitive organisms as well as instruments measuring minute voltage differences. Their work has been continued, in the study of emotional illness, by Ravitz. He also conducted extensive experiments on the states of excitation of the human organism in relation to neurotic states, hypnotism, sleep, and drugs. His work shows that significant changes occur in the electromagnetic field of human beings.

Many experiments with specially developed instruments have measured the energy levels and emanations of living creatures, from plants to humans in normal and pathological conditions. These studies have traced the effects on these force fields of virtually every influence conceivable, from weather conditions to emotional shifts. By 1955, the researchers had concluded that every organism is an electrodynamic system that responds to electric impulses both within itself and from outside. They had determined further that emotion can be equated with natural physical energy. These findings added to the understanding of psychosomatic unity advanced since the 1930s by the physiologist W. R. Cannon, his wife, Flanders Dunbar, and the psychiatrists Franz Alexander and Wilhelm Reich.

Precursors of Synthesis

Reich, in fact, seeded grounds much larger than the field of psychosomatic medicine. His work embraced many disciplines, each interest growing as an organic correlative of the others. As a result, his body of thought supports the ageless hope that humankind will ultimately achieve a unification of all human truths. In this, Reich figures as perhaps the most important precursor of what I perceive as a new age — an era when we may hope to build a universal synthesis of knowledge. I will speak to this hope in chapters 23 and 24.

Reich's panorama outreaches the synthesis of most twentieth century creative investigators, I believe, not only because it joins scientific to sociocultural knowledge, but because it explores the essential nature of being.

One other precursor of the new age has left us an intergrated body of thought that is equally impressive for its breadth and depth. This is the French Jesuit Pierre Teilhard de Chardin. Teilhard began with very different data from those of Reich, but he formed strikingly similar views of human energy. His ontology coincides at many points with the concepts I have reached in part from the springboard of some of Reich's inquiries.

Teilhard was a paleontologist by academic background (he was a member of the expedition that discovered the Peking man) and a student of many other scientific fields as well, ranging alphabetically from anthropology to zoology. In the 40 years of his work before his death in 1955, he developed a phenomenology based on what he called the law of recurrence, or the law of complexity / consciousness. According to this principle, matter groups and regroups itself in increasingly and vitalized evolutionary arrangements, from atomic units upward through the hierachy of living beings.

Evolution, he said, can be classified in four stages. The first three are cosmogenesis, biogenesis, and anthropogenesis, or the birth of the universe, life, and individual human beings respectively. The fourth is Christogenesis, the formation of ''ultrasynthesized'' humanity into an organic convergance — a summit that Teilhard the scientist called the omega point and Teilhard the theologian posited as the mystical body of Christ. Each of these stages grows from and extends the one before it, the last being Teilhard's extrapolation from the spatiotemporal ''drift'' or direction set by the first three.

Teilhard holds that the movement of matter in all the evolutionary stages is spiral. The cosmic mass, churning in a vortex, has produced every existing thing.

In aggregates above a certain complexity, the involuting torsion results in the rise of conciousness. That is, there is a double movement: multiplication and then compression of matter, followed by association and then the interiorization that is awareness. The vortex impulse underlies not only the formation of specific entities but also their sociality, their interaction among themselves and with their group's surroundings, whether we are speaking of humans or cells. In Teilhard's view, therefore, consciousness is coextensive with life. Chapter 1 cited his insight that the singular difference between the lower and higher forms of life is that a higher being knows that it knows — perceives its perceptions — and can direct both itself and its environment. The logical and the empirical conclusion he derives from this has already been quoted: ''. . . universal energy must be a thinking energy.''

Wilhelm Reich arrived at his concepts of universal energy from within the framework of psychiatry. Like Teilhard's studies of fossil remains, his observations of patients led him in two directions: inward into the discrete elements of nature, and outward into the unity of the entire cosmos. His holistic perspective refused to stop at the mechanistic descriptions sought by contemporary science but reached for a fundamental explanation of the workings of the universe. This focus on both specific phenomena and the totality of their processes he termed functionalism.

Trained as a psychoanalyst in Vienna just after World War I, Reich subscribed to Freud's views on the necessity for uncovering the unconscious and dealing with repressed material. But from early in his career, he found himself increasingly concerned with the questions of how sufferers repress and why they resist the resolution of their emotional conflicts. Exploring the dynamics of repression, he concentrated on the negativities that he and his colleagues were finding in patients. These attitudes not only prevent people from forming a relationship with the doctor at the beginning of treatment but seem to strengthen resistance the deeper the analysis goes. This is due, as Reich saw it, to the human tendency to avoid the perception of painful experiences and also being afraid to expound and experience pleasure. He postulated that the avoidance is a function of blocks developed in childhood to dull the impact of punishment or rejection by the parents of spontaneously expressed feelings, both positive and negative. As we have seen, blocks are not only "psychological"; they early become actual muscular rigidities that manifest themselves through body structures in character armoring. This systemic blockage freezes the flow of energy and simultaneously the perception of the flow — the emotions. And as Reich would discover later, it can trigger organic disease.

The key to restoring health, therefore, lies not just in exposing buried memories and ideas but in dissolving the frozen armor. Over time Reich developed highly succesful therapeutic methods for releasing the energy bound up in blocks, which demonstrated that the human being has total psychosomatic identity. (This is a very different thing from the concept of psychosomatic parallelism accepted by many present-day physicians and psychiatrists.) His techniques have been carried forward in neo-Reichanism, bioenergrtics, and core energetics, and I will review some of them in Part III.

Reich's chain of psychiatric theory grew from his observations of human sexuality. Close examination of resistance patterns revealed to him that the inability to sustain the emotions of sex correlates with an inability to achieve full physical discharge. Libido is therefore a real energy flow in the organism. It is self-regulated in the healthy person by laws of energy conservation and release but is blocked in the neurotic by the character armor. This is true of all other expressions of feeling

In the early 1930s, Reich began research on the electrical components of pleasurable and unpleasurable feelings. The results supported his thesis that an orgasm is a pulsatory movement of energy in four beats: mechanical tension, bioelectric charge, bioelectric discharge, and relaxation. By 1939, experiments had convinced him that this pulsatory rhythm occurs throughout the autonomic nervous system, from cells to organs. He found the charge, in fact, moves a previously unknown form of energy, different from electrical, mechanical, and chemical forces. He named this energy orgone.

The laboratory work underlying these findings had already led Reich into the study of microorganisms in the plant and animal kingdom. This study had revealed the four-beat biological pulsation and the presence of orgone everywhere he looked. Over the following years, he progressively extended his research into energetic activity, adding to the findings of established disciplines such as meteorology and geophysics and helping found new fields such as biophysics. In the process, he steadily harvested a monumental synthesis.

Orgone is present, Reich deduced, not only in all living beings but everywhere in the cosmos, including vacuums. It is a universal preatomic energy that makes up all matter, and it is the medium or substratum for electromagnetic and gravitational forces.

Its motion is continuous, and contrary to the law of entropy, orgone does not disperse from but is attracted to concentrations of itself. When streams of energy are drawn together, they superimpose in a spiral, which is the fundamental shape of creative activity: witness the structure of galaxies and cyclones, cells and crystals. The spiral form of orgone movement is visible in human auras and in a blue envelope around the earth, among the radiation from many other "solid" bodies that Reich saw and tested. Everything that exists interconnects because of the orgone network. A single entity is an existential variation, characterized by greater or lesser complexity, of what Reich ultimately termed the common functioning principle.

The common functioning principle makes for a free interchange of energy wherever entities meet: in galactic space or within a living body, between sexual partners or among members of a society. But like individual people, social units from the family to the cultural level sustain armoring. Reich supported Marxian theory (though not Marxist political practice) for its cogent protest against the economic and government repression of people's rights to self-determination, just as he founded sex hygiene clinics in 1929 to help people — including adolescents and the unmarried — protest against the moralistic repression of their rights to self-regulation. The same vision prompted him in the late 1940s and 1950s to investigate ways of helping the geosphere discard nuclear wastes, and these experiments led him into the field of weather control. Until he died, in 1957, Reich anchored his psychiatric treatment and his scientific investigations to the conviction that the health of every energetic mass, whether a cosmic entity or a person or a minute particle of life, lies in its freedom from blockage.

The dissolving of blocks has remained a primary aim of the various practitioners who have carried on Reich's work of healing. His psychiatric followers are not his only heirs. Many streams of the human potential movement owe their basic orientation to orgonomy. For while Reich's controversial claims and struggles against authorities lost him much professional support especially toward the end of his life, his insights have increasingly emerged (often without credit) in established medical and scientific circles.

His psychiatric theory and methodology have been embraced by several other distinct schools that base their techniques directly on his. All of us continue to focus on the autonomic nervous system, leading the patient through both physical movement and psychoanalytic techniques to release the energy and resolve the character attitudes frozen into the structure of the body and the personality. Lowen and I, who began our careers as students and colleagues of Reich, found that while this twofold program is highly effective in itself, it neglected the vital volitional aspect of integral human functioning and proved unable to ensure permanent relief.

Chapter 6
OBSERVATIONS OF THE ENERGY FIELD

Freud observed to Thornton Wilder that creative insight makes many seminal discoveries that scientific inquiry reaches only much later. These scientific insights come very belatedly, if Freud was referring to the long, long voyage from Oedipus legend to the Oedipus complex. Freud opened the perceptive genius of his core to transform the objective accuracy of the Greek myth into a practical therapeutic tool. He also opened his inner will to a principle that has always been understood in the creative arts, though not in the technical sciences: the suspension of disbelief.

Aside from some simple equipment and lighting arrangements, seeing the energy field with the physical eyes needs only the willing suspension of disbelief. The field appears as a light cast or as luminous radiations that pulsate spontaneously and regularly around every mass I have observed, from crystals to living beings, to the earth's atmosphere. The field is not an esoteric or strange property, waiting for the day when the technology produces more delicate devices capable of capturing and analyzing samples of it. Chapter 3 touched on the research of Burr and associates, Delawarr Laboratories, and the Life Energies Institute, among others. I have no doubt that design and engineerig advances will develop increasingly reliable machinery.

At present, I know of no technology that takes accurate, automatic readings of subtle but visually perceptible changes in the fields of exposed subjects, such as trees and waterways. Too many of the extraneous energetic forces at play are registered. And most equipment for testing small, isolatable specimens is reported as depending on some degree of manipulation or input by its operator, as my recording instruments do. Experiments with such equipment are therefore subject to human error.

But I want to emphasize again that I think everyone who has functioning eyesight can, with some training and patience, learn to observe energy fields. The only impediment I have found, in myself and people I have worked with, is transitory or internal blockages to perceiving energy field phenomena. Energy emanations generally cannot be seen when the eyes are projected stressfully and stare hard, or when the body is held in a tight, unyielding attitude.

Instruments and Methods

My own study of energy fields, as I have said, began a little over twenty-five years ago under the tutelage of Wilhelm Reich. He trained me in the use of orgone energy accumulators and other instruments he had built. From these, I moved on to experimenting with devices such as Kilner's chemically coated screens, and then with equipment I designed. By the late 1960s, my body of findings was extensive enough to demonstrate which field phenomena do and do not require mechanical aids for the human eye to see them, and under what conditions.

I had also developed filters for use with a wide range of subjects: individuals and crowds, potted plants and freestanding vegetation, rock formations and small stones, the earth's horizon over land and water, and the skylines above mountains. The filters are necessary for perceiving a field clearly in strong natural or artificial light. The intensity of the frequencies of the spectrum between violet and red, as happens in a soft dawn or sunset or in moderate electric light, must be reduced considerably so that the radiations beyond these two bands can emerge. Exhaustive trials with various kinds of translucent materials and coatings produced five basic colored filters that suppress different segments of the spectrum. A table showing the differences in these spectrums and an illustration of their effects prepared by S. A. Silbey, of the Physics Department at Princeton University, appears in Appendix A.

For my observations, I mount the filters in two ways: over the eyes or over the light source. For the eyes, the filter material is set in goggles designed to fit snugly against the face from temple to temple. The goggles, of course, are portable and can be used to observe energy fields in outdoor settings and lecture auditoriums. In a room, a light bulb, preferably fluorescent because its light simulates the glow of the aura and makes it more visible, can be encased in a filter. All other sources of light are turned out or curtained so that only the filtered rays illuminate the subject.

To look at the energy field of very bright masses, such as a wheat field on a brilliant sunny day, it helps to block out the energy source itself — in this case, the wheat — completely. This can be done by using something like a dark-colored, mat-finished cloth mounted on cardboard. Indoors, I view the subject against either a very light background or a very dark background. The best background for such observation is white, sky blue, or midnight blue that is uniform in both color and texture. For example, with cobalt blue filter, which transmits purple light, the entire aura of a person's body will be visible against a pale backdrop.

Ordinarily, though, no filtering is needed to see the energy field when illumination is controlled. Try this experiment. Choose a room where the light is soft and diffused and the walls are white or pale blue. If they are no other color, a white sheet works well as background. Sit, facing the wall with the light behind you. Raise your hands with the fingers slightly spread and hold them steady with either the palms or the backs toward you about a half-inch apart. Relax your body and breath regularly and deeply. If you catch your breath, bite your lips, or experience other such expressions of tension when concentrating, take a minute or two to try to release this holding pattern.

Now, direct your gaze to the fingers but your attention to the space around the tips. Use your peripheral vision the way one would when looking for something in the dark. You will begin to see a light blue mist in a layer about a quarter of an inch deep. This envelope will project slowly from each hand until the layers touch and then penetrate each other. Next, draw your hands apart slowly. They will leave illuminated pathways the size of the fingers. When the hands are brought together and separated again several times, the whole aura down to the wrist will become noticeable. If you give your attention to tactile sensations, the mist will feel elastic and malleable, like taffy, when the hands are being separated, and like a cotton ball when they are being brought together. In a normal state, most people's auras pulsate 15 to 25 times a minute. But try listening to some stirring music, and watch what happens to the rate of your energy field.

To trace the rhythm and shape of the pulsations' wavelengths, I generally use a kymograph. This device is a rotating drum equipped with a clock mechanism and a paper tape. I hold the kymograph pen in my right hand, which I steady with the left. As I observe the energy field I am investigating, I make a curve on the paper corresponding with its pulsatory movement. I draw the pen upward as the field expands, downward as it contracts, and across as it pauses.

I am very much aware of the variations that a human operator can introduce into experimental findings. But, as I noted, equipment has not yet been designed that can record energy fields independently. Kirlian photography, which chapter 7 will describe briefly, may hold promise if the process can be converted to registering movement, like a motion picture. However, my recordings over more than twenty years have proven relatively consistent. They do make it possible to analyze mathematically. The sections that follow include some of my results.

Energy Fields in Vegetation

The energy of every entity is a beautiful thing to watch. It varies in pulsatory rhythm, layering, depth of layers, play of colors, and other characteristics. The variations depend on the nature of the subject, its condition, its age, its physical and psychological surroundings, its geographic location, the season of the year, and the weather, to name only the salient factors that effect its reciprocal cycle. The energy emanations symphonize in a pyrotechnic of multihued waves, beams, streamers, and fireballs.

The field of plants generally has two layers interacting around the surface. The inner layer, immediately around the leaves and branches, is 1/8 to 1/6 of an inch wide and has an overall light blue or gray color. The layer is structured and can be easily seen. The other layer is much lighter, with an extension of 1/2 to 1 inch. It makes various multicolored, radial movements. Fireballs also shoot into space from the outer layer of the field.

The colors of the field vary greatly, depending on the species and whether the plant is flowering. Flowering plants have a much more extended field, slower pulsation, and a greater luminosity around the flowers. The chrysanthemum, for instance, has a beautiful sky blue inner layer over the flower itself, which is about 1/2 inch wide. In the outer layer, steaming gold rays extend 3 to 4 inches away from the plant. Cactuses display a concentrated, deep blue inner layer and a radiant outer layer streaming several feet from the plant. Orchids have a very dark, narrow inner layer. The outer one is made up of beams and rays that resemble searchlights.

The energy field of most plants pulsates into the surrounding air for 2 to 4 seconds during phase I (expansion) of the energy cycle. The movement reverses for phase II (contraction), and the energy in the surrounding air streams into the plant. Including the rest period, the pulsatory cycles of plants range from 10 to 30 per minute. I believe that this energy exchange plays an important part in the process of photosynthesis.

Observation of energy fields of leaves has shown that the plant's orientation to geographic cardinal points influences the number of pulsations that each leaf emits. For example, in a white snowball plant, the leaves pointing north pulsate about 32 times a minute, but only 28 times a minute when pointed in the other three cardinal directions. Changing the plant's position disturbs this pattern, as the de la Warrs discovered. Following their work, I positioned plants in different directions. I found that the plant will orient itself toward the geographic cardinal points again by changing the pulsatory rate of its leaves to reflect the new directions to exchange energy with the atmosphere commensurate with its needs.

I can see patterns in the field of trees that are harder to pin down in other plants. The tree as a whole produces a pulsatory movement upward from the roots to the leaves. Hardwood varieties pulsate from 12 to 14 times a minute, while evergreens show a rate of 18 to 22. Evergreens have a strong, smoky blue inner field with radial tufts. Hardwoods emit light blue radiation in the first layer and generate radial movements in the outer field that differ among the species.

Flowering trees have a slower rhythm. Each beat is two or three times longer and more sustained than nonflowering trees. And there is an extreme brilliance around the flowering part of the tree. Dead trees, in sharp contrast, have a dull, gray field and a much slower pulsatory rhythm than live ones.

In large wooded areas, the field of each tree merges with its companions' and with the forest's. The inner layers, measuring 3 or 4 feet around each adult tree, flow into an outer layer of radiation which combines with those of other trees and shoots hundreds of feet skyward. The reverse movement, bringing energy from the surrounding atmosphere into the growth, is much more striking in stands of wood than in single trees or plants. These observations led me very early to believe that the oxygen-carbon dioxide exchange is only a fraction of the purifying process that the life force of the vegetable kingdom carries out for the animal world.

Energy Fields of Crystals

All crystals I have tested, whatever their structure and composition, resemble organic matter in the basic characteristics of their energy fields. Pulsation from the crystal's body flow to the periphery and into the surrounding air, and streams of movement enter the crystal from the atmosphere. The energy envelope around the crystal also has two layers, as in plants. The inner layer is about 1/8 inch wide, and the outer one measures about 1/3 inch and is marked by striated shapes. The color variations are as extensive as in human beings, though the field in crystals is not so well structured as are those of animals, trees, and other plants. Here are some examples of the colors and movements:

Crystal	Inner field	Outer field
Quarz	Blue-gray	Yellow; radial movement
Fluorescent quartz	Green	Yellow; streaming
Calcite	Yellow	Yellow, brown, red; streaming, radial
Opal	Blue-green	Mauve; circular

In a series of experiments conducted with some colleagues, we exposed quartz crystals to modulated sound produced by an oscillator. The stimulus proved to be very intense. In certain ranges, the field of the crystals doubled its pulsatory rate and increased its brilliance significantly. Other ranges made the field contract and the pulsations lag.

A crystal's orientation to the geographic cardinal points has as definite an effect on its field as has a plant's. In fact, the shifts are more marked. However, crystals react to the cardinal orientation differently than plants, where the strongest pulsations occur to the north, as indicated earlier. When the leading edge of a piece of quartz points to the south, the pulsatory rate is about 9 a minute. It decreases to 6 a minute to the west and to the north. But it jumps to 14 when the edge points east. The majority of crystals show similar swings as the main edge is pointed in different directions. Moreover, changes occur as well in the formation and coloration of the field's two layers.

Geographical location also effects the pulsatory rates of crystals. On a 16-day cruise fpom New York to Curacao, I took along samples of tourmaline, quartz, sulphur, hematite, and obsidian. For my observations I arranged them so they faced in the same direction, when we studied them, throughout the trip. The ship sailed from a latitude of almost 41 degrees (New York) to 8 degrees, somewhat southward of Curacao. Observing the five crystals four times a day, I found that their pulsation per minute increased steadily to latitude 22 degrees, held this level of excitation to 20 degrees, and then decreased their rates as we proceeded southward. Findings such as these have convinced me that scientific inquiry will be able to define the interpenetration of atmospheric and individuated energy in concrete terms. A future Dobereiner may be able to uncover a periodic law of universal exchange.

Energy Fields Over Topographical Masses

The play of big natural forces have a majesty of scale that both confirms and expands what other energy entities reveal concerning the field phenomena. I began to learn this on a seaside vacation in summer, while I was still in training with Wilhelm Reich. I set out to explore energy pulsations in the atmosphere, over the earth, and in the water. Later years provided other observation stations, such as prairies, mountain peaks and sides, canyons, rivers, and temporary seats from inside an airplane. But none of these combine the perspectives on the three elements of air, land and water in such breadth as does the seashore.

My longest in-depth study of large-scale field phenomena took place in 1968-70, and covered two years of sequential observation followed by analysis of the findings. The place was the New Jersey coast at North latitude 40 degrees 20 minutes. The focuses of the study were the energy fields above the horizon line above the ocean, over the sand beaches, and within the water mass of the ocean. My tools included a series of color filters ranging from blue-green to violet to screen out the various segments of the light wavelength that obscure the visibility of the energy fields at different times of the day and under different weather conditions. In bright sunlight, especially when looking at pulsations over the horizon or from the beaches, I also used dark-toned strips in several widths and depths to block the source of energy from vision. These sources included the water and horizon line or the sand. I recorded my observations on paper rolls on a kymograph. Here is some of what I saw:

Pulsations of the Air Field

The area where the sky meets the sea shows constant pulsatory movement. A misty, blue-grey illumination emerges from the water, swells rapidly, and extends toward the sky. Three zones form successively as the envelope surges upward, as illustrated in Figures 2 and 3. The zones differ in consistency, color, speed of formation, and direction of movement.

Zone A extends 5 to 10 degrees from the horizon line, but is in fact deeper, since it incorporates the horizon, too, which I blanked out with a strip. Its light, blue-gray color varies in intensity with the amplitude of the pulsation, atmospheric conditions, and time of day. On a clear day, the intensity is very brilliant around noon but dulls after sunset or when the sky is overcast with gray cloud cover. The outer edge of the zone usually is fairly uniform at the beginning of the pulsatory movement and becomes fringed or irregular as

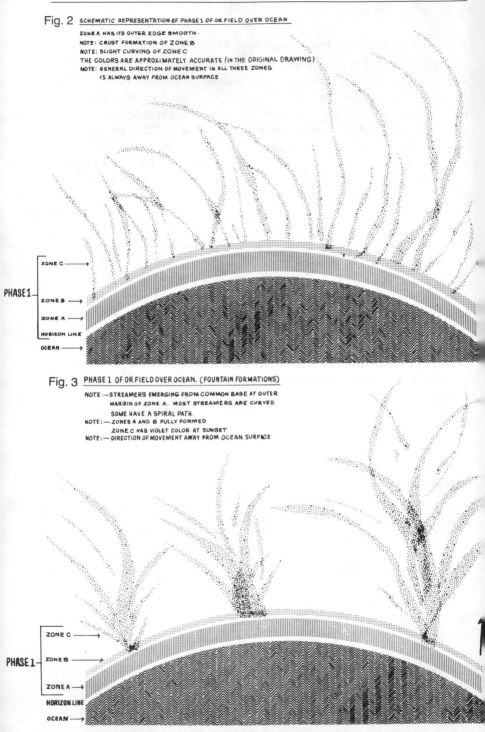

Fig. 2 SCHEMATIC REPRESENTATION OF PHASE 1 OF OR FIELD OVER OCEAN

ZONE A HAS ITS OUTER EDGE SMOOTH.
NOTE: CRUST FORMATION OF ZONE B
NOTE: SLIGHT CURVING OF ZONE C
THE COLORS ARE APPROXIMATELY ACCURATE (IN THE ORIGINAL DRAWING)
NOTE: GENERAL DIRECTION OF MOVEMENT IN ALL THREE ZONES
        IS ALWAYS AWAY FROM OCEAN SURFACE

ZONE C
PHASE 1
ZONE B
ZONE A
HORIZON LINE
OCEAN

Fig. 3 PHASE 1 OF OR FIELD OVER OCEAN. (FOUNTAIN FORMATIONS)

NOTE :— STREAMERS EMERGING FROM COMMON BASE AT OUTER
          MARGIN OF ZONE A. MOST STREAMERS ARE CURVED
          SOME HAVE A SPIRAL PATH.
NOTE :— ZONES A AND B FULLY FORMED
          ZONE C HAS VIOLET COLOR AT SUNSET
NOTE :— DIRECTION OF MOVEMENT AWAY FROM OCEAN SURFACE

ZONE C
PHASE 1
ZONE B
ZONE A
HORIZON LINE
OCEAN

it amplifies. When fully developed, it looks like a sharply peaked mountain range. The consistency of the movement is soft to the eye, cloudlike, and more or less homogenous. On first view, it appears to flow perpendicular to the horizon line and away from it. Closer observation shows that the movement is curved, with a concavity usually toward the west or northwest. A possible reason for this appears in Appendix B. Zone A takes from 1/2 to 1 second to form.

Zone B rises immediately above Zone A and occupies 3 to 5 degrees of space. Its inner margin next to the fringed edge of A, forms tonguelike projections. Its outer perimeter fuses with Zone C. B's outer edges are fringed, too, and its color varies. On clear days, it has a brownish shade, not brilliant, and under all conditions it remains duller than A. Its texture seems coarse, resembling an irregular honeycomb. This layer appears to be formed by condensation, and has the look of a sort of energy crust. Its speed of formation, like Zone A's, is 1/2 to 1 second.

Zone C is composed of luminous streamers surging skyward from the irregular interface with Zone B to a height of 40 to 50 degrees, where it merges into and becomes indistinguishable from the energy movement of the atmosphere above it. The streamers are luminous light blue. Toward sunset, they take the shape of fountains emerging from the ocean surface, as Figure 3 illustrates. Zone C's overall outline is slightly concave, with the center of the curve at the north or northwest in the Northern Hemisphere, where the energy field as a whole moves clockwise from west to east. I have not investigated these field phenomena below the equator.

As with other energetic entities, the energy pulsation surges skyward, in this case through the first two zones to amplify Zone C. This three-level, outward pulsation in the air mass in the expansion phase of the reciprocal energy cycle is followed by the reverse movement of the concentration phase. Energy now streams toward the ocean and all three zones fade out. A rain of vertical or oblique streamers shoots out of the vault of the sky, giving the impression of continuous movement. Various shapes appear. Jets crossing each other's path seem to lean together like bundles of wheat, as shown in Figure 4. Or a single streamer will split into two or three branches. When this happens, the intersection is usually visible at a height of 10 to 40 degrees above the horizon line.

As in all energy entities I have observed, a rest period succeeds the contraction period of the reciprocal energy cycle, when there are no perceptible outward pulsations, downward streamers, or other discharges.

In quantitative terms, the frequency of the pulsations in the expansionary phase is influenced by time of day, atmospheric conditions, and seasonal

Fig. 4

PHASE II (EAST, WEST)

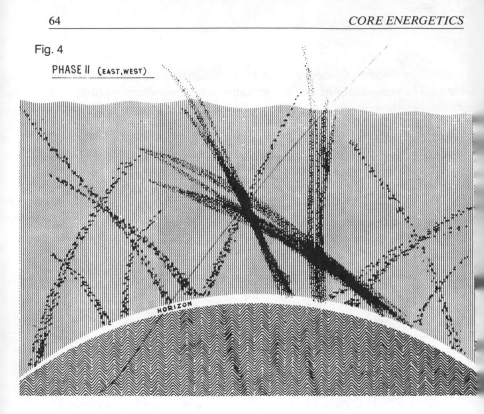

GRAPH I

Fig. 5

RELATIONSHIP OF PULSATIONS —

• • • • P *OVER OCEAN*
━ ━ P *OVER SAND BEACH*
━━ P *WITHIN WATER MASS (SEA WAVES)*

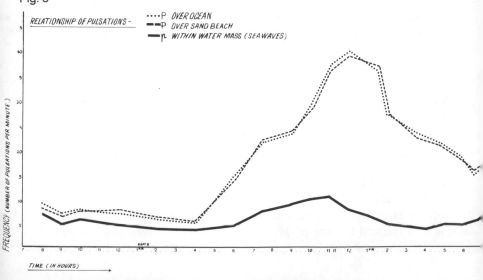

FREQUENCY (NUMBER OF PULSATIONS PER MINUTE)

TIME (IN HOURS) →

changes. Evidence also exists of other dynamic forces at work that have not yet been defined. In general, the pulsatory rate on a clear day increases until about noontime and falls off gradually thereafter, as Figure 5 indicates. On low-energy days, the frequency level diminishes, and specific changes occur as well with the rotation of the seasons. For example, it is higher in summer and falls off during winter.

Field Activity Over Land and Water

For observations of the energy field over the beach, as I have said, I blanked out the same itself with a dark-colored strip to protect my eyes from the glare on brilliantly sunny days. My sightings were taken at close ranges, from 25 to 50 feet. My line of vision was a little above the plane of the beach. The patterns visible in the field above the ocean can be seen from this vantage point as well. The movement of energy again appears in three zones and pulsates in the three phases described for the air. The frequency of pulsations over the land is virtually identical to the rate recorded for the air and is shown in Figure 5.

The pulsation within the body of the ocean is quite different, as would be expected. The water mass captures the freemoving energy from the atmosphere, slows it down, and molds it in the flows, currents, and eddies that shape the waves. I observed the waves across a span of shoreline for their frequency (number per second), velocity, periodicity, amplitude, and width. I tracked the direction of the wind as well. I did not, however, investigate one factor that should be monitored: the comparative force of discharge of the energy captured within each wave upon the beach, measured in units of sound.

On a clear day, the frequency of the movement of average waves rises from sunrise to noon and declines in the afternoon and evening, as the solid line in Figure 5 traces. This is a fairly constant picture when there are no major changes. The rate rises slightly around 10 p.m., and then falls again until predawn. It then begins the ascent that will quicken after the sun comes up until the noontime peak.

The integration of the three pulsatory fields is strikingly displayed in Figure 5. A fuller explanation of the integration of the three fields will be found in Appendix B.

Effects of Mass Energy Fields

People around the world are known to be sensitive to weather. They become excited when it is bright and clear, feel apathetic when it is dull, and sense anxiety or irritation when a storm is brewing. Spring cheers up almost everyone. What underlies these responses is a marked similarity between the behavior of the earth's energy field and the aura of the human organism. When the earth's envelope is intense and pulsating rapidly, the human field is more vivid and active. When the atmosphere is heavy, both fields decelerate and dim. In the springtime, the auras of people in the streets are collectively more brilliant than at any other time of year.

Field phenomena also mold the relationship between people, as several later chapters will detail. Living organisms are resonating systems that respond to each other's vibrations. The rhythmic patterns of a person will affect other people in his or her proximity. Some people can pick up the waves that others emit with very clear definition. There is, of course, a widespread conscious ability to recognize when one is "On the same wavelength" as another.

The interpenetration of fields explains as well the influence — beneficent or baneful — that people can have on other life forms. Here is an experiment that I made with plants.

One day, a patient entered, depressed and complaining, with a whine in her voice. She sat next to a flowering white chrysanthemum plant, which had the typical energy field of its species, which I described earlier: an inner sky blue color of beautiful brilliance, with gold streams on the outer layer. It pulsated 14 to 16 per minute.

As the patient sat there, the pulsations, to my surprise, plunged to two or three minute. The brilliance of the field disappeared, and a slight gray emanation seeped into the radically reduced pulsation. I mentioned this to the suffering woman, and told her that even the plants cry when she whines.

Since this experience, I have made it a point to keep plants in various parts of the office. In sessions where much anger and other powerful negative emotions are expressed, the field of the plant placed next to the person's head will shrink. It will stay contracted until the person has left, when it will open and pulsate at its normal rate. But if the plant stays for three or four hours close to several people who are working out their pain, one after another, the lower leaves begin to wither and turn yellow. Within a day or two, the plant dies. Control plants in the waiting room remain healthy.

To pin down the exact processes that a plant undergoes when exposed to negative emotion, I carried out a two-part experiment with chrysanthemums. The first was a concentrated observation of the field of a healthy one. I recorded the pulsatory movement of its energy emanations on a kymograph stripchart. Dr. Silbey analyzed my findings. His report is quoted exactly in Appendix C, both to show how a physicist interprets my results and to point out some limitations of my research design.

Shortly after receiving Dr. Silbey's report, which he completed in February 1970, I ran the second part of my experiment, using a vigorous chrysanthemum plant whose field was pulsating 25 times a minute in the brilliant colors described earlier. I placed the plant two feet from the head of a bed that people sometimes lie on during their sessions. A man in my care began to speak one day about something that had happened to him that was causing him a lot of pain. While he was talking, I watched his energy field, particularly over his head. Then I saw radial beams from his head directed toward the chrysanthemum. They looked like porcupine quills invading the field of the plant as they penetrated the outer layer. The plant then decreased its pulsations, its outer layer disappeared, and its inner layer darkened. The space between the man's head and the plant turned dark blue. As he started to scream with agony, some of the radial streamers split like the forking of lightning in a storm. Though they seemed to be destructive impulses being given explosive expression, they were beautiful to see, for no energy field in nature, even when depressed or distorted, forfeits its essential and deeply moving splendor.

Evidence of auras and energy systems in humans is not limited to visual observation. In addition to Kirlian photography, experiments by my colleagues and me during 1969-77 recorded energy fields around the human body using sensitive photomultipliers and video processing techniques. The intensity of the signals from human beings recorded by the photomultipliers can be correlated with certain physical and psychological states. In addition, color video displays of subjects indicate a thin pulsating field surrounding the body.

A photomultiplier is a device which responds to extremely small quantities of light by producing a measurable electrical charge. Controlling for numerous factors, we were able to record light emanations from passive individuals. The greatest energy was recorded from people with strong energy-filled bodies. Several subjects could increase the signal of their fields at will. Increased energy output also was recorded from people who were asked to concentrate their energy into their arm, as if to strike a blow. Interestingly, fields faded when people were in an agitated mental state. In some cases, however, the signals remained briefly after subjects left the dark room where the experiments were conducted.

These energy fields can serve as precise diagnostic tools for physical and emotional disturbances, as later chapters will describe. The human aura will be examined in detail in the next chapter. The exchange of energy between individual entities of all kinds and their environment clearly demonstrates the universality of the reciprocal energy principle. Applications of these findings can have implications for human knowledge and welfare beyond their use in therapeutic settings.

Chapter 7
THE PHENOMENON OF THE AURA

One of humankind's oldest desires is to soar free of earthbound matter into space, both the outer space of the sky and the inner space of the "non-material" self. The yearning for airborne travel has populated cultural traditions since prehistory with human and divine personages who are able to fly. The man Daedalus, from Minoan lore, is known to us less for his legendary lifetime of magnificent architecture and sculpture than for a single device he designed: wings for himself and his son, Icarus. The sungod Ra, who was salient in the Egyptian pantheon by the early fourth millennium B. C., is just a prototype of the winged supernatural beings who emerged in the world's high civilizations.

The exploration of inner space has absorbed Eastern peoples much longer and more productively than Western, as Part II discussed. In the West, the evolution of the sciences with their emphasis on demonstrable proof progressively relegated to mystics and occultists the very idea of inner space, our movements in it, and our potential for entering outside space through it. Not until our own century did the technical disciplines turn serious research efforts to these phenomena. Thus, while the investigations are expanding — Chapter 5 reviews some of them — the reports we have that attempt to be concrete come mainly from observers whose work cannot be objectively replicated, such as C. W. Leadbeater, writing about Freemasonry, and nontechnical practitioners like the medium Eileen Garrett and the healer Edgar Cayce.

But the correspondence between inner and outer space is a physical reality, due to the principle of reciprocity, the law governing the movement of internal and external energy within all entities. This pulsatory phenomenon has immensely important implications for the whole direction of each human life, as Chapter 9 will begin to explore. The pages to follow shortly will examine its expression in the human energy field, the aura, where its operation provides essential diagnostic information and invaluable guidance in the therapeutic process.

The aura, to recapitulate, both permeates the solid body and draws external energy into the whole organism. The basic life force composing the person's physical body, aura, and ingested energy is the same substance. These differ only in their vibratory frequencies and cohesive forms. Because the aura's pulsatory rate is immensely quicker than the body's, it telegraphs precisely what is happening within the person on all functional planes: the physiological, the emotional, the mental, and the spiritual. How it does so will be reviewed following the next section. What it telegraphs can be summed up in this way: The energy movements in phase I, the assertive period of the cycle, and phase II, the receptive, partake of each other completely. Therefore, the state of functioning in one phase determines the state of functioning in the other. A localized alteration of the reciprocal energy exchange will reverberate throughout and beyond the organism.

To my knowledge, energy fields provide the clearest demonstration at present of the reciprocal energy movement. However, the conclusions just stated can be drawn with equal firmness from observation of solid physical bodies. For while biophysics and other technical disciplines are too new to have uncovered the exact nature of the universal life force, a good deal of documentation by the established sciences points to the universality of the principle of reciprocity. Before turning to the aura itself, then, let me set out a few of these findings.

The Principle of Reciprocity in Biological Organisms

The continuum of scientific inquiry today ranges in focus from the subatomic to the supergalactic. Each segment of the continuum lends confirmation to the generalization that all entities exhibit a pulsatory rhythm, emitting internal substance on one beat, so to speak, and taking in external substance on the next. At the microcosmic level, Einstein's formulation of the energymatter equation laid a theoretical foundation for the physics of this movement. Atomic technology proved his proposition with evidence that mass and energy are interconvertible.

In the animal kingdom, the forces at work within each body also range from the microcosmic to the macrocosmic. Beginning with small units, we can see the principle of reciprocity at work in Brownian movement, the vibration of microscopic particles in gaseous or liquid solution. Protoplasm, conventionally considered to mark the borderline between living and nonliving entities, contains pulsatory vacuoles whose rhythmic periodicity has been studied closely by Alain Rheinberg and Jean Gata. They point out that each of these tiny bodies is contained in a membrane that contracts and expands "according to a rhythm that depends on the environmental conditions and the state of the cell."

In larger aggregates, the pulsations of cells combine to form reciprocal movements in tissues, which in turn are integrated in to the organs and systems to form rhythmical reciprocal patterns. All these patterns symphonize in a functional whole that vibrates and pulsates as a unity. This natural harmony is assured at the organism's inception. Life, to again use the word's conventional meaning, starts as a single cell that burgeons through countless divisions and permutations into a mature entity. But the organism retains the essential activity of the single cell, the overall pulsatory pattern. This movement is differentiated and modified along with the development of the cells to manifest itself in the different activities of the single-celled processes, tissues, organs, and systems of the body.

Among the single-celled processes, that of the cilia, which line the respiratory tract of mammals, waves back and forth like a wheat field blown by the wind. The combined movement works foreign particles upward and outward, away from the lungs. J. L. Cloudsley-Thompson notes, "Their beat is often continuous thoughout the life of the animal, and the stimulus for this arises endogenously in the protoplasm of the cell . . ." This action may be under neural control, but the movement is regarded as being independent of nerve impulses.

Nerve tissue shows an inherent three-phase periodicity in conducting nerve impulses. The passage of an impulse along a nerve depolarizes the membrane and produces a refractory period during which no other message can pass through it. After a short rest, the membrane is polarized spontaneously to allow for another transmission. The rhythmic firing of cerebrospinal nerve cells maintains muscle tone and therefore body posture. The incredible complementarity of parasympathetic and sympathetic activity directs the internal and the collective movements of the vital organs. Reich attributed the functions of pleasure and anxiety, or expansion and contraction, to these respective divisions of the autonomic nervous system.

The principle of reciprocity operates visibly in biological organisms from the standpoint of their receptivity to cosmic phenomena in their environment. Chapter 6 discussed the responsiveness of vegetation to such factors as orientation to compass points. But again, these interchanges have long been documented from general physiological evidence. The influence of massive natural forces on plants and animals has probably drawn more continuous study over the ages than any other aspect of biological existence.

The transition of primitive social groups from hunting and gathering to agriculture and husbandry depended on some understanding of these forces. Weather changes, mentioned in the last chapter for their effects on moods, were a matter of basic survival until modern times, as they can be still. The bearing of not only the seasons but the climate on fertility in plants emerged over the centuries as farmer-settlers followed conquerors in the wars for empire. By the eighteenth century in the West, incidentally, the knowledge of climate as a determinant in biological life had led to theories about its role in social institutions. Montesquieu's *Esprit des Lois*, for example, analyzed the part that climate played in shaping the differing laws and forms of government adopted by various societies at various times.

The coincidence of the menstrual and lunar cycles was spotted by many peoples long before they grasped the connection between copulation and procreation. But latitude affects the menstrual period as well. The period occurs ordinarily about twice a year among the women of Tierra del Fuego and four times a year among Eskimo women. The onset of puberty is markedly earlier in the tropical zones than in the temperate.

Finally, a plethora of vital functions attests to the impress of the diurnal cycle on the human biological clock. Cultures with control over their food distribution have generally developed a pattern of three meals a day, but in this too, geography influences the timing: the presundown high tea of British tradition precedes the Hispanic dinnertime by some five hours. Humans the world over sleep during night of their particular region. During the day hours, their activism follows the same periodic rises and falls as the earth's field described in Chapter 6. The impact of jet lag has been pinned down thoroughly enough to bring about regulations on the work periods of long-distance flight crews: a displacement of five hours or more from a person's accustomed solar time has been shown to be critical. The exceptional adaptability of the human organism allows it to accept significant changes in the number and timing of meals, sleep schedule, longitude and latitude, and other relationships to global patterns. The fact remains that the balance of our very physiological well being depends intimately not only on its innate condition but also on all the external reality surrounding it, up to and including the forces of the macrocosm.

All these factors are reflected strikingly in the higher vibratory frequencies of humans, the aura. The energy field of the person, like that of every other entity, exhibits the two active phases of movement characteristic of the reciprocal energy cycle throughout nature. But much subtler variations exist within the basic pattern than can be found in any other species. The phases arise respectively from the assertive operation of the person's core and from its receptive operation. The receptive movement passes mainly through energy funnels, which are distributed around the perimeter of the physical frame. While the two directions of flow make it convenient to discuss the intake functions separately from the outbound pulsation in the aura, it is important to keep in mind that the energy composing both kinds of formation is the stuff of all things, the universal life force.

Phase I: The Expression of Inner Energy

The history of a person's whole life as well as the current condition of the organism can be observed in the aura. It can indicate, for instance, a pain as systemic and enduring as a trauma of rejection in infancy, or as localized and transistory as a tooth extraction. An affront of any kind, whether a physical illness or a failed expectation, disrupts the aura in patterns that will be described in later pages. One configuration of blockage in the pelvis, for example, typifies a high risk of cardiovascular disease, a category of pathology to be explored in Chapter 18. For this reason, I closely observe the aura of people with whom I work. I use the information it provides to diagnose the illness, locate the skeletomuscular and characterological blocks that need to be dissolved, and guide the person toward internal integration.

More than this: the aura communicates, sometimes in considerable detail, the nature of the person's unique gifts, the special thrust of the core's creativity in this individual's life, which leads the therapeutic work into helping him or her integrate with the outside world. The reason it can do this, as I said in Chapter 2, is that the core consists of the nuclei of all the energy elements in the organism, from the subcellular components to the tissues, organs, and systems. The core therefore makes up the aura, too. In fact, as human dysfunctions are defined by the distortions of core energy showing at various locations in the energy field, so the person's horizon of gifts is defined by the exceptional charateristics of the aura when functioning is restored. The aura discloses the pattern of intensified luminosity and color, deepened layering, heightened pulsatory frequency, expanded responsiveness to outside forces, and other indicators.

The aura of a healthy person shows as a three layer, cloudlike envelope surrounding end extending outward from the body. Its general condition relates to the organism's overall metabolism of energy, so that its attributes vary with such things as production of heat, level of activity, emotional exitement, and rate and quality of breathing. The word itself comes from the Greek *aúra*, meaning breeze. The person appears to swim in it, as in a fluid sea tinged rhythmically with brilliant colors that constantly change hues, shimmer, and vibrate. For to be alive is to be colorful and vibrant.

The auric envelope viewed as a whole is blue-gray to sky blue, and it illuminates the periphery of the body in the way the rays of the rising sun light up the profile of dark mountains. In phase I of its pulsation, it swells for one or two seconds away from the body to a distance of two to four feet, where it loses its distinctness under ordinary circumstances and merges with the surrounding atmosphere. At full breadth and seen from the front, it has a nearly perfect oval shape with fringed edges, a form it retains about 1/4 second. Then, in phase II, it abates rapidly — in 1/8 to 1/5 second — and disappears completely. The rest period, phase III of the cycle, lasts one to three seconds. The expansion-contraction process then begins again, and in the average waking person, occurs 15 to 25 times a minute.

While this frequency is independent of any other known bodily rhythms, such as respiration and heart beat, it correlates very directly with the degree of excitation in the organism. During sleep, the rate of pulsation slows down, the width diminishes, and the color is weaker. The rate generally reaches its peak about noon, presumably because bodily activity is also at its peak at the time. It is less in the early morning soon after awakening, and falls off again in the evening when the organism is exhausted.

Excitement enhances the aura in all aspects, enriches the color, broadens the extension, accelerates the pulsations. For example, when a person in treatment strikes a couch repeatedly with a feeling of anger, the rate may increase to 40 per minute. Kicking the couch rhythmically will increase the frequency if this is done as an expression of feeling. Kicking as an exercise, without feeling, has no effect on the rate. When the body goes into vibration as a result of deeper breathing and strong emotion, the rate rises markedly to as high as 45 to 50. At the same time, the width of the field extends farther and the color brightens. The same vivid changes occur in a group where there is strong communication: the people's auras reach more than 50 pulsations a minute and move outward toward the walls and ceiling of the room they are in. Then a fantastic thing happens, which Chapter 21 will describe in some detail. Briefly, the heightened movement among the individuals forms a magnificent new energy mass shaped like an umbrella over and around them. A new conciousness develops that is more than the sum of the individual consciousnesses and that spirals into and through the contributors as well, again because energy flows undivided. This new formation can be palpated between the hands of someone standing in its midst.

In phase I, the aura reaches its maximum luminosity, which makes the layers and their complex movements easier to see. The luminescent activity of the energy, like its reciprocal exchange, is also a law of nature perceivable in solid physical bodies. Several groups of creatures are able to emit light as a result of their inner movements and biological processes. These include unicellular structures like bacteria and fungi as well as multicellular animals like flagellates, sponges, fish and fireflies. In higher organisms, it is known that vital functions such as the mitosis of cells, oxidation, and other metabolic activities are accompanied by luminescence. The glow of the aura is therefore a normal expression of the organism's life processes.

Interestingly, the layering of the energy field traces a developmental course in the human being, as do the life processes themselves. The aura of a baby is a uniform and unstructured light blue. Layers begin to take definition between the ages of 2 and 3, and are well-differentiated by puberty.

In the mature organism, the energy field as a whole exhibits the general charcteristics already described. The three layers are schematized, though disproportionately in Figures 6 and 7. The innermost laycr is the hardest to discern because it is quite transparent and looks like an empty blue-black space at any distance farther than two or three feet. From this close, and viewed against a dull, black or midnight-blue background, the observer can see it as a band about 1/5 inch deep at most whose true color is on the borderline between ultraviolet and violet on the spectrum.

The second, or intermediate, layer is complex and difficult to describe as it is made up of multiple shapes and forms. It starts clearly defined at the outer boundary of the inner layer and extends three to four inches. It is bright blue-gray except the head, where a vivid yellow or white corona permeates the layer. We might assume that this is what some contemporaries saw as a halo or crown on powerfully alive people like Buddha and Jesus. But everyone has this crown, though its intensity, size, and other qualities vary according to the condition of the organism.

The intermediate layer has three primary patterns of movements. First, a wavelike form fills the whole layer to its extremes homogeneously, like water on blotting paper. Second, a corpuscular activity appears rather like the Brownian movement of smoke particles under a microscope. Third, white or yellow rays commencing at the inner border of the intermediate layer travel its whole width and extend several feet away from the body into space, almost reaching the walls of a room. In spite of these radial projections, the intermediate layer is dominated in the trunk and extremities by the wavelike movement, which flows distinctly along the surface of the body. Its overall appearance is that of a blue, shimmering liquid extremely rarefied but brilliant. It gives the impression of a stream of fireflies extinguishing their glow at rapid intervals and swarming simultaneously in the same direction.

The ray forms dominate around the head, where they create a fringe effect. Their pattern and outline change with every new pulsation of the organism, like the streamers of the aurora borealis firing toward the sky. Usually the rays move perpendicular to the surface of the body.

The outermost layer is ordinarily 6 to 8 inches wide inside a room, but in an open space, it extends several dozen feet away. Near the seashore, in fact, I have seen it expand to as much as 100 feet. It has an indefinite inner body that begins at the outer bounderies of the middle layer. Its consistency is very thin, almost transparent. It has a delicate sky blue color, shot through with the white or yellow rays traversing it from the middle layer. The salient movement of the third layer is spiral or vortical. It appears as though the particulate or Brownian-like shimmering in the second stratum, finding greater space, expands in all directions outward from the body as compressed gas expands when the volume of its container is enlarged. As mentioned earlier, the outer boundaries diffuse so that the margin of this layer is lost in the surrounding air.

As far as I can see, the three layers move simultaneously, and the various directions of flow combine in two complicated but integrated basic patterns. Facing a person gives a clear view of the first, which looks like a figure 8. Observed from the front the field moves from the ground up the insides of the legs and thighs, and branches at the solar plexus to stream up the sides of the trunk and the outer edges of the hands and the arms. The two main streams rejoin at the root of the neck and cross over to travel along the opposite sides of the head. This is the first segment of the longitudinal flow seen from the front. The second segment consists in a movement down the chest and belly that, again, divides at the solar plexus to descend the hips and the outsides of the legs toward the ground.

The upward and downward flows of energy alternate within each half of the field, above and below the solar plexus. The two directions of movement occur simultaneously in the two halves like the shifts in the upper and lower solid body when a person walks. Effectively, then, the vital force of the organism sweeps in two circuits, which fuse at the midline of the torso to create a figure 8. This formation and movements that underlie it also appear in the aura when it is viewed from the back, and from both perspectives, the two sections of the 8 are about equal in size and vigor in the normal person.

Looking at the field in profile, as in Figure 7, sheds light on the figure 8 shape. From the side view, the energy is seen to pulsate outward like a fountain from the solar plexus, the site of many vital organs. I therefore assume that the basic longitudinal flow rises within the center of the body's cylinder — the torso — probably from the heart, lungs, liver, intestines, spine, and other essential structures, and swirls through them and out of the body into the air. The spiral or vortical pattern seen in the third layer of the field apparently takes its origin from the helical form and spontaneously twisting movements of these parts. The overall shape of the aura in profile is ovoid or like a kidney bean.

The second fundamental formation is visible both in profile and from front and back: a perpendicular pulsation, outward from the body cylinder, also apparently arising in the internal structures but spiraling across the diameter of the organism rather than up and down its length. Energy sweeps out and in, tracing sometimes like a pendulum swing, in two phases of the reciprocal cycle, which correspond with the capacity of the physical torso to expand and contract. The rays from the inner margin of layer 2 and through layer 3 make up a third prominent shape of movement visible in the energy field. Many subsidiary designs appear as well, such as circuits around the limbs and emissions adjacent to major physiological structures, like the heart, the spine, and the large nerve plexuses. The latter formations provide grounds for the assumption that the internal structures are their place of origin.

The physical motions of the body can be reduced to the two summative patterns exhibited in the aura, the longitudinal figure 8 and the perpendicular pendulum swing. Applying force against the supporting base of the cylinder translates into walking or running. A swallow requires both forms of movement. Breathing and digesting depend mainly on the expansion-contraction patterns. Lowen's book *The Physical Dynamics of Character Structure* develops this subject in detail.

The emotions, the specific energetic activities that propel us to unify with or reject external reality, are obviously expressions of the expansion-contraction pulsation. But the figure 8 formation also interrelates with them. The upper torso contains the heart feelings and the lower torso the sexual. If the flow of the energy in the figure 8 is cut off from its top section, then the assertive phase of lovemaking movements can become hard, pornographic, pushy; if it is cut off from its bottom section, the assertive expression can become artifically romantic, sentimentalized, stilted. Moreover, particular emotions make themselves felt most strongly in particular portions of the anatomy and show in the corresponding areas of the figure 8. Tenderness pulsates mainly in the throat and chest, for instance, and anger in and below the shoulders. In general, the soft, gentle feelings vest in the front and the firm to aggressive ones in the back of the body.

Color changes in the aura also identify the emotion a person is experiencing. A deep feeling of love produces a soft rose color around the chest and head. Sadness turns the field over the chest a dark blue. Rage introduces a dark red over the shoulders and upper back. A golden glow suffuses the head when the expressions of feeling is forthright and sincere. The colors of the whole field weaken, as do its other characteristics, when the organism is in a state of pain probably because the action of the sympathetic-adrenal system withdraws blood from the surface of the body.

In its expressive phase, then, the aura communicates all the conditions and processes that make up a human life: sense deprivation or satisfaction, physical illness or health, emotional conflict or harmony, spiritual poverty or fulfillment. And because the assertive and receptive pulsations are generated by a unitary energy system, the evidence in the aura's expressive functions appears as well in its complex of intake operations. These are carried out, as I said, by the organism's energy funnels.

Phase II: The Ingestion of External Energy

Monuments, works of art, and literature from ancient periods show us that peoples all over the world subscribed to the existence of energy centers through which the human being contacts external reality. The references have come down to us in many forms: the crown of the Buddha, the chakras described in the minor Upanishads and Tantric works, the entry points in acupuncture, the Egyptian Eye, and the Greek spira. We cannot know whether those who represented or wrote of the energy funnels saw them physically. We do know that they can be seen, and that observers in recent times have studied and reported on them. C. W. Leadbeater at the beginning of this chapter, has described his findings in much detail, and I will describe some of these in the passages to follow.

The purpose of the centers, as noted previously, is to draw energy from the surrounding atmosphere into the organism to charge it. This centripetal movement reciprocates and counterbalances the centrifugal emanations from the core, as do diastole and inhalation in the cardiovascular and respiratory systems. Again because of the spiral course of energy, the centers are shaped like funnels, or bells, and their action is vortical. Their open ends, or mouths, project outward into the energy body, and their narrow tips penetrate the aura's innermost layer to touch the skin. The tips are hard to see, as is the first auric layer itself, but the cup section can be viewed fairly easily under the same conditions as can the whole of the energy field.

The appearence of the centers is in fact similar to the chakras of Eastern tradition, but they are energy organs, as the kidneys and heart are physical organs, and they are as vital to human health on all vibratory planes, the material and the nonmaterial alike. The energy they draw in is metabolized by the organism and distributed through the body, down to the cell level. The centers also emit inner energy, of which they are composed, along their sides. These emissions vibrate faster than the auric envelope proper.

The basic vortical pulsation in the funnels themselves integrate subsidiary trajectories traced by the action of the energy streaming into them. These flows set up secondary forces at right angles, as a bar magnet thrust into an induction coil, producing a current of electricity that girdles the coil perpendicularly to the axis of the magnet. The incoming energy also spreads radially toward the periphery, forming what look like spokes or adjoining petals on a flower. The radiant beams that originate in the second auric layer probably take their shape from these petal-like segments.

In the healthy organism, the wheels rival the rainbow. Each center, and often each of its spokes, is brilliantly colored. The funnels measure two or more inches from tip to mouth and three to eight inches in diameter when a person is at rest, but like the auric layers, excitement enlarges them and intensifies their movement and hue. My colleagues and I are locating energy wheels all over the body. They are juxtaposed, for instance, to acupuncture points and small structures. The principles and most visible ones are found proximate to the vital organs, to a number of the more important plexuses of the autonomic nervous system, and to some of the more potent endocrine glands.

As Figure 9 illustrates four of these major funnels are feeling centers. They are located in the front of the body: at the throat, the heart, the solar plexus, and the pubis. There are three will centers, these in the back of the body. One is over the small of the back, and acts with the anterior sexual center. The second controls two subdivisions. It is situated directly between the shoulder blades and has a subordinate funnel both below it and above it, at the posterior attachment of the diaphragm, and at the nape of the neck. This triune formation, linked particularly to the outer will, is described in very little of the literature. Above the cluster is a joint will and mental funnel, at the occiput. It is instrumental not only in the person's action capacities, along with the two other will components of the funnel network, but also in the executive mental functions. This center connects immediately with the lower of two other mental organs: the one in the forehead, between the eyes, analogous to the third eye of Eastern theory. At the crown of the head is a vortex that incorporates and exceeds the operations of all the anterior and posterior entries.

The energy centers at the front of the body are located more specifically as shown in Figure 10. The funnel spinning over the throat has some 16 spokes, eight of which are blue and the remainder of which look red, yellow, and green. The bell is two to three inches wide. It functions to receive energy for the whole organism; it relates to the person's capacity to take in, digest, and assimilate. It is associated with the thyroid gland and also with the wind-pipe, and therefore plays an important role in respiratory activity.

The Center at the heart measures three to four inches across and is predominantly a glowing golden color. Its 12 spokes express an undulating motion that carries red and yellow through the gold. It activates the heart feelings — the primal emotional impetus towards opening to the forces of the universe, identifying with the suffering and love of other human beings, accepting the fits and starts of life patiently. This funnel interconnects with the mental centers, and is responsible for the component of warmth in a person's altruistic decisions. Without this element, even the most constructive human actions risk becoming mechanistic and abstracted.

The solar plexus is the site of the third vortex, a beautiful formation three to four inches wide in which Leadbeater sees 10 petals. Half are various shades of red and half have tints of green, and they form a flower configuration like a morning glory or a hibiscus. The operations of this funnel involve all the expansive and receptive movements of the organism. It sustains the person's awareness of not only the pleasures of life but also the truth in the self and the cosmos, so that it nourishes the faculty of intuition and the capacity for wisdom.

The fourth center is located a little over an inch above the midline of the pubis. Its predominant colors are yellow and red, but the petals glow with many shades of blue too. This funnel focuses the person's ability to extend the self in lovemaking with another, to let go, to exchange pleasure, so that it projects a strong connection between the pelvis and the heart. In the reciprocal energy cycle, this funnel has much to do with our giving, while the posterior sexual center is mainly involved in our receiving.

The pubic center, as I said, acts in concert with the fifth funnel, the lowest of those shown in Figure 11. Situated at the base of the spine, this vortex sends energy into the gonads and the adrenal glands. It swirls in four quadrants that make it look like a cone surrounding a cross, and its colors are orange and red. Leadbeater sees a very fast shifting movement along the arms of the cross out to the rim, which measures four or five inches in diameter. He describes the whole as resembling a basket woven around the four arms. The functions of this center are more than specifically sexual. It supports the ability to give and receive spontaneously and to move with the involuntary processes, including those of the unconscious. Its activity thus underwrites the free flow of energy in the funnels higher up the spine.

Above the coccygeal organ is the cluster of will centers, directed by the vortex between the shoulder blades. This rotating wheel measures three to four inches across and contains a great many spokes, which I cannot count. Other commentators give differing estimates. The color of the main will center is yellow to red, and it deepens as the assertive and decision-making functions of this cluster are exercised. Selfhood, autonomy, and other articulations of the ego connect with these vortices. The subdivisions channel to certain of the ego's powers. The one at the nape of the neck fuels self-assertion and the sense of dignity and selfworth; the one over the rear attachment of the diaphragm metabolizes the energy for the outer will.

The occipital center serves both the will and the intellect, as I noted, joining as it does in the operations of the frontal energy organ, as well as the volitional cluster below it. The major activitiy of the occipital funnel is to implement ideation. It supports the ability to decide what action to take according to one's perceptions, and then to call on the assertive expression from the back of the body to take that action.

Over the frontal bone appears the eighth energy center, identified in the East as the third eye. This is a big funnel, too, four to five inches across. Its colors are primarily yellow an blue. Its configuration is complex; two halves are visible in it, and each contains many further segments. Leadbeater believes the whole organ shows 96 spokes. Here too, as in the fifth center, he reports rapid undulations that produce a basketweave effect around the lines between the spokes. The frontal vortex connects with the pituitary body and provides the person with clearsightedness, perceptual ability, a sense of the design of life. And while I catalogue it as a mental center, it promotes the early stages of spiritual development, which is a principal function of the wheel at the crown of the head.

The uppermost vortex is the most resplendent of all. An indescribable array of colors scintillates through its fundamental brilliant purple and the gold that glows at the heart of a secondary interior whirlpool. This nucleus is identical in tone, construction, and shape to the heart center. This points to the union of heart qualities with mental and spiritual abilities and indicates that the crown cone represents holistic integration and activation. Physiologically, it sends life force to the pineal gland and the frontal lobes. The normal diameter of the center in a fully healthy person is an incredible six to eight inches. Its pulsations are so rapid and complex that its segments are impossible to see, but some Indian writings call it the thousand-petaled lotus. I believe that it is the organ of not only our individual fulfillment but also our collective evolution. For as I observe it in people undergoing therapy, it opens and flourishes in the same measure that the core opens and flourishes. And I am convinced, as I have said at length in earlier chapters and will speak of it again, that communication from core to core generates unprophesiable progression.

Part III:
The Dynamics of Dysfunction

Chapter 8
SOURCES OF DYSFUNCTION

Expansion and joy are part of the birthright of humanity; they are native feelings that can soar from emotional health. What, then, takes away this gift?

Until recently, the answers to this question in the West have reflected the dualism of the healing arts that I noted first in Chapter 1: the division of the soma from the psyche, and the extension of this separation within the family of psychological therapies. The separation within the human entity is reflected by the split between the individual and the environment. Unable to discern that the source of illness and healing lies within, the human consciousness thoughout the ages has relied on some outside agency to cope with suffering and to ease pain.

For some 200 years after the advent of scientific medicine, a development of the eighteenth-century Enlightenment, human pathology was considered strictly physical in origin. The insights of Sigmund Freud and his followers into mental-emotional disorders swung the pendulum over to a wholly psychological explanation for illness. But even during Freud's early career, in the early 1900s, investigators on both sides of the professional fence began to see the human being as a psychosomatic unity. Many open-minded practitioners today, regardless of their specialties, will acknowledge in principle that treating a psychological disturbance independently of its physiological corollaries is as incomplete as ignoring the role of nutrition in the formation of a child's intelligence quotient.

From the field of physical medicine, a pioneer in the work to formulate the psychosomatic approach was the great Canadian clinician Sir William Osler. After observing numerous cases of angina pectoris, Osler established that these patients were reacting directly to emotional factor outside their immediate life situations. In the United States, the physiologist Walter Canon did a now-famous study in the late 1910s. He proved that the blood pressure of animals changed in the conditions of fear and rage. He concluded that the sympathetic nervous system responds in two opposite ways under the impact of such intense emotions: by expanding or contracting the whole organism. This activity in turn produces one of two reactions: the flight or capitulation syndrome, expressed in fleeing or in freezing and holding; or the fight syndrome.

In 1932, the psychiatrist Franz Alexander inaugurated further ground-breaking work in psychosomatic medicine at the Chicago Psychoanalytic Institute. Studying many people with particular types of organic complaints, he and his colleagues persistently uncovered a particular psychological landscape accompanying each type. Certain heart patients, for example, showed abounding hostility, a neurotic complex that expressed itself in aggression, the desire to dominate, and an overweening ambition to "achieve". Simultaneously, Flanders Dunbar was making extensive observations that demonstrated the relation between emotions and specific pathologies. Her findings led her to describe "the coronary personality", "the ulcer personality", "the arthritic personality", and others. In that period and since, the Menninger brothers, William and Karl, have furnished overwhelming evidence connecting physical disease with emotional causes.

Over the same decades, these interrelationships were being explored at far greater depths by Wilhelm Reich. As we have seen, he perceived the human being as a unified energy system rather than a composite of psyche and soma, and that when the person denies his or her primal emotions, the energy flow converts into physical and emotional blocks. These blocks distort the whole of the person's functioning and reveal themselves not just in the way suffering people feel and look at life but in how they hold and move their body. As Reich discovered, a person who is not aware of the negative primal movements, and who rejects his potential for destructiveness, will trap a great amount of energy in that denial. The organism's energy slows down, in a sense thickens, stagnates, and then freezes.

But this is not all. Emotions are made from one yarn, for they are moving energy currents. Blocking negativity, therefore, also blocks the positive primal emotions: faith, compassion, joy in others' existence — love.

The concept of psychosomatic unity is gaining increasing adherence among various schools of healing, but the bent toward dualistic thinking remains strong. Geneticists and environmentalists have joined the long nature-nurture debate. The first attributes most importance to genetic codes and the second to environment as the source of neuroses. The psychoanalytic disciplines are being challenged both by behavioral schools that see inheritance alone as the foundation of emotional illnesses and by phamacological therapies.

Each of these approaches has significantly expanded our understanding of given aspects of human illness. Treatment methods based on them, however, necessarily narrow the therapeutic focus from the whole organism to its most visibly afflicted part according to the practitioner's perspective: internal subcellular programming or external life situation; past experiences or present stimuli; the psyche's unconscious or the body's biochemistry.

But illness is a process — or rather, an interruption of the life process — that penetrates the entire person, because the flow of living energy in the organism is integral to the organism. This means that the presenting complaint must be viewed as symptomatic, not causative. It also means that diagnosis and treatment must seek out the effects of the interruption not only at the site of the evident dysfunction but on all the human operational planes, the physical, the emotional, the mental, and the spiritual, and in both the conscious and the unconscious domains.

Chapter 2 introduced observations on how distortions of energy thicken the defensive periphery and how the resultant armoring dims the person's awareness of the outside world and inner reality, of the direct stream of the primal positive and negative emotions. Chapters 9 and 10 will enlarge on the structures and origins of these distortions. First, let me return to the reciprocal energy cycle and summarize its overall relationship to the four planes of vibratory movement. As we will see later, the locus and severity of arrhythmia in the pulsations of energy profile dysfunction throughout its course.

Energetic Aspects of Dysfunction

Assertion and reception, we know, are natural expressions of movement toward the environment by any living thing. An amoeba, for example, performs many outward movements in trying to encircle its prey. This is a totally involuntary process depending upon spontaneous biological activities and chemical responses. A fish, using both the voluntary muscles of its frame and its involuntary pulsatory movement, propels itself in the water in the direction it wants. Because the fish uses a voluntary process, it can travel many miles, while an amoeba can cover only a fraction of an equivalent distance, relative to its size. All animals move on the surface of the earth, countering gravity through their muscular contractions, which also give direction to their movements, usually in the direction of the head.

Humans also move on the earth with the help of their voluntary and involuntary systems. The voluntary movements arise from the decisions we make: to act or not act, to turn our thinking to one subject or another. The involuntary movements beat through the organism. They arise as homeostatic impulse that flow toward the surroundings and make up the primal positive emotions. The sum total of the forward movements of the voluntary and involuntary systems constitute the positive expressions of our existence and our creativity.

The voluntary sector of our perceptions and decision-making faculties generally correlates with what is considered our conscious mind: our self-awareness and self-direction. The involuntary sector comprises the un-conscious processes: our innate impetuses and our unconscious energy for-mations, plus the buried experience of our unremembered past. Integration and creativity require freedom of movement from the innermost reaches of the unconscious to the outermost perimeters of consciousness. Traditional therapies tend to demote the conscious and the voluntary in a reaction to their apotheosis in the Victorian era. In core energetic terms, such ap-proaches embrace at most only two planes of vibratory movement — the metal and emotional, as narrowly defined — and only their assertive phase, their expression into the self-aware mind. The reciprocal movement, from outside reality into the outer and thence inner mind, is omitted from treat-ment; so is the expression of the whole cycle through the physical and spiritual planes of the organism.

Spiritual life does not flower until a person's emergies can flow fairly free-ly from and into the core. For that reason, I will postpone exploring this ac-tivity until Chapter 19.

Healthy people show self-possession in all of their behavior: economy of gesture, coordination, grace, appropriate responses. The voluntary and in-voluntary processes are fused in the fluid expressions, whether these emanate mainly from the body, the emotions, or the mind. The energy of the organism pulsates in and out intensely, each part drawing nourishment from each other and from the larger surroundings and also sending vitality out-ward. The principle of reciprocity balances the aggregate operations as well as those of the energetic components to give the person self-control in the assertive and receptive movements of longterm exchanges.

Control due any habitual restraint on the flow of energy is not self-possession but self-imprisonment. Physiologically, the constriction translates into holding patterns in the muscles, which not only reduce their flexibility but cut off the person's awareness of subtler movements. Sensory awareness is lowered, and the nerve impulses lose strength. The perceptual-volitional functions lose vitality simultaneously, because they are deprived of the energy they should receive in the charging phase of the reciprocal cycle.

In all cases, the ability to act vigorously and react appropriately diminishes. Withdrawal may affect the whole organism, so that its pulsatory rhythm may be depressed. Or it may show most immediately in increasing spastic symptoms that lead to stiffness and pain. The classic stiff upper lip and frozen jaw attest to this. If one section of the anatomy is held tight, another will often overdevelop, and the frequency of pulsation will increase accordingly. The strain of maintaining the holding pattern in one region and sustaining the overstimulated rhythm in another will appear in pathological disruptions and a decrease in the pulsatory rhythm of the aura.

The constrictions of energy, therefore, are not isolated dysfunctions. They are blocks of stultified energy that trammel the physical body in skeletomuscular rigidities, and also disrupt the higher planes of energy, thus affecting mental attitudes. Armoring anywhere affects the entire organism, but the specific locations of slowed movement indicate the specific directions that therapy could take. One can see the blocking in all of the general behavior expressions of the person: posture, gesture, voice, as well as the content of verbal communications. The aura, however, generally provides a significant aid to identify the disturbances.

The slowed frequency of the energy field's pulsations is caused by the deviation that the energy flow must make when it encounters a block anywhere. Vital force cannot stop moving; thus, when it meets a barrier, it must circumvent this or back up in the opposite direction. The result as I said, is an increase in the pulsatory rate of the overcharged area, which is visible in the figure 8 formation of the energy envelope. This inevitably causes an imbalance in the normally rhythmic reciprocity of the assertive and receptive phases, and one principle will come to dominate the character expression of the organism.

Suppose, for instance, that the two halves of the figure 8 in a person should pulsate 20 times a minute but that the movement is impeded in the pelvis. The blockage will decrease the pulsation in the lower part of the 8 to perhaps only 10 times a minute. Therefore, while the energy will still take something of a figure 8 form, the lower section of the movement will be smaller, and the organism will be feeding energy into the upper part of the 8, which will enlarge.

Now, suppose the contraction-expansion movement of the aura shows blockage in the upper back, where the volitional operations emerge primarily and the assertive principle dominates. The overcharge will then move to the front of the body, exaggerating the receptive principle. For a number of reasons, some of them cultural, this often occurs with women who are blocked in the pelvic region. The decreased frequency of the pulsations will express itself in an attitude of extreme submissiveness, the organism will perceive the humiliation of this state, and a hostile reaction will set in. With this character formation, dysfunction may afflict the biologically receptive organ of the uterus. The diseases may take the form of deep tissue changes, such as uterine lesions or possibly tumors, or of functional disturbances in the menstrual cycle.

On the other hand, when the assertive principle is overdeveloped at the expense of the receptive, it becomes aggression and brutality. Many men identify destructive aggression with manhood, mistaking it for independence from parents and for personal creativity. This distortion shows up in various ways, again depending on other factors. It may make the man's sexual expression hard and pornographic, as I mentioned earlier. It may turn him into a barroom brawler. Or it may trigger cardiovascular disease, which is an affliction mainly of men who bottle up their aggression.

The disturbances visible in the outward pulsations of the aura hurt the intake network commensurately. The powerful forces streaming into the person from outside space must be modified so as not to overload the organism. The defensive perimeter, we saw, serves this purpose, working like a rheostat to step down the incoming energy. When the periphery is armored, the organism's ability to metabolize external energy is impaired, and the blockage inhibits the charging phase of the reciprocal cycle by disrupting the vital force of which the intake funnels are made. The energy center may collapse partially or totally and become faint or invisible. Or the funnel may reverse, so that the mouth end cups the skin. Or one or more petals may wither, making the sides of the funnels asymmetrical. The width of the affected wheels decreases to an inch or less, their luminosity fades, their color muddies, and their vibrations become sluggish. The diminution of awareness that distorts inner reality is matched by a decline in the understanding of external reality, so that the energy blockages become a self-perpetuating syndrome — a neurosis or a psychosis. I want to emphasize, though, that all of us exhibit this two-phase imbalance to some extent, because all of us connive to a degree in maintaining our blocks. We thus deprive our core of the vital force it must receive through the energy centers to live and work; and we deprive our intake funnels of the movement they must have from the core to even stay open.

The parts of the organism adjacent to a depleted energy wheel suffer a general depression of activity, corresponding with the fact that each center targets immediately on a specific organic operation. The location of the principal centers is illustrated in Figure 12 as they appear in a healthy person. Patterns of dysfunction will be pictured in the next chapter as they relate to particular character disorders.

The great majority of people exhibit considerable fluctuation in the crown center, the organ of holistic functioning and evolutionary progressions. The reason is that this funnel does not thrive unless all the others are relatively open and active.

A flaccid throat center denotes inflexibility and an unaccepting attitude, a refusal to risk "swallowing" anything and seeming gullible. The defensiveness often shows in an intense face and a weakness in the chest as well as a rigid throat. Chest constriction parallels a depletion of the second center and indicates a stifling of the heart feelings. Closure of the third funnel, at the solar plexus, identifies a diaphragmatic block that likewise inhibits breathing. In both cases, the potential for giving and receiving remains unfulfilled. In everyday language, the person "has no heart" or "has no stomach" for the outside world.

An imbalance in the fourth or fifth wheel, the sexual centers, exemplifies a breach of the principle of reciprocity: When one deflates, the other balloons, and vice versa. The undercharged region will show an underdeveloped musculature and some times fatty deposits. Obstructed will centers correlate with weak shoulders, a tense back, and at times the formation called a dowager's hump at the top of the thoracic vertebrae. The subsidiary funnels often function disjunctively, dominating rather than sharing subordinately in the energy of the cluster, The upper one then supports excessive pride, and the lower one sustaines an exaggerated outer will.

The occipital center denotes the executive abilities of a person to perform both positive and negative ideation. If the frontal center is negative, the occipital center will tend definitely to recreate and execute negative ideas, and therefore bring the person to a negative state of life. When this center is well-developed, as in the person of great executive abilities, it dominates the overall movement, and expresses in some way the will aspects of the personality. However, overdevelopment of the center frequently accompanies imbalance in the will cluster. Underdevelopment will incline the person to maintain and act on negative ideas, which in turn are visible in a damaged frontal center. This combination prevents the person from perceiving life deeply or fully, and it identifies an underlying critical and complaining attitude, whether this is expressed in overt behavior or not.

The center over the frontal bone, expresses the wholeness of the person in terms of his spirituality, mind, and body. The center also has a lot to do with spiritual vision. As with other centers, the functioning of the frontal funnel depends on opening the other centers. When the frontal center is closed, as when excessive negative thinking occurs, the person becomes trapped in a negative attitude toward life, a critical evaluation of others, and, on the whole, an overall doubting and negative behavior that emphasizes the character defenses and negativities. When the center is open, the expression of the personality is positive and cheerful and expresses joy and faith in life. A disturbance of this center deprives the individual of the ability to visualize and comprehend. The person simply lacks the deeper vision about his life and the connection it has with his actions and decisions.

The crown center serves the total integration of the human entity. It is the last center to be awakened and is related to the spiritual advancement of the person's life. The crown center cannot fully develop unless the other centers are open to some degree.

Importance of the Aura

The great value of evidence from the aura and its energy centers, then, lies in its comprehensiveness and its accuracy. Either intentionally or unwittingly, we may misrepresent to ourselves or others what we feel and think, and we may conform our conduct to contingencies rather than to subjective truth. The aura cannot do this. Its movements and formations replicate exactly the conditions within the organism: in the solid body — the set of the skeletal structures, the state of the muscles and softer tissues; in the emotions — the streams of life force relative to internal and external stimuli; and in the mind — the perceptions of the streams in the shape of feelings, the thoughts that emerge from the perceptions, the concepts that frame the thoughts, and the decisions that direct the reaction and actions of the whole. The aura therefore delineates the systemic implications of an illness, whether the primary symptoms surface in physical disabilities, emotional imbalances, or warped thinking.

Under the concept of the core as the wellspring of right energy, illness constitutes a state of estrangement between the defending periphery and the headwaters of the individual's life. The cone shown in Figure 1 of Chapter 2 girdles not only the core but the inner protective capacity as well. This gives us several clarifying perspectives that are useful to review here.

The perimeter, or outer self, is not the real human being but rather the interface with outside reality. The real person lives in the first and second layers, which are made up of the primal positive and negative emotions. I call this person the inner self, with the respective levels representing our higher and lower natures. Let me stress again that the adjectives apply not morally but dynamically. The force of the core has the highest rate of pulsation; this same energy alters in level 2, shifting gears so to speak into a lower frequency.

The pulsatory rate in the perimeter is intrinsically the lowest in an energy entity, because level 3 has the innate function of interceding between the inner self and the enormous range of frequencies in outside reality. The peripheral self houses the ego, which is our faculty of volitional thinking, or our self-aware thought and choice. Human beings tend to identify the self with the ego, for existential as well as experiential reasons that Chapter 11 will take up. It is important to highlight here that the ego's activities incor‑porate our unconscious structures, which are also stored in the defensive perimeter. These are the turgid energy formations we have created out of our numberless exchanges with the outer world. Penetrating all planes of our energetic composition, they constitute much of our armor, our machinery for negating the free flow of vital force into and out of our inner self. The denser they are, the more they block the reciprocal energy cycle. And the more the peripheral self lets them orient its movements, the more it increases its estrangement from the inner being. From the standpoint of our basic substance, then, the fundamental cause of human dysfunction is denial of the natural energy movement within the organism. The dysfunction is expressed in patterns of denial, which exhibit common characteristics but which are uniquely combined in each individual.

Chapter 9
PATTERNS OF DENIAL

During infancy and childhood, each human being seizes upon strategies to fend off pain and suffering and to exert its own will. All of these strategies, however, are counterproductive because they fragment the unitary flow of energy within the human organism. When any part of the energy flow is thwarted, the whole current becomes distorted. Thus, when the infant blocks off the movement of primal negative energy, the surge of positive energy also is distorted, slows down, and congeals into blocks.

While this negation of the energy's flow is the underlying common denominator of all human dysfunction, the more immediate or triggering causes, which will be explored in Chapter 10, carve the specific features of each person's condition. These features tend to follow patterns, for human beings do exhibit similar ways of building defenses against pain, anxiety, and suffering. Freud and his colleagues catalogued the patterns in relation to their point of origin in the person's psychlogical history. Different schools of healing accept these classifications, though they may name sickness according to other aspects of them. In bioenergetics, Lowen and I built on Reich's brilliant analyses of character attitudes and structures to fill in the outlines of five general patterns of defense, and I am uncovering others.

I want to reiterate, however, that the defensive pattern does not define the person. The core does. A person in treatment is not a character type or structure or any other label. He or she is a human being whose functioning has gone awry, and whose soul has an inborn brilliance and beauty that the therapy is designed to release. The pattern summarized in the next pages, in fact, are only overviews, for they show significant variations in each person due to the uniqueness of every core.

They do reveal a major consistency in one regard. All dysfunctional people, whatever the dominant typology of their dysfunction, root their specific characterological configuration in three major forms of denial: self-will — the self-aware and unconscious outer will; pride — not the glad feeling that comes from real accomplishment but the mask feeling of personal superiority; and fear — an essential as well as a peripheral distrust of the movements of life force and of the equilibrium between the person and the environment. These combine, differently with each person, in an effort to

baffle any energy flow from and into the core, because movement is perceived as a threat to the whole being.

The Oral Character

The oral person, in Freudian concepts, has gotten stuck in the infant stage
of development, and does not have enough feeling throughout the
organism. The ego is generally weak, and there is an attitude of demanding
life from the world and blaming outside sources for not having obtained it.
The fundamental message that comes through the mask, the crust of
pretense of the peripheral self, is "Give it to me; you owe it to me." Disappointment evokes bitterness, resignation, and peremptoriness; on the other
hand, the person is elated beyond reality when demands are answered.

The primary root distortion in the oral pattern is pride:"I am better than
you. I am more than other people, and I must outdo them." All the person's
actions are measured and compared with others'. This competitiveness leads
to distancing from others. The boundaries of self-awareness and self-
direction are tenuous and easily collapse or inflate. The predominant
modality of pride falsifies the process of the love feelings, which are mixed
with the extreme neediness to justify the exaggeration of the receptive expression, the "Do it for me" attitude. Self-will and fear accompany the pride.
The first imposes on the energy of others. The second deforms the instinct
of self-preservation into a state of concentration and defense against that
very energy, as well as against the life force from the core.

Figure 13 represents the energy field of the oral person, in contrast to that
of a normal person, shown in Figure 12, Chapter 8. To simplify the descriptions, the energy centers appear here and in the following illustrations with
their mouths inverted toward the skin to indicate dysfunction, though as I
said, a depleted funnel may instead retain its symmetrical bell shape but fade
toward invisibility, or may collapse in one section and become lopsided.

As Figure 13 shows, the core energy of the oral character radiates feebly,
the result of systemic undercharging. The energy field has a low pulsatory
rate, ordinarily less than 15 a minute. The primal negative emotions of
hatred and rage are structured into the third level along with fear to depress
the aura all over the body except around the front and top of the head. The
person is open to the force from the core, which has a limited integration
with the periphery, but cannot marshal energy or sustain a rhythmic flow.
The core can be reached more readily than in other character formations,
however, so that the field can accelerate relatively faster and work more easi-

ly to dissolve the person's blocks. Blockages appear in the occipital area, the throat, the back of the neck, and especially the shoulders, which are usually pulled up in an expression of deep anxiety. The radial movements in the second and third layers of the field are often broken in the small of the back, in the groin, at the knees and ankles.

These obstructions make it difficult for the energy of the aura upward and frontward, ballooning it in the top half of the figure 8. Here, because the field is depressed overall and the throat and shoulders are particularly constricted, the energy pulsates actively around the face and the frontal lobes.

Correspondingly, the energy center in the forehead is generally well developed in the oral person, and the eyes are bright and charged. The activity at this site vitalizes the intellectual faculties and the understanding, which in turn helps the crown center function fairly freely despite the depleted state of the intake network as a whole. The coccygeal funnel is inverted, so that the capacity for sexual discharge is very low. The cone over the heart as well as the throat center is partially collapsed. The organ at the solar plexus is also blocked, but at times it shoots out energy asymmetrically in a radial movement projecting two feet.

This fluctuation typifies the volatility and instability of the whole energy system. The organism is like a limp sack. It sucks up external force at the mouth, the lower torso , the limbs — all over the structure — but cannot metabolize it effectively. The body is in fact often long and thin, and the musculature lacks tone. The major will center is collapsed, so that energy bleeds to its upper and lower sudivisions; hence the underdevelopment of the ego and the exaggeration of pride in the oral person.

The Masochist Character

The masochist contrasts with the oral character. This person was typically hovered over as a child. For instance, the mother may have pushed food on her little boy, demanded hugs and kisses, and in general intruded on his autonomy. Feeling his core abused and violated, he began building a wall that in his adult body appears as a thick accumulation of muscle and fat. Implanted in the peripheral self, the masochist takes on a victim role, viewing any movement from outside as an imposition or a humiliation. The mask says, "I'll be safe only if I control you. I'll put you down; otherwise, you're going put me down." Within the organism, any strong surge of energy is perceived as a catastrophic threat, which broadens the "you" of the outside world to mean also the estranged inner self: "I don't want contact with you. It's too much."

The most notable feature of the masochist's energy system, illustrated in Figure 14, is the overcharging of the outer layer of the person, which suffocates the core. Because of this surcharge, the ego is constantly struggling to make room, to clear away the occlusion it feels from its own defenses. The predominant expressions are hesitancy and fear, which are related to the person's refusal to move. Again, the fear displaces the instinct of self-preservation. It generates a state of unspecified worry and anxiety, which is, so to speak, a trick to prevent the person from allowing energy to flow. Outer willfulness accompanies the salient emotion of fear, taking the form of stubbornness and resistance, spite and defiance. The distortion of pride has two prongs — a superficial attitude of humbleness and unobtrusiveness that overlays a hidden attitude of superiority and denigration of others.

The armor of the masochist shows tremendous blocks in the upper torso as well as the thighs. The energy pile-up in the shoulders and back pulls in the centrifugal movement that should take place through the front of the body and damages particularly the receptive funnel in the throat. Whereas the oral person has an overall low energy rate, the field of the masochist pulsates at 30 or more beats a minute. This excessive rate radically distorts the movement of the field and creates bands of blocks that capture the free flow of energy through the trunk. The buttocks and groin are often as severely bound as the thoracic region, and significant impactions appear also around the knees and calves.

The thick tissue built onto the upper back and shoulders correlates with distortions in the will cluster, whose lower subdivision, connected with the outer will, overacts. The throat funnel, instead of receiving, pushes out, and this transmits a thrust to the jaw that can give the face a prognathous look. The heart center is occluded but active. The throat center of receptivity is closed. Therefore, the heart center cannot expand. Both sexual centers are usually somewhat depleted, though the coccygeal funnel will be more open than the pubic. Overall, these intake organs reflect a general arrhythmia in the reciprocal cycle. The energy moving from the core to the periphery is continuously twisting back on itself. The field over the head is interrupted by a badly deflated crown center and shows a muddy brown color. But the frontal wheel may be open, giving the person foresight and considerable understanding. This activity, however, is not great enough to overcome the masochist's resistance against a balanced evaluation of external reality. This capacity, however, needs relatively little stimulus to awaken because the funnel at the solar plexus is often open and fairly well developed.

The Energyfield of Man
Colorplates

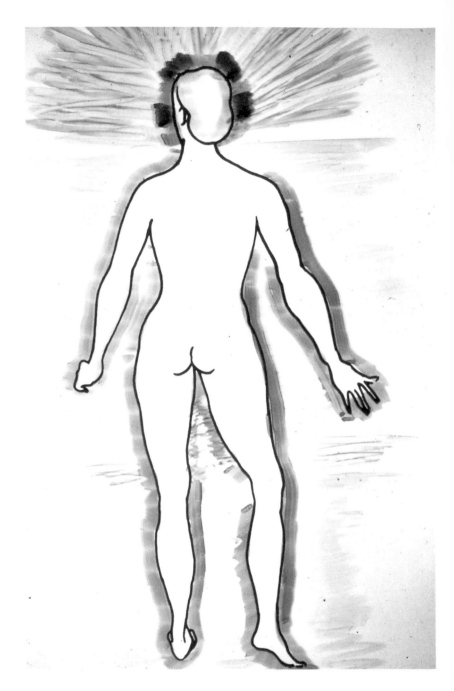

Fig. 6 **The Human Aura (appears in various individual forms)**

Fig. 7 **The Human Aura (side view)**

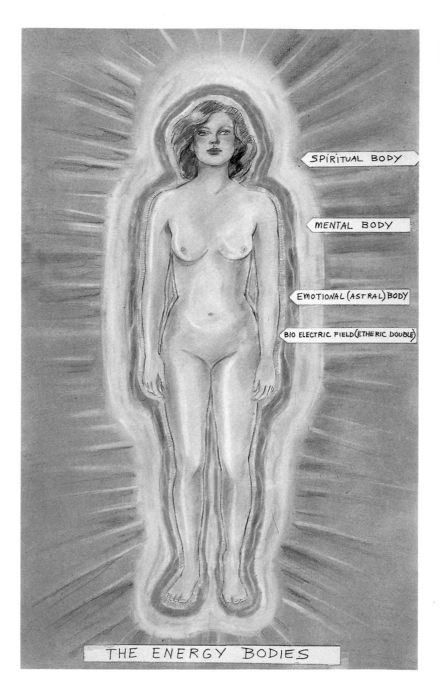

SPIRITUAL BODY

MENTAL BODY

EMOTIONAL (ASTRAL) BODY

BIO ELECTRIC FIELD (ETHERIC DOUBLE)

THE ENERGY BODIES

Fig. 8

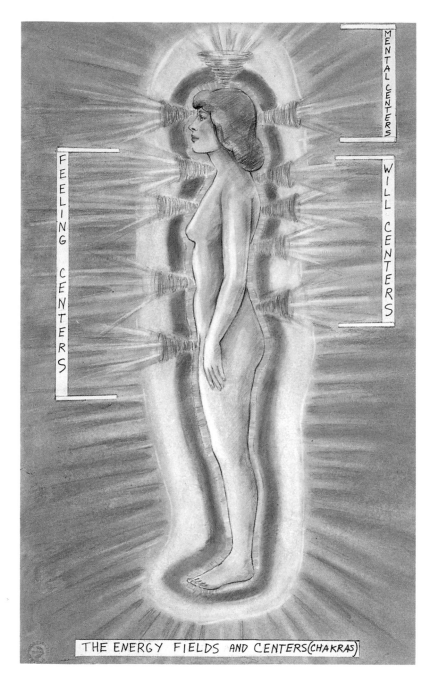

THE ENERGY FIELDS AND CENTERS (CHAKRAS)

Fig. 9

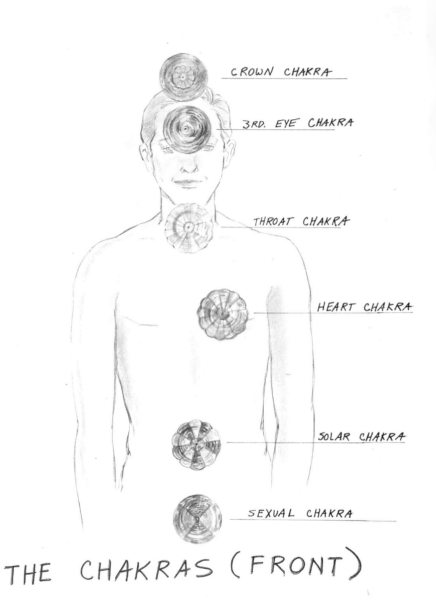

CROWN CHAKRA

3RD. EYE CHAKRA

THROAT CHAKRA

HEART CHAKRA

SOLAR CHAKRA

SEXUAL CHAKRA

THE CHAKRAS (FRONT)

Fig. 10 **The Chakras (front)**
(modified picture from Leadbeater)

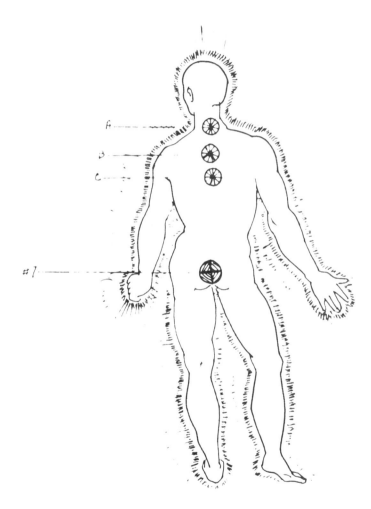

Fig. 11 **Back view. Sex and Will Center**
and it's sub divisions (A, B, C)

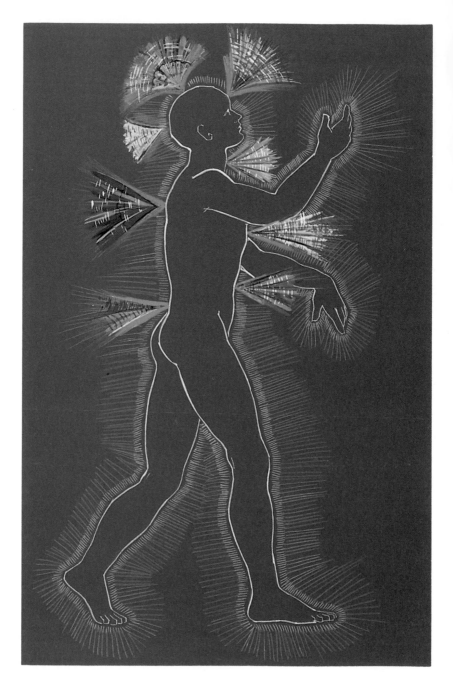

Fig. 12 **Normal Structure**

Fig. 12 **Normal Structure**

Fig. 13 **Oral Structure**

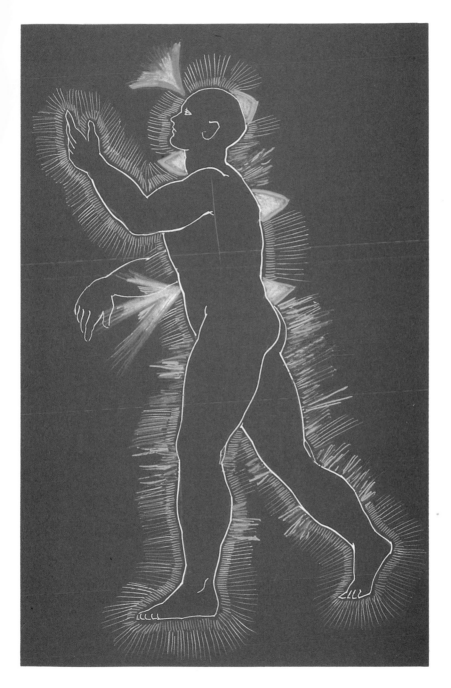

Fig. 14 **Masochistic Structure**

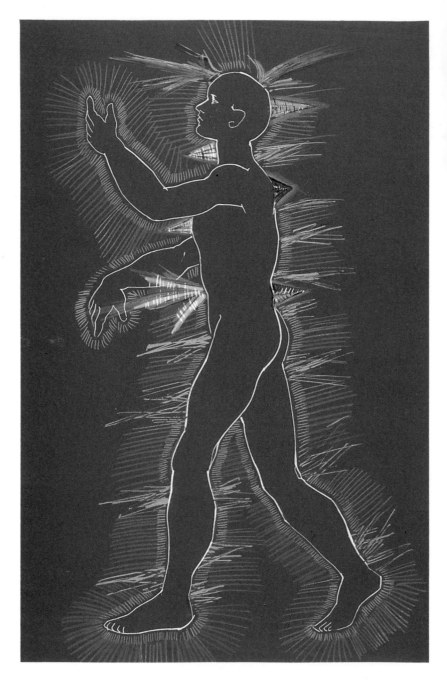

Fig. 15 **Schizoid Structure**

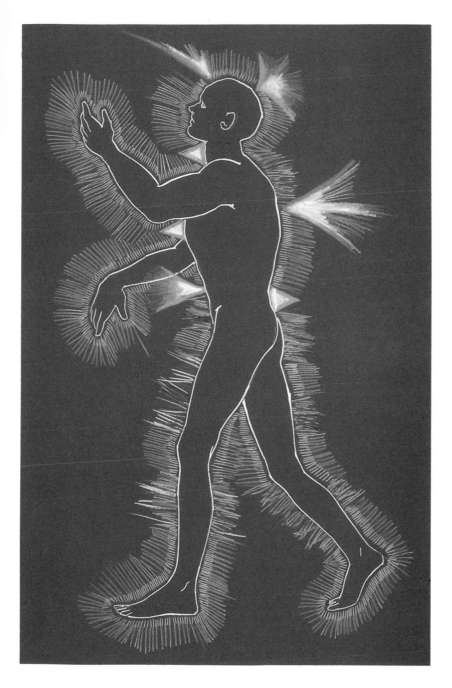

Fig. 16 **Psychopathic/Aggressive Structure**

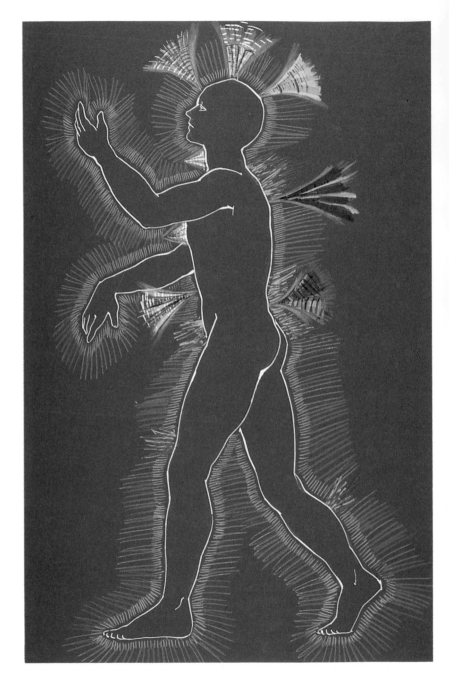

Fig. 17 **Rigid Structure**

Fig. 18 **Aura of a Typical Coronary Case**

Fig. 19 **Aura of a Person Who Had a Recent Coronary Attack**

Notice: heavy blocks in the small of the back and lower back, thigs and legs.
Notice: mulberry like dark cones over breast.

Fig. 20 **Breathing of a Rose**
Four successive stages of the energy field of the rose
(Photos: Joseph Breitenbach)

The Schizoid Character

The schizoid structure classically grows out of early and massive disorientation due to an undecipherable variety of hostile reactions against the child's spontaneous expressions. The adult personality is consequently an unstable composite, like a crack-webbed mirror, liable to turn another fragment to the outer world at any particular moment. The boundaries of the aggregate ego are fragile and collapse easily under the stress of life. The personality's lack of functional integration makes it unable to focus as an entity, which results in discordance and discontinuity on all planes of operation.

The fractures extend to the surface of the mask, whose shifting features the person clings to one after the other in an energy-consuming effort to maintain some sort of balanced facade. The organism can turn inward to draw energy from the living center, but it cannot bring the unified and unifying core to the periphery.

The core is surrounded by unintegrated primal negativities, and the principal protective emotion transmitted to the periphery is fright. This produces extreme distrust grading into paranoia in the various mask selves. Pride in the schizoid structure is often as intense as fear, and understandably, given the person's systemic disorganization, it expresses itself in an attitude of control. Self-will fluctuates, shifting and standing with the different peripheral selves; it has no general cohesion.

When the splits in the schizoid structure are severe, approaching psychosis, the entire energy field rotates 90 degrees and projects at right angles to the length of the body, effectively separating the figure 8 movement into two slow-moving whorls. The less seriously disturbed person also has a depressed pulse rate, below 15 a minute. The color of much of the field is usually lemon-yellow to brown and somewhat murky, unlike the transparent light-blue field that the masochist and the oral person retain between the areas of armoring.

The energy blockages in the schizoid person appear grouped together, as though they were separate compartments in a pomegranate cultivated from past experiences. Many interruptions disorder the envelope, in particular at the joints of the trunk and the extremities. The back of the neck carries major blocks, from which the aura protrudes in a wing shape 2 to 4 feet. The radial forms in the third layer of the field look bundled and uncombed. The aura is sometimes suppressed over the frontal lobes and more often down the face, and in this case, the dulling extends to a degree around the neck and the occiput.

When the frontal energy center is open, however, as it is shown to be in Figure 15, it has a striking development, and provides the person with brilliant insights and intuition. Like the oral person, the schizoid may therefore show a well-opened crown funnel. If the frontal organ is damaged, its petals will be asymmetrical, but it will still exhibit considerable vitality, since the solar plexus center in schizoids functions at least fairly vigorously. The bell at the throat, though, is often inverted, and the heart funnel and the sexual centers are greatly diminished. The rest of the posterior intake cones are usually depleted, too, so that the schizoid person lacks integrated assertive expression.

The Aggressive Character

The aggressive pattern has been triggered by childhood experiences of seductive manipulation and inconsistency in the behavior of close adults, such as a father's alternately welcoming and rejecting his daughter. The conflicting encounters have lodged in blockages that stultify movement in the genital area and displace energy upward into the torso above the waist and into the head, as illustrated in Figure 16. The ego and the faculty of rational thought take prominence, to the deprivation particularly of sexual functioning but generally of all the feelings, those of the inner self and those of other people. The peripheral self is inflated and overcontrolling, and the mask grasps for power: "I'll prove I'm right, and then, my way or else. I don't believe in anything except what I say is real." The obviously dominant distortion here is self-will, expressed in messages similar to those that the masochist sends out — stubbornness, vengefulness, contradiction — but on an angle of attack rather than defense. Also like the masochist's, the ego of the aggressive character is braced against change, but it will, in addition, strike out against movement.

Hence, "I'll stay where I am" is followed by "I'll destroy you if you try to budge me." However, this person has a powerful core blessed by an abundance of energy, executive ability, and wonderful gifts of innovation and creativity.

The imbalance in the figure 8 energy form entails an asynchronic pulsation in the upper and lower torso; the rate below the midline may be significantly less than 15, while the upper trunk will pulsate 15 to even 25 beats more a minute. The personality's aggressive expression, propelled from the back of the body, becomes tremendously exaggerated, and the pelvis and hips are tightly contracted and passive. The person has difficulty receiving throughout the organism. The severest blocks appear in the lower body, around the groin and gut, the buttocks, and the small of the back, where there are radial protrusions in the second and third layers of the energy envelope. The shoulders may be equally armored; the musculature there holds a great deal of tension. The holding pattern may also create obstructions around the elbows and thighs.

The arrhythmia in the movement of the aura as a whole makes the condition of the intake organs predictable. Neither sexual center functions well. The aggressive character denies genital movement, as I said, so that the excessive aggression in the upper body and head contrast sharply with the lack of assertivity (as well as receptivity) in the lower trunk. The heart center is quite closed also, as is the funnel at the throat. The center adjacent to the solar plexus has little or no strength either.

The will cluster, conversely, is even more developed than the masochist's. The main cone can reach four to six inches in diameter, though the upper petals may project asymmetrically over the lower. The frontal center likewise flourishes. But it has a lopsided protrusion, which resembles the horn of a unicorn and can extend three feet from the forehead. Yet in the aggressive structure, the crown funnel remains mostly collapsed, and again, any vitality it displays extends only sections of the cone, not the whole. The systemic dysfunction of the receptive operations is probably the reason for this anomaly.

The Rigid Character

The least disunified character type is sometimes also the most resistant to the full reciprocal swing of inner energy. This is the rigid character, whose core has not suffered the depletion apparent in other structures and usually pulsates strongly, often at 30 beats or more a minute. Hence the generally harmonious and balanced movement of energy throughout the organism shown in Figure 17. This movement provides the grounding for exceptional executive skills and a high ability to perform. But the good overall integration has been achieved at the expense of the soft feelings arising from the core. The heart is not open, so that while the rigid person may handle arm's-length exchanges adroitly — dealing with and exercising authority, completing tasks — holistic relationships are aloof and unrewarding.

The pattern of defense in this character formation rests on a denial of the receptive operation. The peripheral self places much emphasis on success. Therefore, extreme pride and self-will shape the expressions of the mask:

"I'm better than other people, I can do anything I undertake." The ego thrives on one-upmanship, reflecting a fear of vulnerability: "I'll go you one better, I'll make you give way." Overt hostility is less a feature of this person than a narcissistic disregard of others, accompanied by an attitude of isolation and a belief that self-interest necessarily runs counter to that of the others. The motif of activity is to reach and take quickly but not to release or expend, and the potential for giving remains unfulfilled because the potential for receiving is denied. This sufferer therefore feels hollow of meaning, inadequate, dry. Yet the mask, denying the sense of emptiness, asserts: "I've got it all together."

The energy field of the rigid person moves vigorously in both the figure 8 and the contraction-expansion shapes. It reaches several feet out from the body, much farther than even the aura of a healthy person at rest inside a room, and the corona over the head usually radiates some three feet. The specific locations of blocks depend on the processes involved in producing them. Some rigid people carry armoring over the shoulders, so that the field shows a wedge form pointing rearward. The aura may also be disrupted in the small of the back, and often condenses significantly at the groin and thighs. These disturbances are not so gross as in the masochistic or the aggressive structure, but they have the muddy brown to yellow hue indicative of dysfunction.

Because of the resistance to receiving, the energy funnels at the throat and heart are generally damaged and invert to face the skin. The solar plexus organ may be open, but when it is partially closed, it is asymmetrical. Both sexual centers have considerable strength; these are always depleted in the other major patterns of defense. Again however, the pubic cone will function less freely than the coccygeal because of the person's limited receptivity. The will cluster appears normal, as does the frontal funnel. The occipital center shows exceptional development. The crown organ may be somewhat dimmed or extended. And as in all patterns of denial, the degree of development in this key center reflects the intensity of the illness, since the crown funnel is the organism's direct path to the core.

As these descriptions show, the different patterns of denial all relay essential energy deviations and barriers that are fixed in the defensive periphery — the superficial arena of life that is fronted by the mask. When these blockages are severe, they will inevitably turn free-moving energy onto the organism in a whiplash that can drive the person literally to physical death.

Evidence from the tributaries of psychosomatic medicine, reported in Chapter 8, has established that psychic strain relates to many killing physiological diseases. But energy distortions do not stop at the soft tissues;

they reach to the very formation of the skeleton. For example, if emotional illness holds the muscles very tight over a period of time, they will pull together with a pressure that shortens the bones. And a study by surgeons has found that some 15 to 20 percent of people who fall from heights snap their bones before they hit the ground. Energy deprivation that is beyond the person's control can be just as ravaging. Babies have been known to die when they are starved completely of physical contact and affection, desires that rise form the core. The pioneer work in France that defined this phenomenon labeled it "hospitalism", but it has been observed in orphanages, too.

Yet even in these tragic cases, outer reality is not the sole cause, but rather the provocation. The origins of human dysfunction must be traced to the protective operations in the person that erect and then escalate the defenses.

Chapter 10
THE ORIGINS OF DYSFUNCTION

Each living being comes into an environment not of its own making, but from an infinitely complex orbit of concentric systems that encompass bigger and bigger fields of external reality. Nature provides each species with the ability of raise its young to the stage of self-sufficiency in its particular environment. Ethnologists are confirming a theory that observers of our own species have long pondered. Animals who teach their offspring train them to integrate their innate movements with those in their surroundings but otherwise allow them freedom of expression. Much of human teaching trains us another way around: to subordinate our innate movements and freedom of expression to those in our surroundings. We learn from infancy that openly airing our emotions and other natural functions is forbidden or risky. Persistent prohibition breeds the belief that merely allowing ourselves to experience them will bring pain and even destruction of the self or others.

The responsibility for these misdirected understandings, therefore, lies originally with external pressures that work unreasonably to inhibit the freely expressive being. The tremendous living force within us is stifled by restrictive mores, religious codes, and standards of social behavior. This is not to say that these and other value structures have no merit. It is to say that when their advocates do not respect the spontaneous movement of life in the child, they sever the outer self from the inner reality, shatter the integrity of the energetic system, and chain the person to his or her mask.

Organized faiths that project cosmic processes someplace "out there", into an abstraction in the heavens, create an alienation between an individual's core and the universal principle of conscious energy that it embodies. Social proprieties stifle movement when they call down a child's exuberance or reject a loving gesture. And as Lowen and I have found repeatedly, some of the most difficult blockages to penetrate are those of the businessman who enters treatment convinced that personal wealth and the welfare of his corporation are the supreme mandates in his life.

The Stifling of Feelings

Human institutions, then, tend to attack positive emotion that comes from the core because they perceive this movement as contrary to their interests. For the same reason and with even greater vehemence, they oppose the emotion expressed in the so-called negative feelings — anger, hatred, the impulse to destroy. I say "so-called" because, to repeat, "negative" implies that these feelings are empty of life or antagonistic to it. This is not true, for they are our second level of inner reality, and reality cannot be anti-life.

This family of feelings constitutes expressions of life, as part of its duality, and not reprehensible outlets. They channel an enormous amount of movement. If we close them off, we stop our creative processes, we stop our growth. Our energy piles up und our person stagnates, as one car stopped on the highway will halt all the cars behind it. Negative emotions do not block energy; they only alter it. They are not "wrong" in themselves; they are very valuable and precious functions of the person, when they are accepted. Anger, for instance, is the reaction when the core is squeezed, as by humiliation or enslavement. It is a beautiful thing to see anger erupting freely in defense against oppression of the individual.

It is conversely an ugly thing to see legitimate anger blocked, for as I have said, negative emotion will emerge in devious and distorted feelings when it is denied recognition. To visualize the interruption of process between pure emotion from level 2 and the deviation that occurs in level 3, the peripheral self, take the case of an actual slave, such as an African in centuries past. Terrorized at the beginning of his captivity, he will freeze, thinking of nothing but how to survive. The clear emotion, fear, cannot be expressed as inaction, because he will be beaten; he therefore submits to work orders, and his terror on level 2 translates into a submissive attitude on level 3. Later, as he grows familiar with his bondage and feels safer, he can allow himself to feel anger against his captivity and to look for ways of escaping or at least undermining his master. But as he becomes aware of these feelings, which range from a sense of friction to murderous rage, his fear surfaces again because he is afraid his master will discover his anger and punish him for it. Thus, in sequence, fear for survival begets anger against captivity, which in turn begets fear of discovery (in fact, a survival fear) and anger against dependency (a form of captivity). The anger itself is distorted in the peripheral layer into resentment and hostility, the most the slave judges that he can afford to admit of the assertive negative emotion. Unless he is a highly integrated person — that is, unless he can maintain his awareness of his inner self despite its vicious suppression by external reality — his outer self, thickened by unreleased energy, will magnetize his perceptions, and he will be caught in his mask of hostile submissiveness.

The slave is of course an extreme example. The elements of this chain reaction are much subtler under ordinary circumstances, deriving from a family configuration that implants the same cycle. All human beings enter life with impulses to be accepted and answered, which come from the core, and with impulses from level 2 to fight restrictions, which seek to protect the core. The seeds of dysfunction are sown not by external constraints per se but by degrees and kinds of treatment that the child perceives as capricious, cruel, or abusive of the core's innate dignity.

The operative agency in the formation of distortions is therefore the person's own perceptions, rather than the reality that the self acts upon. It follows that while relations with the external world — principally parent figures — precipitate negative inner experiences in a child that can accrete into an armored character structure, they do not create that structure or the neurotic complexes it entails. Parents participate in "fixing" a neurosis, in the same sense (though not in the same way) as a stain fixes a preparation on a microscope slide. But the key to whether a life will advance in relative freedom or bondage is held by the organism itself.

Defensive armoring comes into existence very early, solidifying between birth and the age of 3 or 4. The infant is a vibrating, alive system that demands immediate fulfillment, irrespective of the environment. The ego of the infant has not developed and cannot discriminate between the realistically possible and the impossible. Therefore, his or her needs and demands, expressed in absolute terms, sometimes conflict with the parents' reality, their capacity to give, and their limitations. In interchanges between child and parent, both biological systems react according to the law of reciprocity. Energy waves radiate whose vibrations home in on each other, firing nuclear energetic reactions that somatize in both people and are felt by both. In other words, when there is a clash, both feel it, and when there is pleasure, both experience it.

Rejections of the expansive movements of the baby's higher self and the protective movements of the lower deny the little one's inner truth and introduce a split between personal and external reality. These negative encounters are confusing by their nature. If they are frequent or intense, they prompt the very young child to begin formulating an idealized self-concept that tailors behavior largely to what he or she perceives as acceptable. In Freud's description, the mind internalizes the negative lessons and develops the superego. In Core Energetic concepts, the peripheral self stops the flow of vital force and develops blocks. Fear of external punishment thus distorts into fear of self-punishment, and the inner threat may become so severe that it forces the person to deny the very existence of the rejected feelings.

The defensive periphery takes on armoring gradually, expanding with the organism's ability to direct itself. From infancy into toddlerhood, the baby learns to still inner movements, to withdraw awareness from them so as to avoid the pain of emotional hunger. Here is the onset of negative attitudes. The older child who is prevented from expressing love or anger or other pulsations struggles actively to cut off these internal realities, for the parents are saying in effect, "You are not allowed to have your living feelings." This heightens the already tremendous frustration. The child, forced to misrepresent the inner experiences, little by little finds devious ways to handle the energy flow. Here is the onset of acting out, which ripens by adulthood into a habit of projection.

As the outer mind concentrates on solidifying the defensive periphery, more and more energetic substance piles into the armoring. The personality defenses mire the person, reducing participation in the consciousness of the creative self. The core is buried under rubble in the lower self and its surface crust, the mask. An armored person says, "I keep getting fired because I do better work than my bosses, and they can't stand being shown up." Or, "I haven't yet found a woman who isn't frigid." Instead of recognizing its own negative intent, the outer mind rationalizes and projects its negativities onto others. The mechanism for distorting clear energy into blocks is now complete, capturing both the centrifugal and the centripetal pulse of the reciprocal cycle. When events call for a free movement of energy, the peripheral self receives messages of protest from the primal negativities, the second level of being, but mistakenly blames outer reality for its discomfort. It does not realize that this reaction is caused by its own stifling of the core, its own participation in maintaining the internal armoring and the mask.

The Impact of the Mask

The mask acts like a defensive shroud to make the inner self invisible to both the outside world and self-awareness. It exists in a constant state of pretense about true emotions, whether positive or negative, damping the vibrancy and buoyancy of the life center and sabotaging the integrity of the inner protective levels. Genuine impulses to please others or reject them are both skewed by the mask; so are the meanings of truthful messages from others. The mask can pretend to have the same feelings that the real self is experiencing. It may express love in a controlled and withholding way to cover the soul's actual movement of love, which it finds threatening. Or it may camouflage the true emotion with an opposite expression, as a person does by cloaking a yearning for love in the boast, "I don't need people."

Though the mask can distort in either direction, toward positive or negative meanings, it incorporates negativity in its postures more often than positiveness. There are several reasons for this. One is that the core movements are far more intense; core energy has the greatest pulsatory rate in the organism. The person therefore perceives the emotions of the higher self as more threatening than the emotions of the lower self. Another reason is the gravitational pull, so to speak, of the blocks. The mask is a negatively tuned instrument, as well as being an instrument for denying true negative emotions, so that the slower-pulsating energy of the second level is in a sense more readily gummed to it. Thus, a person will often feel more "himself" or "herself" when being hostile, superior, or aggressive than when warm, admiring, or compassionate.

Whatever the characterological face a person adopts, it implies an abdication of personal responsibility. The mask says, "It's not *my* fault." It acts to alienate the self, and then reproaches other people, fate, or society for a feeling of pain or emptiness. Or it commits the self artificially, and then whines that external pressure cause a sense of stress. In the first instance, take any one of us who considers others to be inferior and indulges persistently in small, critical judgments. We may regard these habits as unimportant. They are not. As they gain strength, they feed a state of hostility as a behavior, which in turn leads to chronic anxiety. We thereby intentionally trap ourselves in the mask-building cycle of negation with which the African slave had to contend. In the second instance, look how we all work, one way or another, to keep up appearances. Under a veneer of sophistication, we act like cautious pragmatists, regulating our thinking and choices according to what others favor, or rather, what we believe they favor. Again, the pursuit of conformity may seem inconsequential, as when a person eats an odd diet or wears uncomfortable shoes because of a current fad. But these indicate the same contradiction of inner being that drove businessmen out of windows in the stock market crash of 1929. Trivial or terrible, the imprints on the mask creates profile of impediments in the defensive perimeter that dam the process of real life, the energy flow between the reality of the inner self and the reality of external creation.

Why do we continue to exist in this state of deprivation, clinging to unhappiness and courting disintegration? The core is there in every human being. It moves by its very nature, pressing for release; it strives continuously to reestablish the processes of life. In a comparatively free society, the adult need not and ordinarily does not remain subject to the external coercions of childhood. On maturing, we gain the experience to recognize the blocks in ourselves that make us stumble. How is it that we ignore the vital power of the core to make us whole, and elect instead to cage the self in the perimeter of our being?

Several motivations immediately underlie the choice to live in the peripheral self. First, the very tensions of the character attitude of negation generate excitement. Forces are pressing on the person, conflicting forces that take the organism in their grip: the movement of energy striking against the structures of blockage. I look at the aura of people when they are actively engaged in denial, and I can assure you that the more they go from neutrality to negation, the more their energy field brightens and the faster it pulsates. Thus there is energetic excitement in negation. This excitement is often misunderstood as a free flow of energy, and is chosen by the person as an alternative to an absence of feeling (deadness) or to pain.

Another readily visible stimulus is a heroic but misdirected grit, a blind determination to plough ahead no matter how grim the adversity. A person who is fighting mightily against internal strife is like a leaking vessel so threatened with capsizing that there is no strength or attention for anything but bailing out water. The self is furiously preoccupied with simply staying afloat, and may have to founder before realizing that the ship must be rebuilt if it is to sail freely.

Fear, Pride, and Self-Will

Beneath these reasons, however, lies the trio of distortions that the previous section described as they operate in the major patterns of illness. These are our fundamental grounds of defense: fear, pride, and self-will.

Chronologically, fear lodges in the periphery first. The child, as I just discussed, learns to fear the flow of the core because this, not the primal negativities, is the wellspring of inner movement. Thus, even if the adults in the child's life overtly reject only the negative expressions, covertly they are rejecting the center of the child's being, whose frustration has given rise to the negative reaction in the first place. The primal positive emotions then become frightening to perceive, and safety lies in denying them.

The original fear, the fear of external rejection, abates as the person grows independent. But the superstructure of negation stays in power, maintained by the primal negativities. The mask does not want to listen to the love and truth of the core, and keeps the higher self walled away in a dungeon, like a dictator who is afraid his regime will be overturned if this unifying force is set free. The dictator may hear his prisoner pleading for release, or the dungeon walls may be so thick that the voice of the core doesn't reach him, and he can pretend to himself as well as the world that nobody is there.

Safety is often the comfortable euphemism we use to deny our feeling of fear. The seeker of security has found a *modus operandi* of sorts within an attitude of negation. The stance of defense lets the person feel protected like a nation well stockpiled against attack. The outer self may be unwilling to relinquish the known, the attitude of negation, for the unknown, the experience of open emotion, because the capacity for risk is held back — surely a widespread human trait. Or the person may simply be unable to conceive of any other way of functioning, a point I will take up in the next chapter. Few of us have the genius for the insight of a Freud, a Jung, or a Reich.

Pride, the second member of the triumverate supporting the mask, converts the core emotion of self-esteem into conceit over one's powers of command. Don Quixote, tilting at windmills, gives us a disarming picture of the contretemps into which such pride can lead, but this distortion is more often dangerous than funny. In the skewed vision of the proud mask, all that does not fall within its perception of right is therefore wrong. We all know the feeling — who is not with me is against me, what I can't be or do has no value. The self dissipates its energies in struggle after struggle with what it defines as "the competition" or "the enemy", these being only an otherness that the core would welcome if allowed to make contact.

The Janus face of outer pride is inner shame. Unless a person is profoundly disturbed, some positive movement will penetrate the mask in each direction. As the flow is felt, though, the outer mind perceives not the real quality of the energy but the self-judgment that the movement is "improper". The lesson, as we saw, is learned in childhood and maintained in the energy blocks. Shame in the emotional realm equates with a mental conviction of unworthiness, which propels the person to believe that a justification must be fabricated for opening the core. This is the basic dynamic, for instance, in people who can't accept pleasurable sex feelings until they've drummed up a big fight with their partner. The fight makes it permissible to make love, because an apology — an expression of open-hearted regret and tenderness — is a "proper" followup to anger.

Fear and pride, then, consort to perpetuate the hardening of the mask that denies the core freedom. But there is another conspirator, the outer will. As I said, this is not just the will in the waking state, though it is involved. It is the composite capacity to act voluntarily, much of which, like the unconscious reason uncovered by Freud, lies below the threshold of immediate self-awareness. It is true that armoring arises originally in response to external events, but for the adult, these no longer shape our lives. We do. We accept our own misbased perceptions. We select our own misguided actions. We are not victims of anybody, though we invest tremendous energy in upholding that conviction. We victimize ourselves, we keep our own core in prison, and we hang on as if for dear life to the key.

Like the apple seed, every human being has a life plan, a design for the fulfillment of the unique potentialities latent in the core. If the hull takes the energies from the germ of the seed and concentrates them on producing bark, the core of the tree and the blossoms and fruit will suffer. Let's say our tree strikes a livable compromise. It sends out some branches, and they bear some fine apples. But the tree doesn't reach its full stature, and it sets about blaming the earth, the weather, and the geography.

Yet all the time, the core is straining against the bark. And one day the tree realizes it is sick. It has a sense of numbness inside, interspersed with episodes of anguish, and it is getting no joy out of life. It is in a crisis, and feels that if something doesn't change soon, it will die.

I am going to say a strange thing now: the crisis is a rebirth, and a cause for great hope. I think that without the threat of impending catastrophe, we who constrict our core might spend our earthly days bound in compromise — growing some, but not so much as we could; producing some fruit, but not so generously as we could. The crisis confronts the outer self, the skewed energy of the armored mask, with the inner self, the right energy of the human center. And the very act of self-encounter is the first step toward the reintegration not only of the person within but of this, our being, with outer reality. The resolution of this crisis will be discussed in part VI.

Part IV:
The Results of Dysfunction

Chapter 11
CREATIVE ASPECTS OF THE EGO

From a cosmic point of view, the ego is the primary faculty with which human beings fragment their unity with themselves and the rest of existence. The abuse of the ego is also the major way that people cut themselves off from their core and create and perpetuate illness. Aligned with the character structure, the ego battles to stifle the mutual exchange of energy between the core and outer reality.

Obviously, this concept of the ego differs substantially from the views held by traditional psychotherapies. Psychoanalysis, for example, regards the strengthening of the ego as primary importance so that human beings can adjust and fit into the environment in which they exist. Core energetics also stresses the importance of a healthy ego. But the purpose of core energetics is to align the ego with the core rather than adjust to the environment. In this way, it becomes possible to restore the ego to its proper function of choosing and discriminating rather than ruling the personality.

From this standpoint, the ego stands guard at the intersection of human consciousness between inner and outer reality. Often, it functions as if it were the only reality of the person, denying both the positive and negative aspects of the inner self. However, the ego functions positively as well as negatively.

Briefly, the ego's positive functions are to assess and interpret outer reality, to make choices, and to adjust the interchange of energy between the person's inner being and what the ego perceives as the "out there" — the rest of the cosmos. However, the ego faculties generally associated with the brain — mind, intellect, and will — seek to be the master of human life rather than the servant, its proper role. Because humans fear, above all else, inner and outer unity, the ego is employed to maintain fragmentation in both spheres, and between them, as the following example shows.

A man may yearn deeply to serve his fellow human beings. But this yearning was distorted by early childhood experience, such as parents who insist that he give materially, or who are themselves materialists. They reject the undivided energy that comes from his core — perhaps feelings of love or desire for physical contact. The rejection causes the child to distrust his own inner unity and his connections with his environment, of which his parents are primary. Out of this experience, the man perceives and comes to believe that his gifts are not wanted. In effect, his ego has been unable to truly perceive the reality of unity, choosing to believe instead the limited reality represented by the parents and their actions.

The resulting beliefs become lodged in the ego and the character structure. All of his life, the man will be driven by his deeper yearning, but his ego will distort it according to its beliefs and he will seek material gain instead. The ego will deny the genuine inner impulses that propel the man toward the concept of service and probably will make him skeptical about others who do give and serve generously.

Chapter 2 described the ego's relation to the inner self, the layer of negative emotion and the core. The ego's positive dynamics will be discussed more fully later in this chapter. First, however, let us briefly explore the development of the ego.

Development of the Ego

The ego's development parallels that of humankind. In Darwinian terms, ontogeny recapitulates phylogeny. This means that the evolution of the individual organism replicates the evolution of its kind of being. Indeed, human embryonic development also replicates human evolution from the so-called lower orders. For example, the human embryo develops vestigal gills and a tail during its development. Darwin's formulation is true both in the natural and cultural development of individual human beings.

Like a vegetable or amoeba, the human embryo begins life's functioning largely with the self-regulatory mechanisms needed for growth — circulation, digestion, and the operation of the nervous system. Until birth, the brain operates instinctively, as did the brain of our hominid ancestors. The power to think, feel, and act expands slowly in company with the child's physical development. These faculties grow as the child's increasing experience of the outside world develops the awareness of self and the ability to cope with external reality. At birth, the child does not possess an ego, which only develops as external reality impinges on the undefended core.

In infant needs no ego as its core movements impel it to seek nourishment and warmth from the mother. If these movements were met with unconditional acceptance from the core of the mother, there would be no need for the ego's interpreting functions; reality would remain undivided. However, such unconditional acceptance is not forthcoming, The mother may be angry, tired, ill, or depressed. She cannot meet the baby's need for unconditional giving. So part of her, at least, will reject the infant's core movements of hunger and need for contact. The infant must interpret this reality of rejection, and the ego begins to develop to do so. Gradually, it becomes aware of itself and its environment, which is represented by the mother. It adjusts its inner movements to account for this reality.

Suppose the mother is ill and cannot nurse the infant or give it sufficient physical contact. If there is merely withdrawal, the infant may interpret that its physical needs will never be met, and the ego of an oral person will begin to develop. If the rejection is perceived as hostile, a schizoid ego may develop.

Broadly speaking, awareness of self and intentional direction of the self make up the human ego. Two other realms of understanding exist that are distinct from the ego but essential forces of human consciousness. One is the emotional, the focus of most psychiatric and psychosocial disciplines. The other is the spiritual faculty, the quality of the core, which includes the faculty of intuition. Much of what is emotional and most of what is spiritual reside in the human unconscious.

The unconscious probably developed among our ancestors and now arises in the infant alongside the ego. The emotions developed to provide a texture against which experience could be interpreted. Both fear and pleasure, for example, were needed for survival. Without the emotion of fear, an organism would have no way to perceive truly dangerous and harmful situations. Pleasure was required to draw the organism into the positive acts needed for survival — nourishment, shelter, and reproduction. Spirituality arose to help explain the unknown. It became a search for unity with cosmic existence, which has led humanity and leads the individual from a state of awareness into one of greater consciousness. Each human being is aware of the environment and of the forces which impinge upon the organism. Evolution of the human species or the individual drives toward an ever deeper understanding of the nature of reality.

Out of this development, then, we have four distinguishable domains of human operations: the physical, the mental, the emotional, and the spiritual. Among these domains, the ego has been honed and shaped by the experiences encountered by individual humans and by all of humanity. Human history shows that peoples have advanced in one or several domains at a time. Such movements continue until they reach an extreme that swings the pendulum of individual and collective development back to a middle position or on to another course.

The agency of direction is the collective and individuated ego. It functions positively and creatively when it works in synthesis with the four human planes and in harmony with the rest of humanity and the environment. The ego functions negatively when it exaggerates one or more domains at the expense of others or of the environment. Chapter 23 describes the spiritual development of humanity, which includes the development of the ego. Here we offer a few brief examples of this collective movement to illustrate the collective development of the ego.

For example, primitive peoples with essentially undeveloped egos gradually developed into the high civilizations of the ancient world where the will and spirit were dominant. Classical Greece emerged from this period, developing the mind to help balance the physical and emotional aspects, but with less emphasis on the spirit. Rome exaggerated the will in the service of conquest, but also made progress in political philosophy. In modern times, the human will again became allied with the mind at the expense of the emotions and spirit. This development led to the industrial revolution and the European conquests of the non-Christian world.

In all of the great cycles of history, the collective and individual ego seized upon the predominant mode to fix and perpetuate the status quo, and to fend off change. The Middle Ages, for example exalted the spirit at the expense of the mind, and the Inquisition was created both to preserve the status quo of established religion and to fend off scientific inquiry which threatened to undermine ecclesiastical power.

All four aspects of human existence contain tremendous positive power when they are working in harmony. But when the ego grasps one or more of them at the expense of others, stagnation results. This is as true of societies as it is of individuals. Rome, for example, exalted will, and to a lesser degree mind, at the expense of emotion and spirit. The monolithic Roman Empire could not adjust to the spiritual and military challenges it faced to the degree necessary to endure. Without the intuitive faculties that come from the spiritual domain, it lacked the creativity and flexibility to meet the new dangers. The same is true with the business executive who relies on will to grasp success and material gain. He cannot cope with change, because he has denied the powers of his spirit and emotions. Therefore, he may deteriorate physically, perhaps with a heart attack or stroke, or will experience failure as he faces the challenge of more creative competitors.

To explore the holistic approach, which core energetics seeks to bring to human growth and development, I will discuss the ego in the existential context and the functions of the ego in health and illness.

Some Concepts of the Ego

As indicated earlier, the ego comprises the person's volitional thinking — self-aware thought and the conscious outer will. It has the ability to discriminate and select, but it does not create. The ego can only collect knowledge, memorize, repeat, copy, sort out, induce and deduce, and make choices. The ego is only a particle of the person's far vaster consciousness of the universe. Unless it is integrated with the greater consciousness, becoming the servant rather than the master, the ego loses its effectiveness and becomes negative. The man in the example, for instance may in his drive for material success ignore the needs and rights of others. He may also drive himself to ignore his own needs in a way that creates illness in his organism.

The word *ego* comes from two Greek roots: *e* meaning "I", and *go*, the contraction of the term for "earth". Numerous metaphysical traditions consider the I to be analogous to the physical eye and seek to develop themselves through the faculty of sight. In a sense, the ego represents the eye on earth, which perceives and interprets reality. The ego in its healthy state becomes the eye of the core and perceives, synthesizes, and directs the flow of energy from and into the core. As the servant of core, the ego steps aside and allows the full force of the core to emerge. If it seeks to ignore the core and become the master, the ego functions negatively, distorting the flow of energy.

In its role as mediator between the core and the outer environment, the ego represents an aspect of the common functioning principle, of which Reich spoke. The common functioning principle explains the process by which we can perceive the unity underlying seemingly different natural phenomena. Thus the ego, which lies on the periphery of human consciousness, has the function of integrating the inner and outer realities of human beings.

The ego's functions are suggested in creative and mystical literature, starting with early history. Greek fragments, even before Homer's time, refer to human self-awareness and self-direction as the part of people which put them in a relationship, and indeed on some footing, with the gods. The idea of an immortal soul having free will, that is, the ego's capacity to choose positively or negatively, made its way into Christianity. As suggested by the analogy of the I of the ego with the physical eye, the child's ego develops along with its capacity to see. Light energy is what the child first perceives when emerging from the womb. The ego develops as the infant's eyesight becomes focused and directed, which allows the child to take in its surroundings more fully and accurately. This vision, therefore, has both an exterior and interior function. Through it the seer can visualize the outside world internally, which provides much of the basis for the person's sense of individuality.

Modern biology and psychology substantiate these intuitive and experiential concepts. Jean Piaget, founder of systematic cognitive research, convincingly demonstrated Freud's theory that the newborn does not distinguish between itself and its environment, that the newborn's consciousness is "protoplasmic" or "symbiotic". This means that the infant understands only slowly that it is a separate entity with an independent identity. Once the sense of separation begins to form, the child begins to develop a very strong connection with parent figures who are seen as the essential sources that respond to the child's needs and desires.

The newborn infant contains everything that the adult personality will become — the best and the worst. The child embodies everything that materializes or which may never materialize during its lifetime. These capacities and potentials remain dormant in the child and awaken only gradually. More accurately, they "reawaken". While it may be academic to discuss here whether a person both in this life existed previously, it is my conviction and experience that no one begins life as a clean slate. If consciousness were viewed as a continuous process, rather than as a disconnected phenomenon, many gaps would be filled, many mysteries clarified, and those who argue the primacy of heredity or environment would be substantiated and unified.

The baby's impulses to reach out arise spontaneously from the personal reservoir of life itself, the core. We saw in Chapter 6 that this essential self was distinct from the outer self, the ego or personality. The core has an inner will, which is the positve consciousness of the core that asserts itself and expects to be responded to in kind. For example, when the baby is hungry, it expects to be fed, no matter how tired or grumpy the parent may be.

In a perfect world, the core would remain open to the ego, which could freely seek the knowledge the human race has harvested. It could allow the core to make its creative contributions as fully as its own potential and outer circumstances permit. But distortions, described in Chapter 10, intervene that divide the ego and fragment both internal and external reality. These distortions — such as the belief that the world is hostile — cause the ego to take on a negative aspect, where under perfect conditions it would function only positively to enhance the person's overall awareness of life. In the individual, as in humanity, the negative aspects of the ego obstruct growth by diminishing communion between the core and the universe, between the individual life force and the totality of life force from which it springs.

I believe that most fields of study have regarded the phenomenon of the ego from an unbalanced and incomplete perspective. Some established schools, such as traditional Buddhism, have minimized its importance. Others, such as conservative psychoanalysis, have presented it as the mainstay of life and identified it with the real self. Even the human potential movement, which emphasizes a holistic approach, tends toward a human-centered world-view and egocentric concepts of the person. Clinical researchers restrict their focus to a cross-sectional investigation of the ego. Many of these schools see the ego as distinct from the outer environment and as the essence of the person.

Yet no phenomenon can be studied apart from its setting. "Setting" means the larger and larger orbits of time, space, and motion around an entity, not only the immediate vicinity with which it interacts. At their best, science and philosphy merge on their frontiers. Astronomy, for instance, makes philosophical inferences about the nature of the universe that go beyond what is known of the material nature of the cosmos. And cosmology has learned not only to rely on the findings of astronomy but to respect ancient religious legacies.

If we study the human ego without considering its setting, it is as though we slice a banana and think the cross-cut fibers represent the total nature of the fruit.

Science has delved deeply into physical and biological evolution. If physical and living matter evolve into ever more complex structures, then it seems logical that consciousness also evolves. Energy and matter have a counterpart of consciousness, as some scientists such as Einstein have theorized. Therefore, ego as an aspect of consciousness must also evolve. Although we assume that we humans are the most advanced order on earth, it would seem folly to suppose that we represent the omega point of evolution.

Humanity has evolved in the nonmaterial domains of intellect, emotions, and spirit as the natural world has evolved in the physical and biological domains. I believe spiritual evolution derives from the gradual releasing of the energy and consciousness of the core. When the core is not negated by the ego, its activity produces the entire spectrum of good feelings, from humor of inspiration, from minor pleasure to consuming ecstasy.

When the ego clasps the lower self, the protective negative layer around the core, it allies itself with the primal negative emotions, which strengthens the defenses and shuts off the full force of the core. The resultant armoring draws more primal energy into itself, much as gravity pulls matter. Depending on the extent of the ego's encroachments, the person becomes increasingly trapped in the mask, the idealized false face that everyone presents to the world. The ego fears integration of the universal and individualized life force as the body fears falling. Since we identify with the ego, the movements of the core seem threatening to us. Perception of the law of gravity on the physical plane parallels the notion that the personality will plummet to the ground and be smashed to nothingness if the ego is not the basic focus of existence.

The human being thus yearns for life movement — core movement — but battles to immobilize the movement. The integrative function of the ego is subverted and our developmental process is derailed when we enthrone the outer self as ruler of our life.

The holistic truth that infuses the human being comes not from the ego but from the core. We perpetuate isolation, distrust, and struggle when we operate from the mistaken fear that identification with the life force will dissolve our individuality. Opening the ego to the core gives us joy, which is only the perceived sensation of free inner activity.

We cannot willfully enter our core. Willpower, used as a separate instrument, is tantamount to an act of aggression against the inner self, which will respond with the protective negativity of the lower self. We begin to reconnect with the core by concentrating on the messages it sends. This takes arduous and persistent work on both the physical and psychological planes, as subsequent chapters will describe.

Humankind has achieved considerable understanding of the organizing activities of the ego. We know that it is the energetic entity in our being that maintains the integration of the physical, emotional, and mental planes of operation. We know that it is the medium by which we master the mechanical as well as the intellectual tasks of life. But the ego should not be confined only to balancing the energy flow in the status quo. Individual human development moves toward larger and larger capacity for comprehension. Our spirituality is the agency which impels us toward unification with cosmic existence. It is embodied in the primal positive qualities of the core and expressed through the ego in actions of love.

The Function of the Ego in Health and Illness

Every person comes into existence with a unique potential to fulfill. This potential resides in and is expressed by the core and is determined by the quantity of the organism's energy. Immediately, a third influence is brought to bear: the environment, first in the womb and then at birth, the outside world. The ego acts and is acted on constantly by all three sets of influences.

A person has continuous chances throughout life to work with these forces to integrate them. The movement toward growth is a creative exercise of the ego. On the other hand, a crisis results when the ego blocks these forces. For example, a financially successful man who keeps going on pep pills is applying the negative aspect of the ego; a man of modest means who takes pleasure in his work without being driven by a compulsion for material gain is applying the ego's creative aspect.

A healthy ego is a strong and flexible medium, permeable to energy flowing outward and inward as objective circumstances allow. The ego can drop its mask and yield to the spontaneity of the higher self. Such an ego sees itself in perspective in the three dimensional setting of earth time, space, and movement. It gives proportion to the expressions of inner reality and seeks avenues for those expressions in outer reality. The ego takes direction from expressions of outer reality and seeks their meaning for inner life. It trains itself to express its intentions positively by focusing on the constructive possibilities in events, even painful ones. It explores the truth about the personality and does not hide from the flaws it discovers, but rather uses its inward eye, its connection with the core, to work them out. The healthy ego takes responsibility for its actions, both by admitting mistakes and by welcoming the expansive feelings of accomplishments. It neither exaggerates itself nor negates itself. It understands that either excess distorts optimum functioning.

For example, the man who finds himself in financial difficulty could blame fate or society and further constrict himself to soften the blows he perceives as unfair. Or, if he allowed his ego to function constructively, he could look at his life to see how he had contributed to his difficulties. In this instance, he would use his ego to look outward to discern the evidences of his problems and inward to explore their causes and to tap the fount of creative energy that lies in his core. In this way, the ego would mediate the inward and outward flow of energy in such a way as to open new possibilities.

This is a rosy picture. Actually, all of us have negative aspects to our ego. The existential conflict that every ego confronts is compounded by life-denying experiences from the environment — parents and other authorities, material surroundings, physical health and safety, and social mores. If those experiences are not resolved on impact because the ego is not able (as in a small child) or willing (as in a negatively intentioned adult) to handle them, the person creates images which distort reality and become neurotic complexes. The mask develops when the core movements are frustrated or rejected.

The man in the example may indeed face outer difficulties, perhaps in a depressed economy. But his perception of his situation can be crucial. That perception most likely was shaped by his childhood circumstances. If his parents seemed unfair to him as an infant and child, he may battle the unfairness he perceives in the outer situation without examining his inner being to find the ways he perpetuates his own difficulties. By identifying with the ego, he has trapped himself in a situation from which there seems no way out.

His inner blockages — the belief in the unfairness of life — turns his ego in a negative direction as it perceives any life situation as dangerous, for example a changing economy that may dictate retraining for a new career. But his life has to flow and adapt to the outer situation; it cannot stand still. To the degree that the life flow is denied, the organism also dies.

His ego, to maintain some form of acceptable reality, fabricates devious and distorted ideas from the real messages of the man's core. And then, in a misappropriation of energy, the ego creates the mask and confuses the real person. In his mask self, the man may say, "I really try hard, but the situation is too difficult for me." The ego further builds the mask with additional stoppages of energy throughout the character armoring. The man may pour more of his energy into defensiveness and hostility, misdirected aggression, or motionless passivity.

Insofar as it functions negatively, the ego is defective and undeveloped. Its imbalance may be caused by a lack of vitality, which makes it underdeveloped or weak, or by an excessive mobilization of energy, which exaggerates and overdevelops it.

The weak ego is incapable of mastering or coping with life effectively. The exaggerated ego is overcontrolling and aggressive, but not strong. Strength entails flexibility and responsiveness, whereas the overdeveloped ego is hard and ungiving, as with the hard-driving personality who battles against life's conditions, even when yielding might be more constructive.

Only when the ego is well-developed does it have both the energy and resiliency to identify with the inner self, which allows the soul to transcend it and the universal life principle to inform it. The importance core energetics theory gives to developing the ego derives from this need for flexible strength. A person who is in difficulty cannot even perceive his or her own mask until the ego applies itself creatively.

I re-emphasize that the ego cannot enter the core by force of will, or indeed by rational thought. No one can force himself to experience the emotion of love, which is the outreaching movement of the soul. Love emerges spontaneously as the person removes the obstacles of misappropriated energy that stand in its way. These include skeletomuscular distortions fixed in the body, misconceptions congealed in the thinking, misdirections frozen into the will — the whole neurotic defense structure which smothers the positive energy movements of the core.

When we strive for happiness, freedom, or spirituality by "putting our minds to it", therefore, we act in self-contradiction. This is true of both the underdeveloped and overdeveloped ego. Self-effacing people sometimes believe that their weakened or suppressed ego is an advantage. They think that it gives harmony to their social relations or releases them from earth-bound interference with their spiritual development. On the contrary, the underdeveloped ego lacks the vigor to integrate the inner self, far less to manage a balanced growth of communication between inner and outer reality. Overly assertive people, by contrast, deplete their inner energy and preempt outer energy to feed the structure of the ego and its control over life. In either case, such people suffer from a truncated and deformed development of the abundant potential of their core. They feed a fundamental selfishness and destructiveness and a resulting sense — accurate in this case — that their lives are empty.

The Ego and the Character Structures

Let us now explore, briefly, how overdevelopment or underdevelopment of the ego unbalances the movement of energy in the five basic character structures. In most, it should be noted, the strength of the ego varies with the degree that energy movement is hindered or freed in any given area of functioning. Therefore, a given type's ego operations may be more dynamic in some regions but more stultified in others.

We saw the main outlines and operations of these character types in Chapter 9, where we cautioned that no person is a type, but has both healthy and unified and ailing and fragmented attributes.

The Oral Character. The ego boundaries of the oral person are tenous, and they easily collapse or inflate throughout the organism. The core of the oral person is undercharged due to deprivation during infancy. The ego of such a person swings, often wildly, between grandiosity and collapse. Lacking sufficient ability to mobilize the core, this person easily falls into a posture of blaming rage or unbounded optimism. The ego is not sufficiently developed to deal with the inflow of energy and experiences that it encounters in its environment.

The Masochistic Character. As we have seen (Figure 14 in Chapter 9) the most notable feature of the masochist's energy system is the overcharging of the outer layer of the personality, which suffocates the core. Therefore, the ego tends to collapse into helplessness or into vindictive and provocative striking out to create the conditions which will justify the release of inner energy in a burst of rage. The ego of the masochist perceives any energy movement, whether from within or without, as a threat and therefore seeks to stifle all such movements.

The Aggressive Character. The ego of the aggressive character is hard, brittle, and threatening. Because the structure is overblown on top and underdeveloped below, energy movements are seen as threats which will topple the massive structure of defense the ego has created. In the face of such imagined threats, the aggressive person adopts the posture of attack.

The Schizoid Character. Because of the fragmentation of this structure, and the deep terror in which it exists, the ego seeks to escape both inner and outer reality. In addition to vagueness, the primary defense of the schizoid structure is cold superiority. The ego cannot integrate the fragments that were scattered in infancy by the hostility the person experienced.

The Rigid Structure. The ego of the rigid structure appears strong, but is cut off from the heart feelings of the core. While on the outer level the ego appears strong, the heart is not open and relations with the opposite sex convey egotism rather than real warmth. Beneath the mask of competence and self-satisfaction is a real sense of inadequacy, dryness, and emptiness. This inadequacy is covered by the masquerade — and the reality — of high order excutive skills and adroitness in dealing with and exercising authority.

These characterological factors are only a sampling of the symptoms found most commonly in the five major types of character structures. A block at any level affects all other levels and the whole organism, as we have seen. That is, a physical block will also affect the mind and emotions as well as overall functioning.

However, each person's dysfunction is unique, because each core is a unique creation. But the myriad forms of dysfunction all derive from the separation between self-awareness and awareness of the whole, a separation that the negative aspect of the ego battles to maintain. This holding state, the life-denying antithesis of nature's purpose, has produced the confused state of humanity and many of its ills.

The progenitors of this confusion, as we saw in Chapter 10, are self-will, pride and fear. The first two are largely conscious. They exist in the mask, and the person will usually take great pains to justify them. The fear is largely unconscious. We fear earthly death because we believe it will extinguish the ego and because we overemphasize the importance of the ego. We fear pleasure, the awareness of free and flowing energy, because we see movement as threatening to the control we exercise with our ego. We fear living because it floods us with invitations to merge with it, to run with it, and to expand with it. Our limited ego is baffled by the multitude of choices. Thus we trap ourselves in fear when we identify with the ego, which is only our instrument of self-awareness.

But the real self is not the ego; it is the core. The human center is the universal life principle individuated in each of us, and it cannot die. It gives and receives generously. It welcomes the invitations of living, for through living its potential is fulfilled. The aim of core energetics, therefore, is to guide the fearful and isolated ego to its vital source, the core.

Chapter 12
THE DYNAMICS OF PAIN
I: ITS NATURE AND ORIGIN

Pain signals the fragmentation of the integrity of the human being. It results when the energy flow is blocked within the organism, and often occurs when one severs the connection between the self and outer reality. Life energy flows in one great stream. When that stream flows unhindered, it produces the sensation and experience of pleasure. Pain is produced by a squeezing, blocking, or contraction that stops or inhibits the flow of energy. The greater the contraction, the more intense the pain. Human beings can produce pain in all dimensions of their being — the physical, emotional, and mental. In each dimension, the conflict between the flow of the life stream and the impediment to its movement creates the perception of pain.

The perception is both objective and subjective. The intensity and speed of pain in the physical body can be measured; the pain is an objective "fact". But consciousness determines how intensely the organism feels the pain, how sustained that feeling will be, or whether the sensation of pain is allowed to flow or made to stop. Therefore, the perception of pain is also subjective. It is an individual experience that alternates with other feelings.

What creates the tightening and blocking that produces pain? In the Greek language, the word for pain is similar to the words for pathos and passion. Pain is related to desire. And excessive desire does create pain through specific mechanisms of the body and the mind, for the human entity desires and fears pleasure. The desire for pleasure assents to and encourages the flow of the life stream; but the fear of pleasure creates the tightening against the flow of the stream to produce pain. Pain occurs when the entity places itself in a state of tension.

This tension occurs in the physical and phychic domains of the human system. Therefore, all pain has two elements — the physical and the psychological. The physical element occurs in the body and can be perceived clinically. It is the product of natural forces or energy. The psychological element contains the emotional and mental elements of pain. In short, the bodily element of pain is expressed through the energy dimension, while the psychological element is expressed through the dimension of consciousness.

We will see later in this chapter how pain operates in each of these dimensions and what is needed to dissolve the pain in each.

The bodily element of pain is easy to experience. As you sit in your chair, squeeze your shoulders, your face, your hands, your whole body. Squeeze very tightly and hold yourself for a few moments. You have created a generalized state of pain by squeezing all the systems of your organism. The squeezing blocks the flow of energy, and thereby creates the pain. Usually the creation of pain is not this obvious, but much more subtle. The personality unconsciously chooses areas of the body, such as the neck, the shoulders, or the pelvis for blocking the energy flow. We experience this after a trying day when we feel an ache in the neck, the shoulders, or the back. We have unconsciously tightened up these areas, in effect, somatizing the emotional tensions we have been feeling.

Although in the natural state human beings seek pleasure and avoid pain, it must be remembered that pain has a very important function to perform. It signals that something is amiss in the organism, for the natural state of the organism is one of allowing energy to flow unhampered. Pain signals that the energy is not flowing freely. It indicates illness — that some part or parts of the system are out of harmony with the natural order. This disharmony is almost always recognized by those who experience pain. They seek relief or a cure through drugs, a physician, a psychiatrist, prayer, a faith healer, or whatever form of healing they trust. The person may seek to alleviate the pain through dealing with symptoms or root causes, but an effort is made to end the pain.

Everybody suffers some pain some of the time, and many people experience pain much of the time. It is a tremendous factor in our civilization. Almost half of the population of the United States has some kind of illness that is associated with pain. About 20 million arthritics are in acute pain. These sufferers take more than 10-15 aspirins per day or anti-arthritic pills. Five of eight million people with heart diseases take anti-pain medications. Millions of others suffer from cancer and degenerating diseases. And millions of others have colds, toothaches, headaches, flu, intestinal ailments, physical tension, and the pain of physical injury.

Emotional pain is associated with but not limited to this array of physical complaints. Many millions of people suffer emotional pain ranging from mild depression to severe distress that can lead to breakdowns and institutionalization. Vast sums are spent on treating these emotional dysfunctions, ranging from individual services to residential care and from simple antidepressants to very powerful medication.

The physical, emotional, and economic costs of pain are staggering. In addition to the billions spent to assuage pain, an estimated $ 30 billion per year in lost productivity is attributed to arthritic cases with lower back pain. If the medical and economic costs of all illness and injuries were added together, the price would be truly titanic. A tremendous number of people use drugs to combat both physical and emotional pain.

It is probably impossible to arrive at a precise economic indicator of pain. However, if a degree of pain and a degree of wellness are assumed in the population, all of the millions of people in the country create a pain-wellness curve. (See Figure 18.) Very few people are at the extreme pain end of the curve. But millions experience intense pain, localized pain, and pain that is generalized as discomfort. They create a big bulge in the curve. And the few people who can sustain feelings of pleasure and wellness most of the time will be found on the upward swing of the pain-wellness curve.

Fig. 18 **Functional Diagram of Pain and Wellness**

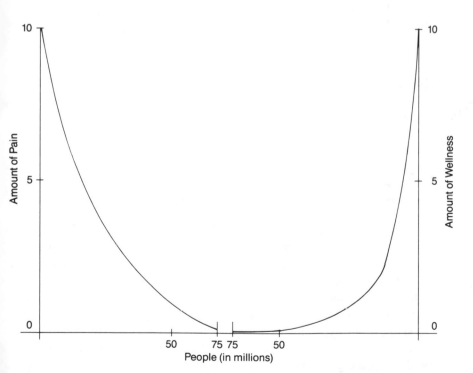

Physical Aspects of Pain

Physical pain also has an emotional component. The physical and emotional aspects of pain are coordinated in the brain, which registers both the physical sensations and triggers the emotional response. The physical mechanism that records the pain is a fantastically complex system, a vast communications network that is condensed into the human body. This system is made up of receivers and transmitters, connectors, recorders, transmission lines, relay stations, and so on. Messages fly back and forth along this system at varying speeds, depending on their intensity and urgency. The system is similar to the communications system that binds our nation and world together.

Physical pain occurs when a stimulus somewhere in the body causes a painful sensation. The stimulus, such as a blow, a jab, or a spasm, impacts on a receptor or many receptors. There are millions of receptors on the surface areas of the human body. The skin contains two kinds of receptors — specialized receptors that are formed like cups, and tendrils which have nerve endings of different fibers. The receptors receive the stimulus, which could be either painful or pleasurable. They transfer perceptions of the stimulus through specific pathways that ultimately connect with the brain.

These pathways begin as two kinds of neurons (nerve cells) which connect the receptors in the skin with the spinothalamic tract — the spinal cord and the thalamic portion of the brain. This tract contains millions of nerve fibers and is located in the spinal cord. The tract carries the pain message (or other sensations) to the thalamus portion of the brain. The transmission of pain uses a complex mechanism of nerves and connections rather than a simple cable or line that carries pain from the point of origin directly to the brain. The numerous neurons and synaptic connections create a pool which connects with other neurons. The pool magnifies or diminishes sensations and creates a very powerful effect of what pain is.

The dynamics of pain are both physical and psychological because the organ that receives the pain message is the thalamus. The thalamus is located in the mid-brain, just above the roof of the mouth. It is a relay center for all kinds of sensor impulses that travel from the receptors to the cerebral cortex. It also integrates sensory impulses. Recognition of such stimuli as pain, temperature, and touch results from thalamic integration.

Many primitive emotions and sensations also reside in the thalamus. As the pain message from the skin is relayed to the other areas of the brain by the thalamus, the pain is perceived in terms of past memories and conditions, the meaning it has to the person, and direct connections with the specific memory points that first register the pain. The way pain is perceived is both voluntary and involuntary, spontaneous and mechanical. Therefore, pain is not a physical sensation alone, but also emotional and mental. When sound comes in, it has to be synthesized and created. The same is true of pain. How it is experienced depends upon the synthesis that is created by the interactions of the stimulus in the brain with other bits of memory, belief, and information.

Types of Receptors

To complicate matters further, four different types of receptors register pain. These are receptors for pain, temperature (hot and cold), light touch, and deep touch. Pain may not result from stimulating the pain receptors, but from stimulating receptors of touch or temperature. Specific pains may be due to a combination of factors. These may include shock, discomfort, actual pain, or a headache. The intensity of pain may vary from terrible suffering to discomfort or malaise.

The distribution of the receptors is not uniform. The stomach and intestine, for example, have no pain receptors. Pain in these organs is produced by pressure and distension. The cornea of the eye, on the other hand, has the greatest number of nerve endings in the body. One square millimeter of the cornea contains millions of nerve endings, which make it very sensitive to touch. The cornea also contains many pain receptors. But some surface areas of the body, such as the ear lobe, have very few receptors. A needle can be pushed through the lobe with no pain. The hand has very thick skin on the palm and is quite insensitive to pain. Overall, the body has a kind of balance, a spreading out of the receptors and how they operate. This distribution undoubtedly is due to the importance of the organ. A tiny prick in the cornea is much more debilitating to the human organism than an identical jab in the hand. Therefore, instead of being uniformly enervated, the body has all kinds of variations and responses to the environment and to the functions of the organs.

Due to these differences in the distribution and concentration of receptors, different kinds of physical pain occur that are characterized in different ways. Neurogenic pain occurs when something has been cut and a nerve severed. The sharp pain of this injury comes from stimulating the end of the receptor. The pain is primarily connected with damage, the perception of which is transmitted to the brain.

Sharp pains are felt right away. The highest speed at which the big fibers transmit pain is 100 meters per second. A meter is 39.37 inches, so sharp pain travels 3,937 inches (or 328 feet) per second. Dull pain moves much more slowly, as little as a half meter per second, or 1/200th the speed of sharp pain. This dull pain is not felt as keenly as the pain of an injury to the eye or to the shinbone, which have many nerve endings. So the speed of pain and its sharpness vary, depending on the thickness of the nerve fibers that produce the pain.

In addition to neurogenic pain, there are pains associated with nerve damage, amputated limbs, heart disease, and muscle fatigue. If a damaged nerve remains outside the body, the pain will be felt as searing heat, instead of the pain of touch or pressure. This pain is called *synesthesia*. The neurons touch so that different perceptions are registered — pain instead of temperature, heat instead of pain.

The pain of phantom limbs is more mysterious. After an amputation, a person will feel like the missing member is being punctured by needles. The person will have specific sensations in the missing toes or in the calf of the missing leg, for example. The pain can be unbearable — searing heat or excruciating pain.

Neurosurgeons can do little about the pain of a phantom limb. They can cut out the endings of the nerve in the stump or put a flap of skin over them to protect them. Or the sympathetic ganglia may be removed or injected with novocaine. I believe the pain of the phantom limb occurs because the energy body remains after the physical limb is amputated. As described in Chapter 4, an energy body occupies the same space as the physical body but has a higher vibration. It corresponds exactly to the various organs and parts of the body. In the case of an amputation, the energy body of the limb is reabsorbed very slowly. If the person is not angered by the amputation, and gives in to and accepts the process, reabsorption will be relatively easy. But the person who feels angry, victimized, or paranoid will maintain an emotional connection with the phantom limb. Subconsciously, the person does not want to let go of the lost limb and does not withdraw the energy body inside of the remaining self. So the pain of phantom limbs, as all other pain, has a lot to do with the person's intentions.

In the case of the phantom limb, the person tightens up. The anger or rejection of the situation causes the person to become tense and to block the flow of the energy back into the body. The tensing or cramping is the source of most pain, including that of a heart attack. In a heart attack, an infarct (dead tissue) plugs one of the main coronary arteries. This plug blocks the circulation completely, cutting off the oxygen supply to the heart muscle. This is similar to the process that occurs when a leg muscle is used extensively. The circulation, especially of the oxygen supply, is cut off or depleted and the muscle becomes very spastic. When the oxygen is depleted in a leg muscle, it will stay contracted until the energy is restored, in the form of oxygen and blood sugar.

In addition, blood vessels have sympathetic nervous system endings. So the heart pain is transmitted directly into the plexuses, which are nerve networks. These networks magnify the pain, which becomes massive. From the sympathetic nervous system, the pain spreads via the vagus and phrenic nerves into the diaphragm and stomach. This is why the perception of a heart attack often seems to begin with pains in the stomach. The pain is so tremendous because the heart muscle cramps.

The Origin of Pain

Today we know that pain is both physical and emotional. It is perceived as the threat of injury to the integrity of the body, its psychosomatic unity. The person evaluates the degree and kind of the threat. For instance, a little child will see a needle and believe that he is going to die; the pain is intense. Someone else who is stuck with a needle for an injection may experience relatively little pain. Freud reports that one of his patients had an operation on a bone in his hip with a brother present. When the doctors cracked the joint, the brother reported that he felt a tremendously sharp pain in his hip also. Freud said this was a psychogenic (emotional) pain. The intensity with which pain is felt depends largely on how one evaluates the threat to one's integrity and safety. This does not mean there is no physical pain or that all pain is emotional. It does mean that all pain contains elements of both.

What is the origin of pain? It is the result of conflict between the life forces and the anti-life forces. As we have seen, the life forces originate in the core, which seeks to flow unimpeded. This flow is hampered, slowed down, squeezed off by the layers that surround the core. The layer of primal negative emotions (see Figure 1, Chapter 2) slows down the core's energy pulsation, but the energy continues to flow, although it is laden now with negativity rather than positivity. The pulsation of both positive and negative energy is met and arrested at the level of the defenses. This arresting of the force creates the pain.

The life force has three dimensions: motility, consciousness or knowing, and experience. Unimpaired, movement and consciousness create a great deal of pleasure. When they become stuck, they create atrophy in the body, stagnation in the mind, and repression and suppression in the emotions.

Atrophy, stagnation, and repression are blocks. The blocks create resistance, which, in turn, creates pain. Resistance in an electrical wire is caused by a kind of metal that will not transmit the current. This resistance to the free flow of electrons creates heat. It is the principle behind the simple electric space heater, or a toaster. In the human being, the resistance creates the pain which is equivalent to heat. Indeed, as we have seen, pain is often experienced as heat.

If resistance creates the pain, what creates the resistance. The ability and willingness to allow the force of life and love to flow is hampered from the beginning of life by the taboos of society. These taboos are reflected in the attitudes of the parents who seek to restrict the child's sexuality and feelings. The child feels the disapproval coming from the parents and squeezes off the proscribed feelings. Thus, the life force, the life energy, the erotic forces in an individual get stuck. The child feels compelled to sacrifice an essential part of its being for the love and approval of the parents.

However, this choice is accompanied in the child by spite and competitiveness, for which the child feels very guilty. The child's anger and hatred toward the parents comes from feeling rejected. If these negative feelings were allowed to flow freely, they could be discharged and there would be no pain because the energy flow would not be blocked. But the negative feelings are also unacceptable. Children are supposed to love, not hate, their parents. So the child covers the negative emotions with a mask of pretended love and compliance.

At the same time that the child is creating the mask of pretense, he is generalizing about all of life from the childhood experience. Often this generalization occurs very early in life. It is done at the unconscious level or is quickly buried in the unconscious mind. Even when the generalizations are conscious, they will be vague because the child lacks the language and conceptual power to precisely formulate ideas. In a sense, the child creates imprints, mental representation, or images of situations in life where certain feelings are not permitted. Therefore, these buried imprints or images keep recreating themselves again and again in adult life. There is an unconscious compulsion to recreate the original childhood trauma.

A boy child, for example, may conclude that it is not safe to have sexual feelings for the opposite sex. These feelings were sternly condemned by the parent. When the child becomes an adult, he may inhibit these feelings with his mate without consciously knowing why, or even that he is doing it. But unconsciously, the adult man believes the sexual feelings are bad or dangerous. Or suppose that the little boy's mother manipulates him, sometimes accepting his feelings and sometimes rejecting them. The boy creates the image that women are not to be trusted. He probably will develop an intense hatred and contempt for the woman. Later in life, when he becomes a man and marries, he has the same attitude. It will not matter if his wife is manipulative or not; she will be seen that way because of his images. And since he believes that women are manipulative, he may marry a woman who does the same things his mother did. After all, according to his image, a woman who does not manipulate him is not a woman.

In another situation, the parent says to the child, "I want you to be perfect. You should be a doctor. I'd be so disappointed if you married someone poor." The child internalizes this ideal and tries to measure up to it all the time during adulthood. The internalized ideal is called an idealized self-image. It can never be fully attained and probably differs substantially from the child's real potentialities. In striving to become the idealized image, the child (and adult) sells out the true self. In effect, the child blocks the free flow of energy and movement toward life through these conditioned reflexes. This blockage is what creates pain.

The child, of course, is not a victim. Each of us brings our own energy and individuality into the world, and these clash with the wishes and desires of our parents. These clashes create the specific conditions and attitudes in us on which we must work for the rest of our lives. As long as the attitudes remain buried, we are out of reality, in a state of tension, and therefore in pain.

So instead of feeling fully the initial pain of the parental rejection, the child creates images, an idealized self-image, and a set of defenses to ward off pain. These defenses embrace pseudo-solutions with which the child seeks both to avoid pain and to get what he or she wants. One child may adopt a pseudosolution of submission and dependency in the belief that this will buy love and approval. Another may cover up the pain with a mask of serenity and withdrawal. A third may seek power to defend against the pain.

The adult person uses these pseudo-solutions in all situations and relationships to the degree that the life energy was suppressed in childhood. Not only do the pseudo-solutions not work — for they are based on wrong and immature conclusions — but they help produce the very pain they were created to avoid. Instead of allowing for the free flow of energy and experience, pseudo-solutions seek to catch, hold, and channel the energy toward desired results. By resisting the natural flow of the life force, the pseudo-solutions create pain. They also create pain in others, by trying to force them to be something other than they are and by hurting and rejecting them when they do not comply.

If we allow the pain to flow instead of fighting it, the pain would go right through us and gradually stop all together. Allowing the free flow of pain permits the divided stream of life to move in one direction. So instead of becoming stuck in a certain area, the stream flows back together and reunifies. The flow can even go in a negative direction instead of a positive one; the pain still would be alleviated because the energy would not be blocked. Many of us have had the experience of bottling up negative feelings until we become almost immobilized. An explosion of anger often can release the positive flow of energy again — at least for a time. There are, of course, constructive and destructive ways and places for releasing negative energy. It is obviously more desirable to pummel and scream at a bed that represents the target of our anger rather than the person in question.

The early childhood experience helps to explain the origin of emotional pain. Its connection to physical pain is less obvious. However, the pain of most ailments and diseases can be traced to the decisions the child made to block off the flow of positive and negative energy. The energy and pain is not only held emotionally and mentally, but it is inhibited in specific areas of the body, as Reich described. For example, a child whose crying is inhibited by the parents will tighten up the chest, throat, and jaw to hold back sobs. Not only is the flow of energy in the form of heat blocked, but circulation is diminished. The adult may have respiratory problems due to the blocked energy in the chest and throat. Often, these problems will reoccur in situations that unconsciously remind the adult of the originating childhood situation. However, the adult probably will not connect the problems to the childhood situation without considerable deep work.

Arthritis is another ailment which is related to childhood deprivation. In arthritis the joints become inflamed, the cartilage is changed, and calcium is deposited in the joints. The joints are under tremendous tension. They are connected by the muscles, which are like ropes. A clothes line hung with a lot of clothes will experience the pressure of the line at the point of attachment, at the ends. The joints, the points of attachment in the body, are points of enormous tension in people who have arthritis. Arthritics feel very wanting, that they never get what they wanted. They have a tremendous demand to get what they want. This demand seems insatiable. The state of contraction mounts very quickly. The muscles tighten and pull the joints, which creates tremendous change in the tissues. In working with arthritics, we find a lot of dependency and unquenchable demands on life. The tension between the demand and its inhibition places the physical system of the body under great stress.

We find then that physical and emotional pain are deeply connected in the unconscious mind. Excavating the sources of pain, in order to provide the understanding necessary to release it, requires extensive work on all levels —

the physical, emotional, and mental. We must call upon the spiritual, both as a source of healing and as a touchstone by which the person can see beyond the current condition. The next chapter explores why the unearthing of the origins and dynamics of pain must be so painstaking.

Chapter 13
THE DYNAMICS OF PAIN
II: THE ATTACHMENT TO PAIN

If the natural order calls for the life stream to flow unhindered and to create pleasure, why do human beings hold so strongly to negativity and pain. Why is it so hard to give up the pain? Why are so many people suffering? Most people would be shocked at the idea that they prefer pain to pleasure. But there are several reasons why human beings cling to their pain. People create pain by stopping the flow of positive feelings as well as negative ones. Feelings of love and expansiveness may be blocked as much as feelings of spite, fear, or the desire for revenge. One part of the person wants movement and pleasure, but another part wants nothing to do with these good feelings. The part that suppresses the feelings of pleasure is unconscious. But the person expresses in other ways the conviction: "I don't want any help. I don't want to have pleasure. I want to stay with my pain." The person prefers pain because it is safe and known. There is security in it. And pain gives a person a sense of limits.

The person may sulk with or rebel against pain, but still feel deserving of it. It is the price paid for something else, or "benefits" that come from taking the pain. People cling to pain as a way to get others to take care of them, to attract sympathy and attention. Witness, for example, the hypochondriac who complains constantly of one discomfort or another. Or pain can be used to punish others. People take secret delight in getting vengeance against others for what they lack. Pain may provide benefits and security, but in a distorted way. The price paid is intense pain and a lot of illness. The point which is being underscored here is that people may have a negative wish for pain. This wish often is not known to the person in pain. The negative wish creates a tension which produces the pain. But due to lack of self-awareness, a gap exists in the person's understanding between the negative wish and the creation of the pain.

The gap creates confusion, because the person says consciously, "I don't want the pain; are you kidding?" The confusion arises because the person does not know that the other part exists. The connection between cause and effect — the wish and the pain — is lost in the gap in awareness. This lack of connection occurs in everyone and creates pain on the physical, emotional, and mental levels.

Sources of the Attachment

The attachment to pain is embedded in the human entity during the early childhood experiences when feelings and sexuality are inhibited by the parents and society. In a sense, the attachment is fixed by the same processes which trigger the pain in the first place. We have seen in Chapter 10 how these parental attitudes affect children, causing them to tighten up and to draw generalizations about life and peoples. In contributing to the block to sexuality, the parents affect the whole person, because sexuality incorporates the elements of love, Eros, and the biological forces, which Chapter 21 describes. The three elements are integral to the life force.

Since to totally block the life stream and the free flowing of the pleasure principle would mean death, the child adopts other strategies. Some of the pleasure principle is attached to negative emotions and attitudes. Often, negativity is accompanied by excitement and pleasure. This is seen most vividly in people with sadistic tendencies. Married couples, for example, may live for weeks or months with deadness and blandness in their relationship. The flow of energy is very low. Then one of them cannot stand the lack of energy and excitement and provokes a fight. Even though the fighting may be destructive, there is life and energy in it. The negativity is allowed to flow between the partners for a while. Then they are able to make up and be loving until the pleasure becomes unbearable again.

In childhood, the blocked energy current produces pain and an unconscious fixation of pleasure to negative attitudes. At the same time, the image or misconception is produced, which also becomes unconscious. When it comes to the surface, the unconscious fixation produces a compensatory attitude of fighting and resisting to maintain the integrity of the child. The defenses are built around the fixation, which also engenders envy, hatred, and competitiveness. The nucleus of these attitudes is, of course, guilt. For such a person to experience total pleasure is very much feared. Why? Because the personality is geared for negative experience and negative excitement. To the degree that there is cheating, impure motives, defenses, guilt, and malice, the pleasure principle must be rejected. The person feels undeserving of pleasure. In addition, the idea is deeply implanted in the unconscious from earliest childhood that the pleasure principle itself is unacceptable. With these attitudes, the person finds pleasure unbearable.

The very peculiar problem in our culture is not the unwillingness to experience terrible negative trials and tribulations as such. The problem is the way we resist the pain of the trials and tribulations and the way we feel unworthy to experience pleasure. A couple, for example, may be willing to go through a painful separation and divorce proceedings. There can be a lot of rancor in the division of property and assigning the custody of children. But the partners may totally resist feeling the pain and sadness of the breakup of their marriage, much as they were unwilling to experience pleasure during their life together. As long as pleasure can be experienced, it does not matter how hard people work or how intense they are. If people give themselves the right to experience pleasure, it equalizes their lives.

The medicine for the pain, then, is to feel the pleasure. But this is difficult. Even if the pleasure is there, people cannot avail themselves of it because they do not believe they deserve it. We all have numerous opportunities for success and for taking important steps in life. But until the place of unworthiness is resolved, there can be no movement. We may find many justifications and rationalizations for failure later on, but the problem is in the unwillingness to experience pleasure, in the fixation on the pain.

An example of how the negative fixation works would be a person who has both positive and negative aspects, which includes everyone. Both aspects are attached to the pleasure principle. If the person is in a relationship with another, the internal conflict between the positive and negative aspects will be at work in the relationship.

In this relationship, Arthur is very creative and open. But Betsy cannot handle this and becomes negative and contracted. She pulls away. Arthur tries to open to Betsy a few more times. She continues to remain contracted and closed. Arthur finally withdraws from the relationship. He feels justified and experiences pleasure from withdrawing. He says, "I tried; I really tried. You wouldn't open up, so it's your fault." Then Arthur starts gloating about Betsy's faults. He puts more energy into his negative attitudes which are attached to his pleasure principle than he does into positive effort. He has become lost within himself by identifying with the negative part of himself. He is unwilling to experience the pain of disappointment. If Betsy then opens up, Arthur probably will close off and withdraw. Then Betsy will start gloating and wallowing in the pleasure of his withdrawal.

This dynamic occurs in many relationships. It shows that there are lots of traps in the way of being able to stay with the positive feelings. When we are wronged by another person, we often gloat over how wrong that person is. We then feel that we must put a lot of energy into covering up that we are being negative also. We lose perspective on life and fall into pain.

It is important, when trying to recapture the capacity for pleasure, to be able to put aside what another person does to cause hurt. In working to eliminate negative aspects, the first basic principle is to take 100 percent responsibility for what has happened. We need to say, "How did I participate in that?" even if the other person contributes 70, 80, or 99 percent to the situation. The matter becomes complicated when people use their perception and understanding to twist and rationalize situations. They justify their own actions and feelings and believe they are rightfully negative, rightfully resistant, and rightfully angry with co-workers, bosses, partners, or spouses. The important point is that the negativities are attached to both the pain principle and the pleasure principle.

In the pain principle, the negativity is attached to the pain to create excitement. When negativity is attached to pleasure, there is a distorted perception of what pleasure is. Because of these intense conflicts buried in the individual, the personality creates in two directions at the same time. One direction is the flow of the stream of life, which contains light, growth, unfoldment, union, and love. Another stream contradicts and stands against the positive flow. The second stream contains darkness, stagnation, withholding, separation, and hate. The clash of the two streams produces tension.

This inner struggle is like two cars, locked at their front bumpers and racing their engines. This tremendous power may move them very slowly, first in one direction and then in another. The power is fully mobilized and almost completely arrested at the same time. If the cars continue for very long, their systems begin to break down from the enormous tension. The same thing happens within human beings. The clash of the positive and negative energy, and the repression of the struggle, creates tension and pressure. This is why pain often is experienced as pressure in the system. In the human system, tremendous forces are captured and immobilized so that they move very slowly and only with great effort.

While all human beings experience this battle of positive and negative forces to some degree, the struggle is most clear in the masochistic character structure. The masochist has tremendous reservoirs of energy that constantly seek outer expression. However, due to an excessive input of energy from the mother during childhood, the masochistic person perceives all energy movements as dangerous and smothering. So the defensive structure reacts to the inner movements by capturing them and turning them back on themselves. The person is constantly locked in an intense inner struggle, which often produces a massive physical structure. If the predominantly masochistic person cannot find someone to provoke an outburst to release the energy, a collapse occurs into a morass of depression and despair. This inner dynamic creates the pain and the person's attachment to it.

Suffering people may think that the pain comes from somewhere else — from sickness, an accident, or an injury. Or they may believe their emotional pain is due to hurts inflicted by others. However, if we examine ourselves and the painful situation deeply enough, we will find the cause within ourselves. This can be very hard to believe. A man has an accident. The other party seems clearly at fault. The victim says, "I didn't want this. Look at these hospital bills. Why does this have to happen to me?" To see how people attract and hold on to pain, we must understand a little more about the tremendous forces at play.

The Negative Force Field

The life stream, which is made up of energy and consciousness, contains tremendous power. It is like a force field or energy field. It contains many seeds of creation. In a sense it creates events, patterns, forms, and very many variations of experience. The field creates the form, nature, shape, and activity of the physical body of each person. If the field is made up of positive energy, the body is balanced and harmonious. When the field is negatively charged, the body will be out of balance and blocked. The shape of the body is an outpicturing of the total entity of the human being — the emotions, the mental processes, and the spirit. The concept of body structure and character formation has been described in Chapter 9. The physical shape and appearance of the body is a counterpart to the psychological concepts of the person.

The way the energy is expressed in terms of its physical aspects, ideas, feelings, and mental processes gives shape and form to the body. The body can be long, short, thick, blown up, or very rigid. It can be mobile and free moving, or inflexible and tight. For example, a child whose parents thwarted his sexual feelings may pull into the upper half of the body, creating a tremendous torso and shoulders, which are perched on a relatively small lower half. Another person may develop layers of fat around the pelvis to smother sexual feelings. Some people block and smother rage with an over-development of the upper back and shoulders. These and many other distorted physical characteristics are expressed in human beings due to each person's distortion of energy and consciousness. In this sense each creates his or her own body.

The human force field is like a fantastic energy vortex. It can almost be compared to an electromagnetic field. But the electromagnetic field has different qualities than the one created by energy and consciousness. The qualities of the human force field have yet to be fully studied and understood. This force field creates in a specific mold that is directly related to the degrees of distortion of energy and consciousness that make up the life stream. Once this mold is fixed it is very difficult to break. The force field perpetuates itself until the energy and consciousness are changed. By creating the field, people trap themselves in repeated patterns which bring them emotional and physical pain.

The energy field both attracts and repels, like a magnet. A person who feels positive about life attracts a lot of good feelings and reactions. People sense the good vibrations, even though the person may not say or do anything. In a negative mood, the same person will attract negative thoughts and reactions. People know immediately when another person is feeling negative and critical. The negative vibrations of a person's force field send out the message: "Stay away from me; I'm angry and negative." When a painful event occurs as the consequence of a person's behavior or attitude, the person does not know what specific attitude or belief created the event. Often, these attitudes are unconscious. The person will say, "Are you crazy? I certainly didn't cut myself on purpose."

It is very important to understand the role of the unconscious beliefs and attitudes, of the images which have been discussed previously. If attitudes and beliefs are conscious, they can be challenged directly and changed, thus changing the energy field. But if they are unconscious, the attitudes cannot be changed. The energy field continues to create negative situations. To the person, the flow of unpleasurable events seems totally outside the area of personal responsibility. All attitudes and ideas can be sorted out. It is the false ideas that create negative events in a person's life. They must be brought to consciousness, challenged, and discarded to make room for new and true ideas.

If we probe our unconscious deeply enough, we will find out how we created situations that we are consciously convinced we did not ask for. Again, suppose there is an accident. Somebody pulls from a side street and smashes into a man's car. He says, "Look at my car. I paid a lot of money for it. This really is an injustice. How can you say I was responsible? This guy pulls out and smashes my car. This clearly is an accident and not my fault."

But if he would go more deeply into his unconscious attitudes, he would find a place where he feels a lot of guilt for owning a new car. He believes he does not deserve it. His unconscious negative attitudes and behaviors create guilt in him. Perhaps he bought the car to impress others or to show that he is better than his friends and coworkers. His unconscious beliefs and desires create an energy that spins and hooks into the energy of another person or condition. In this case the other person in the accident may have similar beliefs and guilts. Their energies spin together, amplify together, and create a crisis. There is no such thing as an accident. We create all aspects of our lives, the pain as well as the pleasure. Often we do not want to take responsibility for either.

The negative energy distorts the force field. The distortion is parallel to the images that are built deeply into the mind. For example, if a little boy has a hateful mother, he forms an attitude about hate in all women. He creates a very deep image in his mind that all women are hateful. The image is, in effect, the force field which he will create later in many circumstances related to women. The image will compel him to act toward women in certain repetitive ways. He may submit to and try to placate women in order to fend off the expected hatred. Or he may become hostilely aggressive.

It does not matter if the particular women are hateful or not. He will see them that way because of his image. His defensive attitudes will attract hatred to him from women. If he is submissive, he will get contempt; if aggressively hostile, he will receive hostility in return. His attitude will become a source of pain, since he also wants a warm and loving relationship with a woman. He will not connect his loneliness or his difficult relationship with women to his image, which remains unconscious.

Human beings strongly resist changing the negative force field. To give it up means giving up the nuclear defensive attitudes within the field — a very difficult undertaking which is quite threatening to the personality. People do not want to change the images and original perceptions. They are the bricks and mortar of the idealized self-image. The images people adopt are made up of perception, sensation, experience, and knowledge. These elements of the image spin a force field like a double vine. The ends of the "vine" rotate in opposite directions squeezing the person in the middle. They pull the energy out of the physical body and trap it in the energy body. The images become knots in the stream of energy. The knots tie up a person's energy in much the same way as one person who is very resistant can tie up the energies of many other people. With one or two such people in a group, the energy of the whole group becomes bound and nobody knows why. The group is being pulled down by the weight of the negativity and the maligning that is going on in the mind and energy of the ones who are resisting.

Physical energy is stopped in the physical body. Mental and emotional energy flows or is blocked in one of the various energy bodies. These bodies correspond to and fill essentially the same space as the physical body. As described in Chapter 7, there are many energy bodies. But we need to deal with only three in relation to the dynamics of pain. While the energy bodies occupy essentially the same space, they vibrate at different rates. The first energy body exactly fits all the organs and parts of the physical body and represents them. Its vibration rate is higher than that of the physical body. This energy body is the one that hurts when a limb or organ is removed. The energy body with the next higher vibration rate is the emotional body, where all emotions are formed. The body which is the seat of ideas vibrates at a still higher rate.

These bodies interpenetrate and exist in the same space as the physical body. When a person is hurt, the pain occurs in the energy bodies before it affects the physical body. If the hurt is resisted and intensified in the energy bodies it becomes somatized. If love is rejected people may feel a pain in the heart and say they are heartbroken or that their heart aches.

The Varieties of Pain

The negative force field traps energy in the energy bodies and causes a great deal of pain. Ultimately the physical pain is created because the person tightens up and stops the stream of life and energy in the physical organism. There are many varieties of emotional and mental pain. They are created by the different images and beliefs that a person holds. For example, a person who believes that love is unsafe or a trap may create the emotional pain of hate. When this person throws out hateful feelings, the recipients of the hatred will contract their bodies and pull in the energy. But the ones who hate also will suffer pain. They have tightened against the energy flow and stopped their own energy. Love is part of the positive flow of energy. This flow is twisted into the energy of hate, which causes us to twist our own energy and physical bodies. Some confusion exists between hate and anger. Anger does not hurt. It can serve as a defense against real hurt from another person. A person often is entitled to be angry. But hate is like a dagger. It lashes out and hurts the other person. Hate is expressed with the intention to hurt, but anger often erupts spontaneously.

Confusion is another type of pain that occurs when one does not understand what is happening. For example, when a therapist tries to understand a client, nothing seems to give. There is no opening. The person argues and the therapist ends up feeling frustrated. The client is confused, the therapist is confused, and both are in pain. While chronic and real, the pain of confusion is not sharp. It is more like disgust or a malaise, a suffering which creates a lot of rage and anger. Often the recipient of confusing messages wants to smash the one sending them. Confusion also is intentional. The person does not want to take responsibility for what is happening, and resists the negative flow of energy, the negative truths that one does not want to face, and thus creates greater pain. In a very real sense confusion is against fusion (con fusion), fragmenting the fusion of energy and consciousness.

Related to confusion is the pain of resisting the truth of the inner feelings. People who resist the best in themselves experience terrible suffering. They may deny that they are resisting the truth for extended periods of time. They may even deny that anything hurts. Indeed, they may be unaware of the pain for a long time. But the more the pain is denied, the greater it becomes. Many people deny this pain for decades. For example, a young woman may yearn to be a forest ranger, but marries because the parents insist. She pretends she really wants to be married, works hard at it, and attains some success. She will totally deny the yearning to be a forest ranger. Year after year the pain of this denial builds up. In addition, she probably will deny feelings of anger, hatred, and revenge toward the parents, whom she blames for the choice of careers. She will have contempt for herself for selling out her longing. Eventually this pain will erupt in physical or emotional distress and illness, perhaps a life crisis that threatens her marriage. The longer the pain is denied, the greater the breakdown when it occurs.

In addition to all the other pains, most people suffer from the very common pain of guilt. This pain results from not recognizing the truth. The truth is that people who suffer the pain of guilt have done something that is not right for them. There is very real guilt for this. But the guilt is often exaggerated and many more guilts are held on to from earlier experiences. It is important for the adult to deal with present day guilts.

Often old guilts are grabbed and put in front of the person as a defense against admitting present guilts. The person says, "I feel so guilty. My father rejected me. My mother was awful. Look how much I am suffering." At the same time, decisions are being made that violate the person's inner truth. One avoids facing the destructive attitudes and making restitution. The guilt cannot be simply washed away. The person must examine it to find the negative intention for the actions that induce the guilt. Why does the person hold on to the ancient guilt? What is being covered up? Admitting and releasing the negative intention gives restitution for the guilt and cleans the energy.

One of the deepest pains is that of injustice. This pain arises when people lack faith in the meaning of life. They believe that life and the universe — God — are chaotic and hostile. These beliefs create a very chronic, very engulfing pain. It causes despair. The person says, in effect, "Why does this happen to me? Why am I being punished? God is cruel. Life has no meaning. I lost my wife. I lost my job. I feel so much pain."

Although the pain of injustice is one people inflict on themselves, they feel that injustice comes from universal, cosmic, or societal forces that are outside of themselves. They believe they have nothing to do with it. However, as we have seen, if any pain is examined very deeply a connection will be found. In this instance, a person may lack faith because of repeated childhood disappointments. These disappointments create an inner image that life cannot be counted on, that injustice is the nature of the universe. The image will create a negative force field that attracts seemingly unjust situations.

All of these mental and emotional pains are created when the life stream is stopped. Movement and consciousness are blocked in some way which creates a cramp, a tension in the person. In the pain of injustice, for example, the person does not trust that the unhampered flow of life will bring goodness and pleasure. When people try to divert or dam the flow of life energy and experience, they seek to ward off the injustices they believe will come. They want the life stream to flow in channels that are safe and known. But in trying to stem the flow, people subtly tighten up, and exert a pressure that conflicts with the energy that is flowing within. The pain is caused ultimately by the belief in an unjust universe.

Chapter 14
THE ANATOMY OF EVIL

"Evil" is a word that has been used and overused, thrown at us for millennia by organized religions and philosophies. We are allergic to it today; it makes some of us anxious and turns some of us deaf. But I think we should listen to this word and examine what it represents, for the concept of evil is as old as man, and there is a continuity in human perception.

Ours is an age of alienation, many say; we have lost touch with the universe and with each other. We are so "busy", we worry so about bills, we have so many fears that our minds are closed. But people also are struggling to reach their own and others' inner selves, and there is a new awareness that we must unravel the phenomenon of evil to open a vital source of truth in us. All the contributions of the past have a bearing on this task. Ours, therefore, is also one of unification and integration.

Philosophers, religious fathers, and thinkers from the dawn of civilization have grappled with the concept of evil. Men have generally believed in a God or Gods, conceived of as a beneficent force from whom all creation and the good flow. Yet there is a contradiction in this belief, for how can God, who is good, create evil? The paradox has led many philosophers to compromise. Some have adopted a monistic view of evil and others a dualistic view. Monists have held that evil has no existence of itself; dualists have asserted that the principle of evil is as eternal as the good principle, the principle of God, and is either equally powerful or only relatively weaker.

The oldest dualistic view was propounded by Zoroaster, who flourished in Persia in the sixth century B. C. His followers represented the good by the entity of Ormadz and evil by the entity of Ahriman. Dualism is found in the third and fourth centuries of the Christian era in Manichaeanism, which believed in a basic conflict between light and dark, between God and the devil as equal principles. The monistic approach was expressed in the philosophy of Plato, who reported Socrates as saying that evil is the result of ignorance and has no real existence, and therefore wise men should disregard it.

The Judeo-Christian tradition has assimilated both approaches but with the emphasis on monism, for Platonism was taken in and reworked with

Christian ideas in particular. The Old Testament teaches that evil is a consequence of rebellion against God. The Book of Genesis presents Adam's fall as man's revolt against his creator, an act that made all humankind — originally destined to live forever — mortal. The Books of Judges, Samuel, and Kings say that if Israel can obey God, it will heal its wounds. There is a primitive concept in the early Judaic tradition that good is rewarded by good and bad is punished. Later, in the pre-Christian Second Book of Maccabees, it is written that God will punish and reward, not necessarily in this life but in the next.

An Old Testament theme attributed to the prophet Isaiah recurs as the central teaching of the New Testament. Isaiah's mysterious servant of the Lord suffered for his people, predating Jesus' redemption of sinners by his suffering and death. Thus when suffering is united with love, it will repair evil and lead to redemption. In the Christian tradition the presence of evil is related to man's free will. Physical evil is seen as retribution for sin; and except in certain latter-day Protestant churches, punishment for serious sin is believed to persist through eternity.

Among the early church fathers, Origen, a theologian of the third century, conceived of evil as the deprivation or negation of the good, and asserted that all men and all spiritual beings will be converted to Christ eventually; therefore, he rejected the teaching that evil is eternal. Saint Basil, a Greek father writing in the fourth Century, said that evil has no substance of its own but arises from the mutilation of the soul. In the same period, Saint John Chrysostom — "Chrysostom" means golden mouth, and a tremendous orator he was — taught that evil is nothing but a turning away from the good. His contemporary Saint Augustine agreed: Evil is not a substance, he argued, for it has no god as its author. And the thirteenth-century philosopher Saint Thomas Aquinas said that the name evil signifies the absence of good.

Philosophical thinkers and men of letters have added other perspectives. Immanuel Kant wrote in the eighteenth century that the good is a categorical imperative, and anything that contradicts it is evil. G. W. F. Hegel saw good and evil as thesis and antithesis of the forces of nature and the universe. And Wolfgang von Goethe, in *Faust*, has Mephistopheles say, "I am the spirit that denies, and rightly so." Five centuries earlier Dante, in the *Divine Comedy*, had described man descending the inverted spiral of progression into the depth of hell, where lies a frozen lake. The devil, frozen up to the waist, bats his wings and grabs other entities around him and chews them up. People are frozen in his lake in different degrees — up to the ankle, up to the knees, up to the neck. Evil is equated with the frozen state of man.

The psychological thinkers from the turn of our century have, of course, searched for the meaning of evil in terms of its function in mental illness. Freud wrote in *Totem and Taboo,* ''Concerning the evil demon, we know that he is regarded as the antithesis of God and yet is very close to him in his nature. His history has not been so well studied as that of God. Not all religions have adopted the evil spirit, the opponent of God.'' It does not take much analytical perspicacity, said Freud, to guess that God and devil were originally identical, and that this single figure was split into two figures with opposite attributes. He also developed the concept of ambivalence, the conflict between the positive and the negative in a person.

Jung, in his explanation of archetypes, identified the first of these as the shadow. It has been believed that the shadow is the source of all evil. In actuality it consists not only of reprehensible qualities but also of normal instincts, creative impulses, and realistic insights. Eric Neuman, in *Origin of the History of Consciousness,* opposes the dualistic concept of God and devil, suggesting that the devil is part of the creative abyss of every living personality. He is the antagonist, the shadow, and he appears persistently in myths as a twin whose double is called the companion.

Wilhelm Reich has given us an overview of man that combines the perspectives of the scientist, the psychiatrist, and the philosopher. In his book *Ether, God, and Devil,* Reich said that the devil has an essential function and is expressed in the neurotic, armored animal in ways discussed in Chapter 5.

All these thinkers who have gone before us have provided a profusion of explanation for evil. We see that same conflict. Those who consider that evil is an illusion, for example, gainsay those who claim that it is an observable fact for anyone who faces reality. Who is right? It will say a paradoxical thing: each of these concepts of evil is true if it does not exclude the opposite approach. Any one of these postulates is incorrect when seen as the only truth. To understand how the opposites come together as a unitary whole, we need to translate the concepts into our own lives. For unless they permeate the whole of the personality — the physical, the emotional, the mental, and the spiritual, which together form the identity of man — they are abstractions.

Evil as Separation

Let us start from an overall view of the universe. Try with me to encompass creation. If you look up in a dark, clear night, you see billions of bodies of matter, organized in nebulae and clusters of pulsating stars, some at an evolutionary stage as red giants, some as yellow dwarfs. Physicists hold two views on the creation of the universe. One is the Big Bang Theory, which argues that all of existence was created at once; the other is the Continuous Creation Theory, which sees being as still coming into existence. The two schools are battling back and forth, but they agree on a centrally important point: all this tremendous creation moves, vibrates, and is made up of pulsation energy.

The pulsating energy is the quantitative characteristic of creation. When energy forms great masses, they start organizing, multiplying, recreating their own species, their own kind. There is a creativity behind the movement of energy, and behind the creativity there is something that knows. This something is consciousness. Once Wilhelm Reich, holding a pansy in his hands, said to a friend, "Look at this. It has a face; it knows somehow, it expresses." The expression is the qualitative characteristic of energy.

In a creation that is unified, consciousness and energy are one. For instance, in the human body, the organs know what to do, how to create equilibrium of the chemical, the physical, and the electric forces that make them up and that move among them. Man, an entity made up of billions of cells, is able to be more than this emission of this organized matter. But in a disunified creation, consciousness and energy are not necessarily one. For instance, energy can be an impersonal or mechanical force, like electricity or atomic energy, that does not seem to be or contain the expression of consciousness. Energy by itself is totally alien to consciousness, to determination, to self-knowledge, to everything that distinguishes consciousness.

Consciousness, then, is the attribute of creativity. It is not only the power to know, to perceive, to feel; it is also the ability to create and in man to will. Man is the first entity on the evolutionary scale who can deliberately create with his consciousness. Now, consciousness can take two directions, as our lives can: it can go downhill or uphill. Freud's concept of the unconscious profoundly altered the classical categories of reason and will, for it uncovered a natural power in the human being that can make him a victim of himself. I say that man's consciousness has a positive or a negative movement, it contains unconscious content, and he either wills this movement or does not will it. This does not mean that the dynamic forces of the unconscious are not operating. The whole organism functions as a unity.

As I mentioned earlier, man today tends to exist in a separatist or dualistic state. He has created the illusion that his life as it moves, as he moves, is different from his consciousness — that they are split. Let me give you an example. Very rarely, when we go on vacation perhaps out in the country or to the seashore, do we encompass creation in our body and in our mind. We walk in the woods and admire nature; or we swim or go boating; or we watch the ocean waves — we perceive their beauty. Yet even at these times, we have no idea, no sense that the same nature operating there, "outside" of us as we say, as inside of us — that life outside and the life within are one. So we trample on it, we block it, we kill it. Man does the same thing with God. We put God "out there". We are supplicant, we pray, as though to a separate entity; or we deny that there is a God. In either case, man cannot really see that what is "out there" is inside — that God, whatever is meant by the concept, is within us all the time, and that man indeed is God.

Some people say that they experience the universe, the cosmos, or creation as supreme consciousness; others say than it is purely an energetic phenomenon. Both are right, of course; and both are wrong if they claim that their view is the only correct explanation of creation. For thought is movement and energy — mental thought, feeling thought, even dead thought, though this last is a short circuit. Feeling thought is energy felt, energy perceived by our consciousness. Something moves in us; and it is impossible to separate thought from energy, consciousness from energy, though they may appear separate in their manifestations.

Now, let us explore the concept of evil by approaching it from its opposite — the good. In health, which is the good or the truth of life, the reality of the human being, energy and consciousness are very much unified. Man feels this unity. Recently a musician who came for consultation said that when he plays from his inner being, the movements of his organism just flow out spontaneously; it is they that are playing the instrument. They come free, they coordinate, they create beautiful sounds. When man is in a healthy state, his life is a constant creative process. He is inundated by feelings of love, of oneness with other human beings. The oneness is the awareness that he is not different from others. He wants to help them; he identifies with them; he senses that anything that is happening to them is happening to himself. A healthy person has a positive direction in his life. He wills his life in a positive direction, and he is successful — in business, in his thinking, in his feeling of contentment with himself. In that state there is little or no sickness and no evil.

The first characteristic in the diseased state is distorted reality — the reality of the body, the reality of the emotions, and the reality of the true nature of other people and their actions. Evil, then, is a distortion of facts that in themselves are natural. Because the sick person does not perceive his own distortions, he feels that the ills in his life and functioning come from the outside. The sicker he is, the more he feels that his troubles are caused by outside forces. A person who is in a state of psychosis, for example, sees the world as hostile. He sits on a chair and he looks at the walls and he says, "They are doing it to me. They are going to kill me, they are going to poison me." He completely abdicates his personal responsibility for his life and his actions. He feels that everything happens to him from the outside. A healthy person is able to a great degree to do the exact opposite.

What happens in the sick person? His consciousness and his energies change in some way. His consciousness has changed its mind, as it were. It turns life into a distorted version of itself in him, and then his energy alters its manifestations. His thinking is limited. His feelings are expressed by hate and brutality and cruelty, fear and terror.

Reich said that the armored person shuts himself off from nature, specifically by forming barriers against the impulses of life within his body. The armored body stiffens up and is inaccessible to feeling, and the organ sensations are diminished or subside. Then the person becomes lukewarm; he hates, but he doesn't even know it. He is ambivalent.

In the armored person, between the core and the periphery, there is a Maginot line. When the impulses of life strike the fortifications of the armor, the person is in terror, and he thinks he must suppress them; for if they surface, he is certain he will be annihilated. To him, his feelings — especially his sexual feelings — are terrible, dirty, bad. When aggressive impulses held inside this nucleus hit the armor, they make it quake. And indeed if they break through the Maginot line, the person is absolutely brutal out of his terror. He is terrified because he cannot tolerate his feelings, the movement and possession of life in him, the sweet hum of emotion, the pulse of love. He acts against himself and against other people, becoming antilife. He does not perceive that the armor is a deadness making the core of life inaccessible and that it is this armor which is ugly and hateful. In the armored state, then, man is divided — the mind from the body, the body from the emotions, the emotions from the spirit.

Amoring may make a person a mystic, because he can't embrace the fact that God is in him. He looks at God "out there", and he says, "If I purify myself, I'll solve all my problems." But this is never possible, because a person who goes into spirituality without having worked out his negativities — his ego defenses and his resistances — flies high like Icarus, but when he reaches the burning sun, he falls into the sea, the sea of life, and drowns. It is only through transcending and working through the obstacles to life that the human being can rise into realms of creation and spirituality.

Reich said another basic thing: we must dismiss the concept of the antithesis of God and the devil. We must expand the boundaries of our think ing. The manifestation of evil is thus not something that is intrinsically different from pure energy and consciousness; it is only creation that has changed its characteristic. In essence there is no evil, but in the realm of human experience there is.

The Effects of Evil

What does evil mean in relation to energy and consciousness? In terms of energy, it means a slowing down, a diminution of frequency, a condensation. The person feels heavy, bound, immobilized. We know that when we feel hateful, dead, or in any other way negative, we feel very heavy. With power we feel the opposite: vibrance. We take a walk in the woods and we say we fly. So the energy of the body slows down and condenses.

In terms of consciousness, the slower the frequency of the movement, the more the distortion of the consciousness, and vice versa. The heavier and more negative we are, the less creative we are, the less feeling, the less understanding. We can reach the point of blocking all movement and staying in the head; at this extreme, we become obstructed, and then nothing matters. Religion and every other organized ethic has presented all the negative attitudes like hate and deception and spite and cheating as evil, evil, evil. Religion sees these states and the actions that express them as the result of a distorted consciousness of what is good and bad according to its codification.

In the Bible Jesus said a sentence that in my interpretation makes a very important point. Speaking to his disciples he taught, "Do not resist evil" (Matthew 5: 39). Let us examine this. The resistance itself is the evil. When there is no resistance, energy is unobstructed and flows. When there is resistance, movement stops, backs up, and stagnates the organism. Resistance suffocates the emotions, deadens energy, and kills feelings. Resistance is bred of caution, a thinking mechanism — thinking not in the sense of abstract thinking but in organizational thinking.

The consciousness in some way is responsible for the energy flow in the organism, as consciousness in a cosmic dimension is responsible for the energy flow in the universe. When I say "responsible", I do not mean "guilty"; in psychiatry we avoid ever holding a person to blame for his negative actions or unconscious content. We try always to see them as the result of a dynamic state created in a way that the person is not aware of and is therefore not to be blamed for. When consciousness is negative, the person is resistant to the truth. There are resistances that are conscious, that a person uses intentionally with awareness of what he chooses to do. A man whose wife has hurt him could choose to open up his love feelings and forgive her or to keep up the negative and destructive feeling and get even with her. Not all of it is a result of unconscious behavior, though much of it is, and for the unconscious propulsion he is not accountable.

Evil, then, is a far deeper thing than that which the moral codes conceive. It is antilife. Life is dynamic, pulsation force; it is energy and consciousness, manifested in many ways; and there is no evil as such unless there is resistance to life. The resistance is the manifestation of what is called evil. Energy and consciousness in distortion create evil.

When we look at people, many times we can observe the distortion in the character expression, as we say in core energetics. We see that the character expression of one person is to be aggressive, for instance, or of another is to deny. One says, "You owe it to me!" Another says, "Go ahead, hurt me." Still another says, "I will show you!" These messages need not be given directly, in speech; they are written in the physical expression of the body and the expressions of the emotions.

The resistance to chance, the battery of defenses, is based most often on the fear of pain or the fear of annihilation. When these defenses take over, there is a negative intentionality in the human being. The person says, "I do not want to know the truth. I am satisfied as I am. Don't bother me." Let me repeat that he is not to be blamed. Nonetheless, we must realize that the resistance, whether the person knows it or not, has a willful element.

When the fear of pain or annihilation overwhelms a person's total being, it maintains the state of evil in him. This fear generally takes one of three dominant forms. One is pride, resistance to oneness with others. The proud person says, "I'll never admit I can be hurt." Another form is self-will. Self-will says, "I resist any other way but my way. I must not be hurt, so I'll attack you first before you attack me." The third form is direct fear of life. The person who is afraid says, "If I am hurt, I must perish".

On the contrary, the person who maintains his defenses fosters misery, ruins his life, ruins his health; for nobody can escape the laws of creation. If we violate them, in the long run we break down physically, we break down mentally, or we suspend ourselves in a state of void, a state of emptiness, which is the state of hell, like Dante's frozen lake.

Fear breeds resistance, and resistance breeds fear. Life is perceived in a frightening way. There is no openness to the greatness of the creative forces, to the benign nature of the universe, to the amplitude of life, even in the physical functions of the body. We use only one-fourth to one-fifth of the capacity of our lungs. We have tremendous resources, and yet we continuously abuse them, many times because we do not know, we are ignorant. Fear is a wall, a defense erected against looking at the truth of a situation, the truth of the expression on other people's faces. The inside of the wall is made of fear, and the outside is made of negative feelings. When we put up that wall, we give other human beings our negativity. Fear is distrust, of ourselves first, and then of others. It is basic distrust of allowing things to be, of experiencing things.

The three major forms of resistance that I described are all connected with the feeling, "I do not want to be hurt". All are distortions, exaggerations of reality, because it is a fact of life that hurt must come and must pass. People must experience pain as they permit the flowing movement of their energy to come through to their bodies and create life, movement, and joy.

Often people who have a highly organized and so-called good life want to hide from basic truths. The time will come when there is turmoil in their life, and the whole edifice they have created may collapse. Life brings the destruction because a building that is constructed with rotten bricks is a tottering building, in danger of falling if any stress is put on it. A collapse is not a sign that nature is baneful; the ultimately benign design of creation is demonstrated again and again to us. A devil like Hitler, with all his scheming and manipulations, at the end is destroyed. The destruction of destructiveness is a creative act. The destruction of our negativities, even if we collapse, is a creative act.

If the building does collapse, the flowing energy is released, and it can reorganize on the truth that is left to help the person build a truly good life. People hospitalized for a psychotic break can function better after the episode if they are given adequate help and good direction. A negatively oriented person may recognize the shakiness of his building short of collapse. Such people begin to thrive quickly when they come into therapy. They enter treatment very aggressive or very resistant, but the moment their initial attitude wears off, they are caught up in the movement of their energy, and immediately there is a flourishing in the personality. The crisis in us should be accepted and understood. The wise man accepts the crisis and works it out. As Jesus said, "Do not resist evil."

I said before that a person dominated by fear projects outwardly, believing all his difficulties come from the outside. The further a human being is developed, the more he perceives his own resistance. If he is able to admit it, he is more in truth and less inclined to act out his negativity indirectly. When we do not admit our resistance, we will act it out indirectly sooner or later. There are many ways we do this. We can put on a nice smile and then put down others, calling one person stupid, another too short, another a crook.

However it is expressed, indirect acting out is destructive. The more we own up to our resistance — and evil is rationalized resistance — the better we dissolve it. The more we feel the pain, the more we accept it, the less we feel it.

In core energetics, we put the patient in uncomfortable physical positions and have him kick and scream, urging him to continue when he wants to stop because of strain. One of the reasons we do this is to help him accept the state of tension in himself, to stay with it and not be afraid he will die because he has discomfort or achiness. In the same way, the more we accept our hate, the less we hate; the more we accept our ugliness, the more beautiful we become.

When we accept the hurt we feel deeply, it gives us a sense of dignity, regardless of what other people say. These are inexorable laws of life. For when we rid ourselves of distortion of our energy and consciousness, we rid ourselves only of antilife.

Part V:
Dysfunction in Everyday Life

Chapter 15
AGGRESSION IN MEN AND WOMEN

Our life today is characterized by a state of excessive movement and intensity that keeps us in constant agitation. It is very hard to settle down and go deep within ourselves to discover our real needs. This intensity forces a mechanical attitude in our actions and takes away from us the deep experiences of which we are capable. But why do we engage in this overactivity, this struggle? What are modern man and woman trying to escape? Through movement and experience, they are trying to fill the vacuum in their lives and their relationship to the cosmos and the deeper meaning of life. Both men and women act out their expected roles in our civilization, thus avoiding the deeper search.

Modern society provides men and women with a unique opportunity to transcend their traditional roles of male mastery and female subservience. But our fast-paced age finds many people wavering between dominance and submission. Women struggle to achieve a new status of equality with men. Men seek to redefine their place and their processes in relation to women and to other males. Disturbances arise among some people as they struggle to integrate the new social dynamics into inherited and socialized ways of being. Conflicts express an exaggeration of one phase of the reciprocal energy cycle of assertion and receptivity: Either the assertive principle becomes aggressiveness, or the receptive phase declines into passivity. Whether the overly aggressive person is a man or a woman, the result in both cases is a distortion of the basic mode — the gender identity with which nature endows each person.

Assertion is active doing and receptivity is allowing inner forces to take their course. Assertion involves the deliberate use of a person's forces, while receptivity is relatively more voluntary. Activity moves toward a changed condition. Receptivity moves within the existing condition and receives the change. Classically, assertion has been called the masculine principle and receptivity the feminine principle.

These concepts are valid because both principles exist in every human endeavor, every physiological movement, every creative act, every interaction. Both genders embody both principles, though in different proportions and emphases. The scientist asserts in creating hypothesis and doing experiments, but is receptive in allowing intuition to make new connections or to allow new insights to emerge. In a relationship, one seeks actively to express wants, needs, or desired behavior in the other. However, one then allows the other to respond in accordance with her or his own way of being, doing, and expressing.

The healthy, integrated man does not represent the active principle exclusively; nor does the healthy, integrated woman express the receptive principle only. *Both must express both.* However, the emphasis differs between women and men in regard to the areas in which both creative principles express themselves or apply.

Considerable confusion exists today about where a woman stands. Is she, for example, the victim of male chauvinism? Individuals and the mass media exploit the confusion by presenting the problem of modern woman as only one of exploitation by a patriarchal society. The problem arises due to the splitting of the active and receptive principles in both men and women. This division creates a state of disunity and the exploitation of women by men who have over-developed their activating principle at the expense of their own receptivity.

Marion exemplifies the distorted passivity which produces such exploitation. A 55-year-old woman who migrated to the United States from Europe, Marion complained that she was a slave to her husband's wishes and her children's needs. Although well-educated and capable, she resigned herself to a subservient position to her husband's authoritarian rule and became totally dependent on him. She submitted even though she had several opportunities to become active and to exercise her talents. She recognized this state of affairs in her late forties when she developed a series of physical ailments and was referred to therapy.

Our culture contains examples of both men and women with identical patterns of false activity (aggression, hostility, violence) and false receptivity (passivity, subservience, submission). The one grasps too much power and responsibility, the other denies self-responsibility. Both men and women face the same problems, but they interact in a complementary way, rather than identically. No self-realization is possible unless each person becomes a full man or a full woman in the deepest possible sense. This is why human problems always are concerned primarily with the relationship between the sexes. This is the area where the distortions of the principles are most likely to be expressed. No matter what other problems exist, they are deeply connected with each person's masculinity and femininity.

These principles are expressed in the sexual life of the woman who can love and harmonize her own activating and receptive principles with those of the man and vice versa. In essence, this harmonization permits mutual surrender in which the woman is able actively to receive and the man to receive through his assertion. The woman encourages the full selfhood of the man, but not by competing or rejecting his masculinity because it threatens her. Nor does the man threaten the woman out of a false need to dominate. The woman's receptivity must not be confused with paralyzing passivity, which is a distortion of true receptivity. The man avoids over-aggression, which equally is a distortion of true assertiveness. For the woman, the pulsating activity of letting be in the state of self-surrender becomes a vibrating force that contributes to her mate's manhood and strength, and, of course, leads to harmonious and deeply pleasurable life. The man's self-surrender lies in truly giving the woman his activity and manhood, which frees her to feel and express her womanhood and her own strength without subjugating herself to the man.

The basic goal in individual situations, as well as with social issues, is to blend these two aspects — the male and female principles — in members of both sexes.

For centuries, the pattern of the dominant man and submissive woman remained mostly accepted as natural by most men and women. The inner dynamics of the relationship lay hidden in the unconscious. However, the Freudian age radically challenged the attitudes of a rigid, class-conscious Victorian society. Psychoanalysis probed the deepest sources of the psyche and discovered the unconscious mind, which uncovered the factors underlying the enslavement characteristics embedded in the relationship between men and women.

Freud's famous pupils, Carl Jung and Wilhelm Reich, went divergent directions. Jung pursued human spiritual development and values. Reich explored the physical aspects of the body related to illness and health through the concept of psychosomatic identity. Our age, with the disintegration that accompanies social change, has demonstrated that none of these pioneering developments — not Freud's discovery of the ego and the unconscious, nor Jung's spiritual philosophy, nor the psychosomatic work of Reich — can alone resolve the plight of human beings in our increasingly complex society. All of these approaches must fuse to create a unitary and harmonious expression of life. Today, many women consciously and unconsciously seek liberation through embodying the aggressive characteristics they see in men.

The male aggressive structure corresponds to the aggressive woman. The male aggressive structure is one in which the upper body is blown up, overdeveloped, and the lower half contracted. The aggressive man believes he is superior to others and needs constant validation for his effort to prove that he is always right. He considers lack of validation as a catastrophe which threatens not only his overblown position, but his very life.

He moves continuously to create his own reality by mastering every situation through manipulation of others. The woman becomes a pawn in his game of dominance, which leads the aggressive man to very focused manipulation of the woman. He uses the woman as a tool for his own ends to hide the tremendous terror and fear related to his uncertainty about his authority as a man. The aggressive character holds an abusive attitude toward the woman, which includes contempt for her softness and feelings. He chooses a woman he can dominate, who thereby does become a mere object to satisfy his will and desire.

Though the real problem in the aggressive man is one of authority, aggressive women do, on certain occasions, become the authority to the aggressive male.

The Aggressive Woman

Like the aggressive man who tends to over-control, the aggressive woman has a need to dominate the opposite sex and her environment. Her contempt for the man is equal to the contempt the psychopathic man holds for the woman. Her need to dominate is reflected in her life experience as well as in her body, as described below.

The Physical Characteristics

What are the physical characteristics of the aggressive woman? They are exemplified by Betty, a woman in her middle 40s, whose body was tight and held in the lower half, but well-developed and muscular. The entire lower half looked like an instrument of holding together. She stiffened her legs, cut off her sensations and could not feel the ground. The well-formed upper body had well-developed breasts and square shoulders. Her face was alive, vibrant, and vivacious. Her friends thought her handsome.

Betty's physical structure illustrates the aggressive woman as described by Reich and other authorities whose observations are reported by Alexander Lowen in *Physical Dynamics of Character Structure*. The body of the aggressive woman, like that of the aggressive man, is split into two segments. The lower half tends to be bulky and blown-up in the woman, with excessive fatty pillows on the side of the thighs. Often, the skin on the back of the knees has not formed and has the quality of baby fat.

A woman of this type even looks like a baby from the back when you observe the area above the knees. The bulkiness of the thighs and buttocks presents a holding feeling. The energy trapped in this region immobilizes it in a state of chronic tension. Often a ring around the groin acts as a tourniquet over the pelvic joints. The ring prevents energy from freely flowing into the legs. The person frequently is shorter than normal and cannot ground herself or feel her feet. A number of variations of this body type range from the extreme condition of over-developed buttocks (steatopygia) to subtle holding formations that are difficult for the inexperienced eye to detect and differentiate. Generally, the lower half of the body gives a masochistic impression. According to Reich, it holds the body energy within a system that is blocked. Therefore, outside pressure must be exerted to release the accumulated tension.

The lower half of the body usually is hairy. Coarse skin covers the front of the thighs in contrast with the baby fat back of the knees and on the sides of the thighs. The upper thigh is the focus of tremendous tension, which extends to the knees. The calves are over-developed. Such women are "calf-conscious" when they stand on the ground. They use the calf muscles as if to hold themselves together. The feet usually are small, contracted, and square, reflecting the person's inability to feel grounded in her legs and feet. The gait is heavy, angular, and rather awkward.

By contrast, the upper body usually is fairly well-developed. The aggressive woman frequently exhibits considerable energy and movement. She is vivacious and active and appears to accomplish many things. She usually has a pretty face, sharp eyes, and a lively expression. Her voice often is harsh and rather deep. The individual can scream without difficulty.

The upper body is tightly drawn. The shoulders are either pulled forward and contracted or held in a position that slopes downward. This produces the impression that the woman is being hung up by the shoulders. The arms have a limp quality when flexed and rigid when extending. The tricep muscle appears in a state of constant tension. As with the knees, the arms have fat behind them. These women usually have well-developed breasts and are able to breastfeed their babies. By contrast, the oral structure's tight upper body may not be filled out adequately, while the hysteric structure displays typically female expression, with voluptuous breasts and a rounded-out chest.

The two halves of the aggressive woman's body create an overall structure that is in conflict. The lower portion represents passivity, while the upper half expresses movement, and exaggerated activity, and therefore accentuated ego developement. When the person favors the ego expression, she must tighten the lower half of the body. This dynamic draws her energy into ego functions, which prevents her from surrendering her ego to the sexual feelings when she tries to feel her lower body.

The Development of the Aggressive Woman

Numerous case histories show that the family constellation of the aggressive female centers on a mother who is primarily concerned with the physical needs and care of the child. However, the mother lacks feeling and has many problems with her husband because of a lack of emotional and sexual satisfaction. Her attitude toward her daughter often is harsh and compulsive. In reaction, the little girl turns toward her father, with whom she develops a close relationship for a year or two or longer. In this relationship, she enjoys the contact and feelings exchanged between them. But the father cannot sustain the open relationship. He may be afraid of his own feelings or a sibling may arrive. Whatever the cause, the father withdraws from the little girl and rejects her around age four or five. She, of course, is terribly hurt by the rejection and feels betrayed by the male. She also fears her mother, whose position she has tried to usurp through her relationship with her father. The little girl develops the idea that her father is genuinely interested in her but has turned off his feelings because he also is afraid.

Jane, a 28-year-old artist, was very close to her father until age four, when he withdrew from her. She said, "I was in despair. I could not understand why he became so withdrawn and distant with me. I was left alone — kind of orphaned since my mother was cold and constantly nagging me."

During her work, Alice, another aggressive woman, acted defensively, constantly blamed her husband for her sexual problems, and expressed feelings that she had to be in control since she was always right in every situation. She rationalized her inability to surrender to her husband on the ground that he ejaculated prematurely. Her husband, the patient of a colleague of mine, explained later that when he had intercourse with his wife, her vagina was so charged that his attitude changed to one of assault, which gave him the feeling of raping her. Thus, he brought himself to climax very quickly, but did not feel he ejaculated prematurely.

A creative writer, Alice would not maintain a constant state of productivity. At one extreme, she could deliver a tremendous outflow of material; at the other, she would become totally unproductive for long periods of time. She expressed bitterness and spite toward many persons of authority, including members of her family and colleagues.

Alice's inability to ground herself and accept her role in the problems with her marriage and work was the outstanding keynote of her work on herself.

She could not accept her limitations. It became clear from her description of her behavior that she felt overwhelmed by hidden feelings of shame and worthlessness. Often she said, "I feel like nothing and would like to pull everyone down with me". At other times she said, "I need power; I must be powerful. I must be more powerful than men. I have to be right."

The little girl is aware of the reality of the relationship with her father. However, she feels that she is right in maintaining her feelings for him and that her father was failed her. She becomes extremely unforgiving toward him and refuses to adjust to the new situation. In school, she becomes competitive with boys. She relinquishes her feminine identification as being the weak one in a relationship. She unleashes on her brothers all the violence and hatred she feels toward her father.

In later life, the aggressive women often is successful in her work and career, and particularly creative in the arts, letters, and science. However, she selects a man she can easily dominate. This drive for domination, which parallels that of the aggressive man, is exemplified by Isis, a woman in her early 30s. She would say, "I have to control the situation. I can't surrender myself to a man. I must have the power. When I explode in temper, I feel alive and good. My boy friend loses his strength and becomes numb."

The woman's relationship with the man is based upon her need for his strength, which conflicts with her desire to subjugate him. Mrs. Hindley-Smith of the Therafields Institute in Canada, coined the term "paranoid-paranee relationship", to describe how one person — here the woman — feeds on the energies of another to sustain her functioning. The opposite also applies. The man may subjugate the woman in a relationship. The following cases from my clinical practice illustrate vividly the aggressive syndrome in women.

Examples of the Aggressive Female Structure

ALICE

Alice, a woman in her late 30s, had been brought up in a highly restricted Italian environment. She entered work with me because she could not release her sexual feelings, which caused anxiety and depression. She said her husband was passive and that she had her own way. Superficially Alice behaved differently. She worked hard as a housewife and believed she was a victim of raising the family.

Physical examination revealed a short woman with a large pelvis and lower body. Her thighs were fatty, her calves hard, and her feet small. Her upper body was tubular and somewhat contracted. Alice had well-formed breasts and vivid eyes, but a somewhat masculine face. Her jaw was locked, with the lower teeth located well behind the upper teeth. In most essentials she demonstrated the typical physical structure of the aggressive woman.

Following a year of work on herself, Alice was able to accept the truth of her inability to surrender and allow herself to participate in her sexual role and functions. She still expressed contempt for men, though she was motherly in her attitude toward homosexuals. She persisted in dominating her husband and children. She had breastfed her children, but viewed them as extensions of herself, so that she possessed them completely.

BETTY

Betty, whose physical characteristics already have been described, asked me during the first interview if I was strong enough to control her, or would she take over the work, as she had done previously. She had been in treatment on and off for several years. Widowed, with two grown children, Betty had found another soft, yielding man. She wanted to dominate him completely, to possess him body and soul. The man endured the situation for a while, and then broke up the relationship by gradually withdrawing. He feared he would be utterly annihilated by her. In the two years prior to therapy, Betty had not been able to establish a relationship with a man, for which she found various excuses. She tried to justify her loneliness by citing her early family situation. As with most aggressive women, Betty had a very warm relationship with her father until she was eight, when he withdrew. Her mother, a black sheep in her own family, tormented the child, until Betty revolted. The mother usually dressed in men's suits, and Betty actually was brought up as a boy in her early years.

Throughout her work on herself, Betty demonstrated her need for power and control: "I need to control men. I must have the power, have it over them. If I don't they will annihilate me. I must be right because if I am not right then I cannot be worth anything." She would continue, "When I control a man, I feel that he loses his power and strength and I get it. Then I despise him and reject him or demand more." Her drive to capture the man's energy for her own exemplifies the paranoid-paranee relationship between the sexes.

As the aggressive woman often is, Betty was extremely successful in her work and felt it was the only endeavor in her life that was worthwhile. She threw temper tantrums during which she threw things at men, but was mild and soft in other aspects of her relationships. People thought of her as a well-behaved, sweet, and agreeable little girl.

ISIS

Isis, whose drive to dominate we saw in the development of the aggressive female, had an extremely beautiful face. In her leotard during the first interview, she displayed the typical physical characteristics of the aggressive woman — a blown-up belly, and excessive fat on her pelvis and lower thighs that were disproportionate to her upper half. She had no ability to ground herself in the legs. She held her knees stiffly and raised her shoulders. She tried to avoid attention on her body through excessive talking and attempting to occupy my attention and interest in her life and problems.

Isis' upper body was constricted and tight. She had a domeshaped chest and a developmental defect on the left side. Her shoulders were square and her neck was relatively short. She had well-groomed hair and dark, expressive eyes that reflected deep sadness and dissatisfaction with life. Isis' inability to commit herself to any man was reflected in numerous love affairs and several abortions. She always blamed her sexual problems on her boy friends. Characteristically, she took over the relationship and forced the man to serve her, up to the point when he committed himself to her. Then she lost interest and went on to another affair. She probably had experienced depression and at one time had contemplated suicide.

In her attitude toward me she demanded special attention, which made it clear that she felt somehow unusual and outstanding. She conveyed the feeling that she was doing me a favor by involving me in her problems. Isis found all sorts of excuses for not paying the fees, claiming extreme hardship. In early sessions, she could not accept any of the physical work that is an integral part of Core Energetics. Examining this block further, I was able to get her to reveal her shame in showing her body. She felt that her pelvis contained worms and dirt which she could not expose to anyone's sight. She wanted people to look only at the upper part of her body, particularly her face, which was alive and at times radiant.

After a year of work, including physical work, Isis did gain some feeling of security and grounding. She decided to marry a man who was very mild and whom she could control and thus feel at ease with. She exhibited a totally unrealistic attitude toward marriage and her logic often defied definition. She thought the man was there to serve her. She held on to the same attitude she had toward her father, whom she accused of rejecting and deserting her without reason. When she argued with her husband, she often broke furniture and actually attacked him. He retaliated by refusing to have sexual relations with her. She claimed she wanted sex but he was unwilling. She sometimes assaulted him while he was sleeping, demanding intercourse. But when her husband expressed a desire for intimacy, she refused, on one pretext or another. Her aggressive behavior approximated psychopathy. Isis demanded her rights, asserting her power in every situation.

The Meaning of the Structure

Two questions arise from examination of these cases and others that demonstrate the functioning of the aggressive female structure: What is the meaning of the structure? And how can the passivity in the lower portion of the body be reconciled with the aggression in the upper half?

In a few instances, the structure may reflect an attempt to unify genetically-based male elements in the physical makeup. Far more often, however, the androgynous characteristics of the lower body — the hairines and coarseness of skin — are, imposed by a masculinizing of the personality. This physical anomaly has many variations, but generally the aggressive woman rejects the lower part of her body and accepts the upper half. She identifies with the functions of the ego.

The attempt to unify the aggressive woman's active and passive elements creates tremendous turbulence and conflict in the personality structure. This turmoil rises constantly to the surface. The woman assumes a defensive position at the expense of her feelings as a female, feelings which she rejects. She prefers to identify with the man's aggressive role to gain what she desires in life. The disunity between the active upper part of the body and the lower passive part reverberates in her relationships with men. Psychologically, she uses temper tantrums to subjugate the man and at the same time creates feelings of victimization, of being used, so that she can indulge in self-pity. The cases I have cited show how the aggressive woman blames the man for her problem and feels sorry for herself.

The irrational unconscious often is expressed in deep therapy in such statements as "I want to get even with the man. If I don't destroy them, they will destroy me." Or, "I'll be annihilated in the weak position he puts me in by rejecting me." Or, "The man must submit to me. But when he does, I despise him. If he doesn't, then I feel he is abusing me and I become the victim."

These women are terrified of surrendering, which means taking a chance of being deeply hurt: a re-enactment of their early experience with the father. They repeat this pattern in adult life, curiously, as if nothing has happened between their early development and the present. These patients fail to realize that current reality cannot be fully experienced if they hang themselves on the hook of childhood frustration. Nor do they understand the great strength and control that they exercise over men in their adult relationships. This misconception is reflected in the faulty judgement that if they are not right they are worthless. Power is equated with security, acceptance, and worth. The problem is compounded, of course, by the fact that many of these attitudes and beliefs lie buried in the unconscious.

Aggressive Women's Relationships

Now let us examine the position the aggressive woman takes in her real-life relationships. As with Alice, Betty, and Isis, she selects a man whose basic posture is passivity, one who does not assume responsibility for his aggression, but conceals it, only to let it out in indirect ways, such as sarcasm.

This woman expresses her aggression in her ego functions and in her upper body. The passive man capitulates, behaving like a "good boy", but he reveals his aggression deviously by withdrawing his feelings or by cruelty in hard sexual behavior. The man usually withholds his love, his pleasure, his tender feelings from the woman. In this way, he subdues her and forces her to submit to him in the sexual act. At other times, he fears the woman's menacing behavior and abdicates his assertive role — his manhood-totally. He thus descends into a state of passivity on every plane. The relationship then is doomed either to fall apart or to reduce the man to a satellite revolving around the woman.

The two partners alternate roles. Externally, the woman is aggressive with paranoid traits. The man adopts the role of paranee and becomes mild-mannered and conciliatory. But they reverse their roles on a deeper level. The woman submits as the abused paranee and the man becomes the paranoid aggressor. Such a couple seem like people chained to a seesaw, one swinging up on aggression and the other down into passivity. Then they reverse positions. In the process, they become parodies of true masculinity and femininity, exhibiting only the distorted aspects of the two principles.

The only therapeutic approach that can effectively interrupt the destructive pattern must deal with the patient's problems on both the structural physical dimension and the emotional dimension. First, the woman must be grounded in her feet. To do this, her energy movement needs to be opened into the lower half of her body from the upper region. Failure to provide grounding and to open the energy flow to the legs will perpetuate the woman's imbalance and its manifestations in unsatisfactory sexual relations, feelings of depression, a conviction of unworthiness, self-victimization, and confusion. Nor can work on the psychological aspects of the structure be truly effective if the patient does not believe she can sustain the insights through a solid connection with the ground.

The importance of describing the aggressive female's character structure is that a majority of the women in artistic, literary, and scientific professions whom I have treated exhibit this split in physical and emotional development. The number of women pursuing such careers is growing rapidly. These woman have great value to our society because of their creativity and their ability to change the unequal position of women in the world. But simply acquiring more power, strength, and rights does not give the divided person herself more satisfaction and happiness. She can savor the pleasures of living fully only when her ego functions and body feelings are harmoniously balanced.

The Aggressive Man

Bill is a 35-year-old artist. He is a tall, burly man with large shoulders, a thin waist, and contracted buttocks. His eyes are very alive in an intense face. He constantly examines others and must put himself "ahead of the game". He takes control of a conversation and tries, so to speak, to pull himself up by calculating important contacts and constantly manipulating others. He feels very unhappy unless he has a retinue of people who obey him and who respect his beliefs.

Bill's relationships with women are poor. He uses them to get what he needs. Recently, however, he developed a relationship with a woman who "knows him", criticizes him, and punctures the bubble of his grandiose ideas by putting him down. He feels trapped and frightened of her. She is the only person who reminds him of his mother. Therefore he feels incapacitated but remains in this relationship, not knowing what to do. He continues to be aggressive and manipulative with other people, but becomes passive with the woman.

The origin and development of over-aggression in men and women has similar roots. When others, such as parents, teachers, or other authorities, prohibit or hinder the positive expression of life, deep unconscious negativity develops as a result of blocking the forward movement of the person. Violence results when the negative, aggressive movements are stopped or denied by being blocked through fear, rejection, or the imposition of perfectionistic ideals and goals. The violence comes from failure to allow existing negativity, aggressive feelings, justified anger, and healthy assertion into consciousness. The person loses contact with his own voluntary and involuntary movements. The energy piles up behind the muscular blocks. A minimal amount of provocation bursts these blocks at the seams, and all the repressed negativity and hate explode violently. The loss of control may lead to destructive actions. These dynamics produce the aggressive character in the man.

The aggressive person is the same as the psychopathic structure described by Reich and Lowen. The word psychopathic has two Greek roots — "psyche" and "pathos". Psychopathy, or over-aggressiveness, thus is a suffering of the psyche. Unfortunately, psychopathy also connotes criminal behavior, and indeed, many criminals do exhibit the characteristics of over-aggression. It is for this reason that I have chosen to call the structure aggressive — a less culturally loaded term. Criminal behavior might better be called sociopathic.

Like all structures, that of the aggressive person is defensive and expresses the main problem of the individual. The other character structures all have their typical modes of defense, as we have seen in Chapter 9.

But all human beings tend to defend, to protect, and to hide certain aspects of the personality as the guardians "of their safety". Of course, each person develops this guardianship based upon past experiences to protect himself or herself from pain, fear, und collapse. Part of each mind believes that only such defenses can protect the person from collapsing into the chaos of those past experiences. These beliefs are based on early images that are etched in the human mind. These early beliefs and images are based upon sensations, experience, knowledge, and the composite of everything that goes into forming beliefs. For the aggressive man, for example, these beliefs may be formed out of the seduction and subsequent rejection by his mother. He feels he must aggress or be subdued and humiliated, which to the child feels like annihilation.

These beliefs are different in nature for different types of personality. Since the person guards them so strongly, because they are equated with security, integrity, and selfhood, they become the major resistance to the integrative work of making the unconscious conscious. The beliefs serve to block the releasing of neurotic complexes and transforming their energy so it can be used creatively. In effect, this holding on to the guardian ideas, images, and beliefs is the aggressive person's problem.

The Physical Characteristics

The male aggressive structure results primarily from displacement. As in the aggressive woman, the physical structure is divided. The displacement of energy, the center of activities, and the center of thinking all got into the upper body in service of the person's self-importance. This is reflected in the "V" shape of the body itself. The shoulders, chest, and whole upper body are over-developed. The lower half displays a somewhat contracted pelvis and masochistic holding. The person constantly favors energy movement to the upper half, reaching the eyes, which become intense and very sharp. The eyes constantly pierce, observe, register, and classify other people's reactions. They do not allow the receptive element of other's emotions to penetrate the aggressive defense and touch the core.

The upper half of the body, especially the arms, is extremely active. The arms and hands overactively, but very creatively at times, move constantly toward life, arranging, controlling, and ordering people, events, and circumstances. The aggressive personality, in effect, captures life with his bare hands and subjugates others with his intent and will. He seeks to enslave others about whose own wills, minds, and attitudes he feels doubt, ambivalence, or uncertainty.

The Psychological Dynamics of the Aggressive Male

The physical structure and activity of the aggression personality is reflected in his psychological functioning and stance toward the world. The aggressive man seems motivated by a tremendous force from within that becomes apparent in every expression. He never relaxes into surrender or yields into life's receptive principle. Rare attempts in that direction are quickly overcome by his enormous will and drive to control. The man appears to be wound from within with a tremendous force that constantly activates him, directs him, moves him according to his will. To exaggerate for purposes of illustration, the aggressive man acts like a robot with a computer set in a certain position that keeps the robot regulated in a direction and position that produces control, domination of others, and having it his way.

The aggressive man's main problem, therefore, expresses itself with tremendous intensity. In this intensity lies an illusory perception of reality, which is vastly distorted. In effect, the aggressive man has this problem because he values his being only when he is on top of the world and right. His posture is one of superiority. His safety and self-respect lie in his demand that the world do things his way. He must always win and get his way. When this does not occur, he experiences enormous terror that he will be destroyed, humiliated, and rendered worthless. His twofold illusion that his safety lies in being on top and right, or that he will be destroyed if he is not on top, is totally self-defeating.

Reality contradicts these distorted beliefs. The aggressive person is confronted daily with situations that contradict his feeling that the world should always accommodate him. His stance toward the world creates a monstrous phantom that is fed by the illusion of superiority, on the one hand, and the terror of collapse and defeat on the other. Thus a vicious circle is created that leads to a constant development of destructive ways to attain his illusion. The destructive behavior produces more terror of collapse and fear of the self-guilt which place a tremendous burden on the aggressive man's life. If the stressful conditions of life exaggerate these dynamics, the person may sink into doubt, distrust, and finally insanity, the ultimate phantom he fears. Thus the vicious circle is perpetuated, and there seems no way out.

In other character structures, with different belief systems and defenses, the aggressive reaction is modified in quantity and quality of expression. The main defensive reaction of the oral character is , "You must give it to me; you owe it to me." The oral personality demands from others rather than accepting responsibility for his own life. The demand for power is modified to seek to fulfill his needs. In the masochistic structure, the main defense is, "I distrust you, leave me alone. You are going to cause me pain." Here, the aggressive component expresses as the distrust of the outer world, inner isolation, secretiveness, and spite, that underlie the whole personality. For the masochist, power comes from withdrawal. The rigid character actually obtains power because the structure is organized enough to be successful. However, the rigid person constantly experiences constant struggle between the mind and emotions, the intellect, and the heart. Though power is gained, the person constantly fears collapse into the emotions and surrender to the woman. The schizoid's defense is one of constantly holding together. Because of the splitting and fragmenting of the personality, it cannot tolerate energy coming in from the outside. Each fragmented aspect struggles with and fears dominance by the other. The aggressive dynamic in the schizoid person manifests in distrust of each and every aspect of both outer and inner reality.

Working with the Aggressive Male

To deal with the aggressive element, whether it is dominant or subjugated to other characteristic postures, it is important to find appropriate ways to help the person who is firmly stuck in the behavior pattern. First, the person must be shown that he is maintaining in his very depths the world picture of superiority over others and that he has tremendous emotion invested in his position.

As I worked with many people, I noticed that when I handed them a globe while we were trying to work out their problems they felt very comfortable about holding the earth in their hands. They said they were very much at home controlling, dominating, and wanting to impose their will on millions of others. It is essential in the treatment to articulate clearly the concrete feelings of superiority over the world and the secret, vague feelings underneath, namely that when they are powerful they prove they are good; if they are not they are bad. Only in this way can the person focus on the absurdity of his attitudes of omnipotence, which are based upon similar previous feelings in infancy.

To come into present-day reality, the aggressive patient needs to discuss in detail and evaluate the world as it is and look realistically at his relationships with other people: his family and his coworkers. He must very carefully be made to understand the reality of his present conditions. Many of these attitudes are buried very deeply in the unconscious. This material has to be brought to the surface by systematic work.

Once new energy and consciousness are released, the aggressive male should experiment with his new reactions, with accepting the reality of his life, and, very importantly, understanding that the reality in no way weakens him. Nor does it devastate his value or selfhood. Rather, reality makes him stronger and wiser. New experiences should be used to test the person's developing capacities along with the solution needed to cope with his difficulties. It is of paramount importance to show the aggressive man that his old ways are unrealizable and, in effect, make him an infant, wasting time and valuable life energies. He needs help in understanding that allowing him to win will defeat him in the long run. Catering to his feelings of omnipotence and his self-will can create overall distrust, paranoia, and perhaps in extreme cases actual breakdown.

The aggressive person should be presented specifically with how his conscious and unconscious negative attitudes force him to accept illusion as reality, which destroys his integrity and creates real and justified guilt. The insistence on "my way" creates real guilt and an inability to recognize one's true aims. If the person recognizes his guilt, he will be able to make restitution for it.

The aggressive man can gain overall security and sanity only be re-educating himself and forming new reactions to present-day reality. In short, the person ceases to try to be the omnipotent infant and seeks restitution for his real guilt toward those with whom he is involved. The recognition and restitution of the guilt will eliminate the noxious components of self-depreciation and humiliation, and establish in the person self-respect and a feeling of dignity and independence. The problem of over-aggression is very difficult to handle, because those with suffering psyches defend with all means against revealing the problem, and because many of the attitudes are hidden in the unconscious.

The aggressive personality afflicts all people to a greater or lesser degree. According to André Leitis thesis "Transference and Countertransference", it has a specific meaning for each type of character structure and attitude. The main expression of the attitude, however, is the feeling of superiority over others. In a deeper sense, aggressive superiority is one of the elements of evil: the confusion that aggravates the personality. When Mephistopheles was asked by Faust, "Who is he?", he answered, "I am the spirit of defiance, and justifiably so." The rationalization of the mask of superiority and its justification make the problem very difficult to handle. Therefore, the work with the aggressive personality should be directed primarily at the workings of the mask by enlisting the creative inner resources of the higher self of the person to help in re-organizing, re-integrating, and re-constructing new healthy approaches toward handling life.

Chapter 16
AGGRESSION IN THE UPPER BODY

The upper body is an instrument of reaching out, of asserting, of making contact with others. The child reaches for the mother with all of its upper body. When this natural aggression is blocked in infancy, the natural reaching movements become transformed into defensive structures. Aggression is hindered, and the face, the voice, and the upper extremities become blocked and frozen. Each person freezes the natural assertiveness in characteristic ways. Much work needs to be done to re-energize and mobilize the upper body to restore healthy aggression and movement.

An infant seeks to make contact with the mother through natural movements of the mouth, arms, and eyes. The infant also makes a very specific movement of thrusting the head forward and reaching with the lips to find the breast and nipple. This movement, though very soft and rhythmic, is forward and aggressive toward the source of food. This rooting movement is present in the young of all mammals. Rooting helps the infant reach toward the breast, find the nipple, gain physical fulfillment, and make contact, energetically and emotionally. The child becomes confused when the rooting function is blocked when the mother withdraws, becomes anxious, or behaves inconsistently (allows contact at one time and withdraws from it at another). The child reaches with a wave of feeling, of pulsatory quavering, and meets a negative response. The breast is cold or there is no milk. The child experiences deep frustration.

The frustrated pulsatory movements of the mouth are constricted into impulses to bite and scream. The feeling and its energy, which is not discharged through pleasurable sucking, seeks discharge through violent actions. This change from tender aggression to violent aggression occurs spontaneously whenever the former meets with frustration. Unfortunately, the child's anger also meets with frustration. Few parents understand, or tolerate, the intense reactions in the infant that express rage upon meeting frustration. They respond with anger, disapproval, and withdrawal of love and contact.

With all forward movement thwarted and rebuffed, the natural movements of the child's jaw, tongue, throat, and arms become frozen. The mouth may freeze in an expression of bitterness; the jaw may become set to meet the expected frustration; the tongue contracts and the throat constricts; the arms and shoulders move upward into a frozen defensive posture of holding. The normal movements of sucking and reaching become distorted and weak. All functions which depend upon a free and deep response are adversely affected.

The emotional response is frozen stimultaneously with the physical one. The situation is tragic because the blocked functions and structures persist into adult life. The childhood traumas remain locked within the musculature of the adult, which inhibit the healthy and positive aggression which each person needs to lead an effective and productive life.

Michael, a 38-year-old scientist, exemplifies in the adult the dynamics of the frustrated childhood aggression. He has had difficulty in his recent marriage. His wife complains that he never kisses her and wants sex on demand. His grim facial expression is portrayed in a tight mouth and stiff upper lip. He has a monotonous, dry voice and avoids any facial expression of emotion. He has been unable to cry.

He describes his early years as follows: "My mother kept me at a distance. She was cold and not affectionate. She demanded that I be proper all the time. I never knew what to do on my first date at 17. My warmth was dead and I was deeply embarrassed. My mother never really held me and shamed me if I expressed any feelings. I must have been angry because I tried to burn her house down. My father was never around. He was often away traveling on business and I had a hunch that he had other affairs."

Michael is of medium height with an intense attitude of holding. His shoulders are elevated, his body rigid. He complains of pain in his knees and walks stiffly like a robot, with a mechanical quality in his body movements. It is obvious that his early childhood experiences had a decisive effect on the formation of his defensive attitudes as expressed in his personality habits and especially his physical body attitudes. These experiences and the defensive reactions have produced an overall stiff, rigid body and a masklike facial expression of deadness. This expression represents a specific character attitude. There are several others depending on the interaction of child to parent and the environment. Knowing these dynamics is very helpful in seeking to restore healthy functioning to the individual.

Aggressive Functions of the Upper Extremities

A child reaches for the mother with his arms. When he's accepted, taken in, and given love, his arms feel connected to his body. They are able to express the reaching and aggressive movements naturally. But when the reaching and aggression are blocked, the arms separate from the body, freeze at the shoulders, and become disconnected. Their movements become mechanical and lose emotional expression. The energy of feelings does not flow freely from the body, through the arms, and into the hands. The skin of the hands becomes dry, and the person loses the sense of touch as a caress. When the flow of feeling through the whole body is free, the shoulders are completely relaxed. They are not elevated, held back, or bent forward.

The arms are instruments of action and expression. They are used primarily for extending the contact of the body or bringing desired objects close. They also serve to ward off undesired objects or advances and to express angry feelings by scratching, hitting, tearing, or just menacing. The arms extended with the palms up express asking and openness. The closed fist indicates a negative or hostile attitude. When the palms are brought together, the attitude is one of prayer, because the person is making contact with himself. When walking and swinging the arms freely alongside the body, a person excites the energy field, which gives a feeling of pleasure.

In my work over the years I have observed that when many people lie on their backs on the couch with their arms extended, I noticed that the hands hang limply like wilted flowers. This posture indicates an inner attitude of despair, a feeling of "What's the use?" If one asks them to reach with the arms and say, "Mama", they often break into deep sobbing and crying. Others, however, refuse to reach and say "Mama", because they feel the expression is meaningless. When the gesture can be made with feeling in the voice and arms, it indicates that the person has not lost the ability to reach out to life. The infant still lives in the heart of all of us, and the feeling for Mama never completely vanishes.

The ability to reach out with the arms is a measure of the strength of the ego. A schizoid person cannot reach out. The oral personality reaches out only when assured that the environment is supporting. The masochist reaches out hesitantly and pulls back. A rigid person grasps, and the aggressive personality strikes out aggressively. The inability of these persons to reach out fully is due to chronic muscular tensions in the upper back, shoulders, and arms which developed out of the need to suppress violent, aggressive movement toward the mother. Children are often told strongly not to raise their hands to their parents. As a result, they literally cannot raise their arms fully as adults.

The suppressed violence locked in the chronic muscular tensions of the upper extremities must be released if the arms are to regain their natural functions of reaching, taking, and giving. Core energetics patients are continually encouraged to release this violence by striking a bed with their fists, a tennis racket, or a foam rubber bat. They strike from a standing position with their arms reaching upward and backward as far as possible. The quality of the blow depends on the degree of stretch and the coordination of the movement. Constant practice with this movement will free the shoulders and develop a sense of ease in all aggressive actions. When well done, the movements also yield an immediate reward in feelings of pleasure and satisfaction. Such expression of suppressed and repressed violence hurts no one and benefits the patient immeasurably.

The shoulders usually become blocked in one of three positions. Elevation is an expression of fear. This is common in children who feel anxiety and panic. They raise their shoulders to hold themselves together. Shoulders held in a downward position indicate a tremendous amount of tension and a pushing down of feelings. In women, bending the shoulders forward indicates feelings of shame, an attitude that develops early in life in an attempt to hide the breasts and femininity. The tension in the shoulders inhibits the striking movement, which is needed to unlock the tension, release the energy, and restore natural mobility. The inability to perform the physical movement indicates difficulty in expressing the particular feelings. The physical channel is blocked and the feeling, therefore, cannot run along its pathway. The blocked channel is like the obstructed bed of a river.

Assertive Expressions of the Face

The face is very important in the expression of aggression. When an emotion does not break through into the appropriate facial expression, it generally is blocked from consciousness. The schizoid person, for instance, may be full of rage and violence, but the stiffness and coldness of his face prevents him from being conscious of his aggression. The compulsive smile of the masochist defends against feeling the anguish and violence locked inside this personality structure. Similarly, the face of a passive man portrays a benevolent, kindly person, which hides from himself and others the rage and anger in the deeper layers of his personality. In working with these individuals, it is necessary to mobilize the aggressive expressions of the face to bring the buried violence to the surface in a therapeutic way.

In other people, the face and manner express constant aggression. The aggressive woman has a sharp, hard face. She seems always prepared to attack or to bite someone's head off. This hyper-aggressivity can be recognized as a defense against the fear of yielding to her feelings or becoming submissive to others.

In the aggressive personality one often sees an extreme intensity of expression in the face, especially in the eyes. The eyes seem to fixate a person and hold him at arm's length. The aggressive individual cannot contact another human being with his gaze. He uses his eyes defensively or to scrutinize others. This seeming aggression is really a pseudo-aggression developed to protect the person against strong inner feelings of weakness or helplessness. These feelings stem, in turn, from the suppression of violent aggressive impulses in the person's early life. It is equally necessary in aggressive individuals to mobilize the face in order to release the true aggression.

Most patients find it very difficult to make a face expressing intense anger. They cannot easily snarl, bare their teeth, or narrow their eyes. Some cannot fully thrust the jaw forward; others cannot retract their lips. Many people's eyes become wide with fear when the lower part of the face assumes a threatening expression. They were not permitted such expressions as children and now are incapable of executing them. Usually, considerable work is needed on the tight muscles of the jaw, the lips, and the floor of the mouth, before the actual movements become possible. Patients can overcome the tensions by practicing aggressive expressions in front of the mirror or face to face with the therapist. Through practice, they gradually lose their fear of facing others with a consciously aggressive and hostile attitude.

One of the best exercises for mobilizing the repressed violence and aggression in the upper body involves the use of a rolled-up turkish towel. The patient grasps the towel with both hands, about four inches apart, and twists it with all his strength. At the same time, he bares his teeth and voices whatever thoughts come to his mind: For example, "I hate you", "I'll tear you apart", "Shut up", or "You son of a bitch". The patient should hold the towel tightly twisted for at least one-half minute to allow the breathing to deepen and the feelings to rise to the surface. The patient can also shake the towel while demanding, "Give it to me". This helps greatly to bring the aggression to the fore. In some cases the patient will spontaneously bite the towel also.

I want to make clear that individual exercises or movements have no meaning without converting the suppressed emotions dynamically to the characterological aspects of the personality and should be used simultaneously with the expression of those emotions.

Aggression in the Mouth

Mobilizing the sucking reflex is one of the most important and difficult tasks in therapy. The tensions which block this basic prenatal function stem from the earliest experiences of life, and are deeply structured in the body. Some people cannot reach with their lips. Suzy, a 35-year-old unmarried woman, was unable to have a relationship with a man. She had difficulty relaxing her lips and bringing them forward as if kissing. She said she felt afraid that something will happen to her if she kisses. Extensive work with the sucking reflex helped her remember the beatings she received from foster parents who beat her, heaped abuse on her, and left her to almost die from starvation.

People like Suzy maintain the familiar stiff upper lip. In others, the lower lip is tied to the jaw. When one asks such patients to reach with the mouth, the lower jaw protrudes in an expression of defiant negativity.

But even when the lips are relatively free, the mouth is blocked from participating in the reaching movement due to chronic jaw tensions, which refuse to soften. The full sucking movement also embraces the throat and upper part of the lungs. Reaching out to suck literally comes from the heart. The movement is cut off, therefore, by the rigidity of the upper chest (manifested by the protrusion of the first ribs), by a ring of tension about the base of the neck, by contraction of the throat muscles, by retraction of the tongue, and by a constriction of the floor of the mouth. One can appreciate how strong the defenses against the sucking movement are, when it is realized that the movement literally opens the heart.

All these tensions contain negative impulses. The protrusion or retraction of the lower jaw suggests inhibited biting tendencies. The retracted tongue denotes the opposite, namely, the desire to suck. When patients are asked to extend the tongue in a tender, caressing gesture, it often quivers with fright. The tight, constricted throat muscles hold back screams of anger, rage, and fright; or a sobbing so deep that it sounds like anguish.

The sucking movements cannot be opened up until these negative and violent impulses are released. But patients are afraid to bite. They are afraid to hit, and, also, afraid they will be hit. One core energetic technique is to place a folded towel in the mouth of both patient and therapist, and to direct the patient, using his head, to pull it from the mouth of the therapist. The therapist bites on the towel and pulls it away from the patient. When this exercise is first suggested, many patients remark that they are afraid their teeth will fall out.

At other times, I ask patients to bite lightly on the soft, fleshy part of my hand. Many are afraid to do so at first. But when they allow themselves to bite, they learn that the bite can be controlled to prevent hurting someone. And they overcome the deep anxiety relating to hurting others. The person who fears to bite would hesitate to put his hand in a dog's mouth, for he projects his own unconscious biting impulses upon the animal.

An excellent exercise to release the tongue is the childhood gesture of sticking it out as far as one can. I assure patients that it will not be cut off. The therapist can also take the tongue between his fingers, using a face towel, and simply hold it in an extended position. This opens the back of the mouth and allows the person to feel fully the air flow through the throat.

Finally, one can encourage the patient to make the actual sucking movements by making an audible sound as he breathes in. The breathing quickly changes the body and may set it into vibrations. However, the sucking movement cannot be fully released until the patient can identify with the infant within, and reach out with his arms, mouth, and heart for his mother. When the patient can do this and work out the dynamic meaning of these energy blocks, he frees their emotional counterpart.

Breathing and the Voice

In the beginning was the Word and the Word was God. The Word could not have existed if it were not for the uniqueness of the human voice. The cat meows, the dog barks, the lion roars, but the human being voices. And he voices words. Words carry ideas as well as the expression of feelings. No two voices are exactly the same. Each person has a very special way of expressing or withholding his feelings. For instance, a petite middle-aged woman who has a need for asserting herself may speak with a husky sergeant's voice; or a bulky, tall man who is afraid to assert himself may use a thin, feminine voice. In both cases, the voice gives the characteristic flavor to the impression we have of these people. It is an expression of their personality.

According to Paul Moses in *The Voice of Neurosis*, the derivation of the word "personality" shows that originally there was a deep understanding of the connection of voice and personality. The latter word comes from the Latin *persona*, which is the mouthpiece of the mask used by actors. The word gradually came to mean the sound of the voice that passes through the mask. The term then shifted to mean the actor himself — the person and his qualities — his personality. Over the centuries, it lost its connection with the voice. We will now seek to reconnect the voice with the personality.

Though voice has lost its conscious connection to the personality, it still carries that connotation. Humans voice their feelings and thoughts. They express themselves through the voice and make their wills known, primarily through the voice. One has a voice in Congress, or has no voice. In fact, vocal expression is a record of the history of the human race. There are 158 nations represented in the United Nations. Many nations may have hundred of dialects, idioms, and regional characteristics. There are 3,000 distinct languages on earth. Each represents a unique way of expression of human feelings and culture. Life begins with the sounds and body movements which gradually were abstracted over thousands of years into words and mental concepts that formed the cultural expression of spoken and written language. Artifacts found with the fossils of early man help date language back to a million years or more ago.

Primitive people used songs and rhythmic vocal utterances in cultivating the earth, in festivities, and in war. The ancient Egyptians used vibrant sounds such as Arr-ou-urr to enhance their feelings during worship ceremonies. Body movements and dancing accompanied the festivities. The ancient Greek throbbed with songs and dances of love in their Bacchanals, shouted battle cries in war, and moaned with desperate, piercing voices the doomed hero's death in their tragedies. The Romans and Byzantines developed a code of law based on words.

In the middle ages, Giovana de la Porta, a Florentine physician, attempted a systematic analysis of the voice in terms of the emotions. In our times, Freud, Abraham, and Ferenczi studied the symptoms of neurosis and described their meaning in the conscious and unconscious expression of speech. But it was Wilhelm Reich and Bio-energetics who pointed out the significance of the way we talk as an expression of our character structure. Finally, Paul Moses states that it is possible, with proper training, to diagnose a patient from the voice alone.

The voice is an instrument of assertive expression. Because of that, it is of great importance in shaping the course of a person's life. The voice is used to express positive or negative feelings. It pulsates with love and is chilled with cold hatred. Positive or negative aggression can be recognized easily in the voice: the positive aggression by decisiveness and affirmation; the negative by a voice which is flat, restrained, and covertly hostile. The aggression indicates the specific character disturbance. For instance, when the aggression is stopped in the oral character, the voice is flat and says, "Give me more". The voice of the schizoid character becomes mechanical, saying, "I don't know where I am". The masochist whines, which expresses, "I blame you".

The voice and breathing are intimately related. One does not ordinarily consider breathing as an assertive function of life. However, good breathing, like a strong voice, is very aggressive. One literally sucks in the air which leads to the active intake of energy. In poor breathing, the sucking movements are absent, and the expiration of the lungs is a mechanical process. It lacks the emotional quality of desire. In this instance, one doesn't breathe because one wants to, but because one has to. Most people breathe mechanically. That is, they cannot incorporate the sucking reflex into the mechanical breathing movement. The sucking reflex contains the inner pulsatory movement that makes the breathing a pleasurable experience. Without the sucking reflex, breathing becomes a mechanical function of expanding and contracting the chest and the muscles of the chest, throat, and mouth. The feeling of flowing pleasure in the body is lacking. The person eventually breathes shallowly, which diminishes the intake of oxygen, which further depletes him of the energy necessary for the basic processes of life.

Development of the Voice

Life begins with the first cry. At birth the doctor awaits the cry. A strong cry indicates vigor. A weak cry foretells lack of vitality in the infant and the possible onset of complications. The cry is, in effect, the basic pulsatory movement of the entire organism of the baby. It also expresses his vital needs.

One can observe the close connection between breathing and the voice in the fact that the first cry initiates spontaneous breathing. In our work with people, we find when the voice is blocked, breathing is limited; and when breathing is restricted, the voice is weak. One therefore has to work with both the voice and respiration to mobilize each of these two aggressive functions.

Before going into this, however, let us examine briefly the development of the voice in the human being and some of its dimensions. This will help give a clearer understanding of the disturbances that occur and the methods needed to deal with them.

In the infant, crying is coordinated with breathing, which is of utmost importance in the infant's total functioning. The rhythm is characterized by fast inspiration and longer expiration. This is the prototype employed later in normal speaking. However, when one is frightened or anxious, the coordination between voice and breathing is deeply affected, which disturbs the rhythmic pattern of vocalization.

By the fourth month, the voice becomes musical and the cry purposeful.

It can express fear, rage, and love. Fear is expressed by catching the breath and puckering the lips. The sound is O — AAAA. Fear is expressed in a state of contraction. Rage is expressed by holding the breath until the face is crimson. This is related to the possible onset of asthmatic reactions later in life. The holding of rage leads to violent release in crying. Love is expressed by the soft sounds of cooing, gurgling, and smiling. The sound is OOOO — A. The organs of speech have a discharging function. They pulsate and release excitory waves from the core of the organism. Breath-holding is like constipation of the gut leading to skin rashes, which express the protest of the infant against the mother's handling.

At about six months, the baby often makes the sound, la-la-la, and experiences pleasure in performing motor rhythmic movements with the mouth. This is the beginning of coordination of motor, sensory, and auditory experiences in preparation for volitional speech. Children who are not permitted to vocalize freely and are shut up develop severe disturbances in the breathing pattern. Their voices become mechnical, dry, or limited in range.

Around age one, adults place pressure on the child to learn. If the breathing is free, speech and the articulation of words are superimposed. Free, pleasurable vocalizing is subordinated to the meaning of words. The voice serves only as a background to speech, like the music in silent movies. Emotion splits from the meaning of abstract words because the child's natural movements are suppressed. The parents' angry voices shock the child. Later in life any unpleasant vocal intonations trigger withdrawal as a conditioned reflex and establish the neurotic pattern. Sounds create motor associations. When the child is emotionally blocked, he attempts to resolve his difficulty of understanding the meaning of words by excessive motor activity, a characteristic of schizoid children. Many times such children find release in dancing. When the child becomes familiar with words, he has the tool needed to influence his environment.

In school, the child enters the world of words and adopts or rejects new patterns with irritability. A child sometimes spits words at the listener, which may be the beginning of stuttering. Or the child may revert to baby talk, or refuse to utter words. The voice of the child is like a complicated engraving. When vocal expression is disturbed, the respiratory function is affected and total emotional expression is basically altered. The blocking of the throat due to holding emotions, such as anger, protest, and rage, becomes a neurotic pattern stamped in the individual's character structure.

At puberty the growth process gives room to differentiate sexual characteristics. The process of general voice change from child to adolescent is called mutation. The change begins with signs of disorganization, huskiness, and unsteadiness. As the vocal apparatus grows by one centimeter anteroposteriorly (Adam's apple in boys), disturbing and altering the light of the vocal cords. Sometimes the speaking voice drops by a full octave in the boy. David, who had an adolescent conflict between his mother and girl friend, had a masculine voice when talking to his girl friend and a high-pitched and childish one with his mother. A female patient told me that the ominous and threatening tone of her voice was an attempt to control her demanding mother. She said that voice began at the onset of puberty.

Disturbances of Voice Production

Any chronic or acute tension state affects the position of the larynx. This organ is suspended in a balanced state between two groups of muscles above and below the hyoid bone. There are three dozen muscles in all. Any unbalanced pull in these muscles would distort the voice. If the group above the hyoid bone tenses up, the larynx moves to a high position and the voice becomes throaty and high-pitched. The mucous membranes also become dry, which causes a "catchy feeling" in the throat. If the muscles below the hyoid bone pull, the trachea (wind pipe) becomes compressed and the voice becomes low-pitched and "chesty". In anxiety, the diaphragm contracts, which results in increased diaphragmatic pressure and a trembling or quivering voice. The contraction also can produce explosive speech. In acute fear there is aphonia (loss of the voice). Depression limits vocal range and produces a dull expression.

The greater the flexibility of the voice, the better a person is equipped to experience and express feelings. When a person is neurotically fixated, this can be detected in the voice, which is an expression of character structure. Following are the major disturbances of the voice:

The Flat Voice. This indicates that the expression of feeling is suppressed and kept within a small range. The voice lacks depth. The rhythm is monotonous, the resonance poor. The oral character falls into this category. He indulges in a lot of "empty talk" to gain affection. One of my female patients talked incessantly with a flat, monotonous voice at the beginning of therapy. She admitted subsequently that this was a gimmick to gain affection and to avoid going deeper into her emptiness.

A Voice Limited to One Register with Narrow Range. This voice is predominantly high-pitched from fear of contacting deeper sexual feelings. This is partially the case in hysterical structures where there is an abundant supply of energy and a blocking of emotions. Also, female-role homosexual men generally have high-pitched voices as if they were keeping the emotion away from the chest and abdomen. The passive-feminine has a soft, high-pitched voice that sounds almost feminine. It says, "I comply; I am aware of you; don't hurt me."

The Mechanical Voice. This voice lacks resonance, is monotonous, dry, and cold. Schizoid people talk this way. Their breathing is split and the diaphragm and abdomen are severely contracted. The range of the voice is extremely limited.

The Affected Voice. The individual with this voice attempts to artificially modulate the voice to cover lack of feeling. The voice has an artificial quality. Many people assume consciously different roles to avoid expressing their true feelings. A patient told me that he started talking with a strong British accent to "elevate his low status" and impress people with his "cultural development". The masochist uses this vocal strategy to express constant complaints and whines in order to provoke a reaction and to release locked emotions.

Core Energetic Therapy for Voice Problems

Releasing natural breathing and vocal expression are important elements of core energetic therapy. By getting a person to use his voice in sustained yelling, using an expression of either "Ah" or "No", we find breathing deepens spontaneously to provide the necessary air. The voice should include all ranges of expression, from yelling to crying to pleading to screaming. It will extend from a soft whine to a scream of such pitch and intensity it feels like an electric current through the whole body.

More specifically, to work on the voice the patient is asked to breathe heavily while lying with his shoulders on the stool. The pressure is at the level of the nipples and the arms are extended holding the rungs of a chair. The feet are on the ground, toes turned in, with the knees flexed and the feet a foot apart. The back is dropped to form a curve. The patient is instructed to breath in heavily, sucking the air with a grunt felt at the base of the throat. Then, the air is expelled powerfully. The phases of inspiration and expiration are approximately equal. He is then asked to scream in a sustained, high-pitched range, increasing the diaphragmatic pressure and releasing the neck. This is followed by a deep breath and another scream, over and over and over.

This process can uncover many problems. Patients who are not accustomed to deep breathing quickly get dizzy and have to repeat the process many times. If the throat is blocked, they choke and cough. If the pulsation traveling downward during the expiratory phase is blocked, the movement stops and the voice collapses and cannot be sustained.

Considerable work must be done to release the tensions in the jaw and at the base of the head before proceeding with the specific work of opening the voice blocks. One can deal with these problems directly by placing the thumb of the right hand one inch below the angle of the jaw. The middle finger is placed at the corresponding position on the other side of the neck. The scalene and sternocleidomastoid muscles are grasped and pressure is applied steadily while the patient vocalizes at a high sustained pitch. The same process is repeated several times as the pressure is applied at the middle point and base of the neck in different voice registers. Many times this leads to agonizing screaming which develops into deep sobbing. One can hear real emotional involvement in breaking the holding and surrender. The sorrow is expressed in clonic movements, and the whole body vibrates with emotion. The voice becomes alive and pulsating and the throat block opens up.

It is striking to discover what is hidden behind the facade of the stereotyped voice. A young woman with an assumed, highpitched voice, acting the role of the little girl with her father, broke into a melodious, mature feminine voice. A man with a flat, dry voice changed his register after this release to a deep masculine voice, challenging his "oppressive father". I was deeply moved with a schizoid female patient who was hiding herself behind an ominous-sounding dry voice, after opening the throat blocks, started singing a melodious, poignant song like a little girl of six.

A person who blocks the throat also blocks the pelvis. It is interesting to note that the jaw and the pelvis correspond in movement and structure. When one opens, the other may close. A male patient told me that when his voice and head started clearing up in therapy, his belly tightened up with cramps. Many people are afraid to open the voice for fear of opening up sexual feelings.

It is obvious, therefore, that the problem of voice therapy is a complicated one because the whole organism has to come into action. Since the voice is the expression of feeling from the core of the person, like the musical sound produced in the center of the wind instrument, the longitudinal flow of movement has to be established by removing the obstructions on many levels and permitting the pulsatory wave of respiration to flow freely. Anchoring the feeling in the feet to root the person on the ground is of great importance. Core energetic therapy is effective in changing and broadening the voice, according to the experiences of many professional singers, because it unifies the rhythmic, spontaneous pulsatory flow of the organism, of which the voice is an expression.

Each person is a unified, organic whole. In restoring natural, positive aggression and expression, it is important to work with all of the structures that were blocked in infancy.

Chapter 17
THE CASE OF THE BROKEN HEART

Heart disease in the United States has reached appalling proportions. It kills four times as many people today as in 1900 and more than twice the number that cancer does.

Why?

This question preoccupies nearly every definable sector of American society from the federal government to the general practitioner in a village of 700 souls. It has crucial meaning for the successful business or professional man in his early 40s or 50s, because actuarial profiles show that this person is the prime target for any of the coronary incidents known popularly as heart attacks.

In 1973, two cardiologists at Montefiore Hospital of the Albert Einstein Medical School in New York City asked me to evalute ten patients under their care. All the patients were men, their ages in the critical range. Eight had had one or more coronaries and two had angina. The cardiologists wanted me to see if the auras of these patients — the energy fields surrounding their bodies — gave specific indications of their disease. While the findings were preliminary, and many more evalutions are needed before they can be utilized confidently, I was fascinated by the observations. I will present them in some detail toward the end of this chapter.

To place the observations in perspective, I will now summarize some of the principles of my work in core energetic analysis as they relate to the human heart and circulatory system.

Life, as we perceive it in our three-dimensional reality, is movement that makes itself known through the pulse — the beat of the heart. Most of us at some time have gathered up a bird lying motionless on the ground and listened for its heartbeat to find out whether it was alive. But the movement of life is composed of a far more essential substance than the physiological elements of blood, chemical secretions, neurological impulses, and the like. Man, like all creatures, lives by the movement of energy, which is received from within and outside of himself. And the heart is the unique organ for transmitting this movement, for regulating and protecting life throughout the organism.

Heart disease, then, needs to be conceived of not only as a failure of tissues, an invasion of the organ by hostile microbes, or an effect of strain due to another illness or abuse of the body. It needs to be seen as a pathological implication of energetic dysfunction.

In the pages which follow, I will develop this perspective through a review and interpretation of several very large studies of heart disease as well as my own small sample. In discussing these cases, I will present aspects of cardiovascular illnesses: some psychological manifestations, the body structure of the sufferers, and my observations of the energy fields of the aura corresponding with the physical pathologies. Let me begin with the heart itself and its action.

The Heart and Its Pulsatory Movement

In human development, or that of any animal in the upper evolutionary scale, a few cells of the protoplasmic mass, which begin dividing at conception, differentiate. They assume the special function of maintaining the essential movement that later becomes the pulsatory activity of the whole organism. These cells come from the ectoderm, our outer layer, of the new creature. But they form what will becomes an interior organ, the embryonic heart. They involute in their growth to shape a spiral, wound mostly counterclockwise, and to create two subdivided sections. Thus, the fully formed heart has four chambers that consist of a muscular membrane of fibers. They expand and contract and are encased in the pericardium. The organ also is equipped with doors, or flaps (valves), that open and close by the contracting and releasing of the heartstrings (tendons called chordae).

A special grouping of cells, called the bundle of His, regulate the heart's pulsation. They originate within the right chambers and spread throughout the organ. They have nuclei that fire like batteries, making a fusillade that permeates the whole musculature of the heart and creating its rhythmic movement inward (systole) and outward (diastole). If the pulsation is charted on an electrocardiograph, we can see that it is composed of many different rhythms, which come from different parts of the heart to make up the whole organ's rhythm of about 60 beats a minute. And this exceptional organ never ceases its pulsatory movement until the entity it serves leaves three-dimensional reality.

The heart's physiological function is to propel the liquid substance of man, the blood, through the arteries to the ends of the body and back again through the veins. In its course around the circulatory system, the blood picks up and distributes countless particles of energy — biological, electrical, and chemical energies — to the very small channels of the vascular tree, the arterioles. These minute blood vessels pulsate, too, operating on signals from the autonomic nervous system. This system controls not only the body's involuntary functions but is also involved in primal emotional activity. Therefore, when people experience emotion, it is translated all the way down to the arterioles as well as to the heart through the bundle of His. The cardiovascular network, then, bears the strain both of pumping and channeling nourishment to the entire organism and of coping with emotion-related impulses that can, as we shall see, literally break the heart.

The heartbeat itself replicates the pulsation observable in the whole of nature, from the rhythmic movements of single cell animals to the cylical patterns of vast biological phenomena. While the pulse-and-rest timings of myriad life forms differ, rhythm as such is an innate characteristic of life. Birds in their flights follow the rhythms of nature to find the routes of migration. There are many theories about how they do this. One is that they trace the pulsatory movements of the magnetic lines of the earth. Another holds that they are responding to the rhythmic changes in the atmosphere.

Other massive biological clocks in nature, repeating rhythms continuously and perpetually, ally with the generative activity of living organisms. In Mexico, for instance, a small gopher-like animal is drawn to the sands when what is called the paint-brush tide is at its fullest. The animals stay for a day, proceate, and then go away again. They do not visit the shore at any other time. And of course, the most important rhythmical event in human biology is the menstrual cycle in the woman.

Reich has pointed out that the common functioning principle in a process repeats itself from the highest to the lowest unit. A tree, for example, replicates its shape from its largest to its smallest limbs. The major branches have the same structure as the trunk. So do the thinner branches and the littles twigs. In the same way, the heart, which specializes in transmitting pulsatory movements of life throughout the organism, represents the common functioning principle in man. Rhythmic pulsation can be found, not only in the arterioles and every cell, but also in the basic building blocks of organic matter, such as deoxyrebonucleic acid — DNA. This molecule, moreover, has the same helical shape as the heart. Thus, the heart is the organized ensemble of pulsatory movements that flow through the smallest components of the physical body.

Cardiovascular Disease and Energetic Dysfunction

Disturbances of the assertive and receptive principles disunify the person and disrupt health. In core energetics, we can see the disturbance physiologically in blocks that indicate the site of energetic dysfunction. This imbalance is apparent in all illnesses, including those of the heart and the circulatory system.

In terms of organic medicine, cardiovascular ailments can be divided broadly into four categories. One consists of diseases of the flaps or doors (valves) and the strings (chordae). Heart murmur is such an illness. Another form of this category, which often comes early in life, is rheumatic heart disease. The valves, as well as the pericardium, become inflamed from infection, which damages their ability to close tightly and breaks down the heartstrings.

Diseases of the substance of the heart comprise the second category. These involve the muscle. They are due to degenerative changes. inflammations, or acute vascular accidents such as a coronary occlusion.

The third set of diseases afflict the heart's rhythm. These frequently accompany and may endure beyond the term of the ailments in the first two classifications, especially those of the heart muscle.

Finally, there are diseases of the circulatory system, such as high blood pressure. This condition permeates the whole vascular tree and can begin in early years. At the outset, high blood pressure fluctuates. Later in life, it becomes chronic. The immediate cause, as explained in medical books, is the constriction of the arterioles, the tiny end tubes that take care of the outflow of blood. Sometimes the arterioles have vascular lesions, but not necessarily so. Most high blood pressure is technically known as essential, or idiopathic hypertension. Both modifiers simply mean "of its own nature". This is a fancy way of saying that the causes of the disease are unknown. Actually, the causes are known, as we shall see.

People's dread of cardiovascular diseases of all kinds revolves naturally around the incidence of abrupt deaths that they can provoke. Circulatory illness and heart cripplers such as rheumatic fever can issue in a fatal and relatively unpredictable attack on the heart, as can any single big affront like a coronary occlusion. According to medical understanding, the mechanism of sudden heart failure can operate in several ways. The parasympathetic nervous system (a subdivision of the autonomic), which slows down the heart, becomes dominant. This produces a state of bradycardia, or a very slow heartbeat, shown by a wide interval between peaks on an electrocardiogram. Ultimately the beat ceases. Or a blood vessel may break or a clot hit the heart, stunning it and stopping its pulsation. But these and other physiological explanations are basically descriptive. The question remains of *why* the arterioles are constricted, *why* the parasympathetic impulses come to dominate, *why* a clot forms. Not until the advent of psychosomatic medicine did the functional causes of most cardiovascular disease begin to be unearthed.

As we saw in Chapter 8, medical science began to uncover the psychosomatic nature of human illness. The works of Osler, Cannon, Alexander, and Reich established the links between physical and emotional wellbeing or disease. Chapters 19 and 20 explain the methodology for treating emotional and physical dysfunctions in different realms by working with the unifying force of the core.

From this expanse of research and experience, a picture has emerged of the cardiovascular patient as a person caught in a vise between unremitting hostility and fear. Each emotion breeds the other in a vicious cycle that traps the organism. Ultimately, the stress of this conflict simply exhausts the heart or irreparably damages the arterioles through constrictive pressure.

In core energetic terms, the source of these ailments is the same as that of uterine disorders in women: the arrest of healthy, open movement of energy in the organism. The blockage is in the pelvis, and the excess energy dammed in the upper torso blows up the ego, a conceptual faculty based in the head. The inflated ego propels its host into aggressive behavior aimed at achieving, accomplishing, and elevating the person's status in life. The ego seeks to appear admirable, indeed, even superior to others. This is the ego of the man who drives for success, equated in our culture with power and money. And this person is the prime target for cardiovascular disease.

Obviously, not all physical pathologies follow the gender pattern that shows men sustaining heart attacks and women suffering illnesses of the sexual organs. I have seen many cases of the rheumatic heart among women, for example. Generally, the onset of the disease came in puberty, right after the young girl's heart had received the shock of rejection by the father. The parent abruptly cut off the tremendous movement of love between him and the child. He probably could not deal with the signs that the flow of her energy was now focusing not only in her heart but in her sex as well. So, to protect his own lopsided equilibrium, he withdrew his affection and tenderness from her, breaking her heartstrings. The damage did not always stop with the heart. Several of these patients had succumbed to tuberculosis soon after developing the rheumatic heart. The whole chest had become involved in the unresolved longing for the father.

A second possible departure from the gender rule is the aggressive female patient I describe at some length in Chapter 15. She is a professional woman, usually gifted in the arts or sciences, who has entered the competitive realm of career making. Like her male counterpart, she amplifies the assertive principle at the expense of the receptive. She is unable to open her heart feelings. Her behavior is predominantly aggressive. This proves in therapy to be a mask that covers her ricocheting between fear and anger, another wearying rat race. I do not have enough evidence to demonstrate persuasively that this character configuration makes a woman prone to heart and circulatory affliction. But recent actuarial tables provide some disturbing testimony. The number of women with cardiovascular disorders is rising rapidly.

There are other exceptions to the gender pattern of course. Some men develop cancer of the testes or other diseases of the sex organs. But, in general, the blockage complex that breaks a man's heart breaks a woman's uterus instead.

Profiles of Cardiovascular Cases

The early findings on the emotional origins of cardiovascular diseases have been confirmed and expanded by study after study in the intervening decades. But two recent sets of research stand out for their innovations in classification. One project was initiated in 1960-61 by Meyer Friedman and Ray H. Rosenman. It has been carried forward since and originally comprised 3,500 male corporate employees aged 39 to 59. The second, reported by George L. Engel, analyzes 170 cases of sudden death, mainly from cardiovascular failure among people of all ages and both sexes.

Friedman and Rosenman have categorized their subjects according to two broad behavior patterns that they call Type A and Type B. Type A is characteristic of the action-and-motion man who struggles excessively to obtain the greatest possible possessions and power in the shortest amount of time. He drives himself hard. He grapples with any challenge and grasps for any advantage. He is rarely introspective or sensitive to the needs of others. In a word, he is aggressive. Type B takes it easier. He is less addicted to a self-image of success and lives a generally less pressured life.

The author's seminal findings in their study of these two groups is that Type A people are two to five times more prone to developing various cardiovascular disturbance than Type B individuals. And one followup of the original sample, done in 1967, shows that 22 of 25 deaths — or 88 percent — from coronary heart disease ocurred among Type A's.

Type A's are the quintessential aggressive character. Also the rigid character types seem prone to heart ailments because they are emotionally and energetically cut off from their hearts, generally speaking. The masochist, however, is more prone to cancer, because of the massive holding of energy.

Medical assessments of Type A people show an anomalous biochemical picture. They include increased cholesterol and increased insulin in the blood and an excess of norepinephrine — an adrenal secretion — in the urine. Also, the hormonal balance needed for proper heart functioning has been thrown out of whack. So these people stress their heart in their struggle against the tremendous swing between the fight and flight syndromes.

Reviewing the people I work with from the standpoint of the Type A and B classifications, I find that Type A people show a very similar profile in their work lives and social settings. This is contrary to the lack of correlation between status and behavior type observed by Rosenman and Friedman, a difference due probably to the specific sociometric traits that define the psychiatric patient population. Type A's whom I have treated have been accomplished people who held important jobs. They were financially well off and socially well respected. They have tended to dominate others, using speech as a means to this end. They have disliked sharing authority.

Their behavior toward women, however, has been generally less aggressive. They have been exemplary husbands, superficially at least. How much they enjoyed sexual relations with their wives is debatable. All have had secret affairs, which gave them intense, overt anxiety. This part of the pattern corresponds with the family constellation of the Type A's. They generally retained a lot of hostility toward their father and a fearful attitude toward their mother.

The mother had been the authority figure and a smothering sort. The father had shown the child hostility, either by withdrawing from him or abusing him. The wife of the Type A has tended to become the boss in his household. In this way, the marital relationship has perpetuated both the dependency needs and the hostile reaction to them that the man has carried forward from his early years. There is truth in the classic cartoon that shows the big corporation executive in the office giving orders to everybody and then entering his own front door as timid as a mouse. In common with Rosenman and Friedman's comprehensive sample, these Type A's have thus had an aggressive and a submissive element in their behavior. These elements reveal the Type A's to be gripped between a chronic, free-floating anxiety and tremendous repressed hostile impulses.

Engel's study concentrates on people who have died abruptly under the impact of intense emotional experiece. His age division, by cases from birth to 60, confirms the gender pattern of cardiovascular disease. The ratio of males to females is 18 to 1 for the age group 41 to 50; 26 to 6 for those 51 to 60 and the peak periods occured among men aged 45 to 55 but among women 70 to 75.

Opening his article with a long view backward into the history of medicine, Engle cites instances from sources as disparate as the Bible and military annals to show the different emotions traditionally thought to cause sudden death. When Peter the Apostle accused Ananias, "You have not lied to man but to God", Ananias fell dead. So did his wife, Shapphira, on learning of his death (5 Acts 3:6). The Roman Emperor Valentinian is said to have collapsed and died " 'while reproaching with great passion' the deputies of the German tribe". Chilon, King of Sparta, supposedly dropped dead from joy while "embracing his son who had borne away the prize at the Olympic games". So did a doorkeeper of Congress in American Revolutionary days, according to the contemporary American physician and patriot Benjamin Rush, on hearing of the capture of Lord Cornwallis' troops at Yorktown. Pope Innocent IV and Spain's Philip V number among many figures in history who died on learning that their armies had been defeated.

Current cases in the practice of Engel and his colleagues, as well as press reports, led him to classify the causes of death into eight categories. Four relate to the loss or threat of loss of a close person. The relationship may be only symbolic. For example, the 27-year-old army captain who commanded the ceremonial divisions at President John F. Kennedy's funeral died ten days later of a "cardiac irregularity and acute congestion". Three causes concern a present or even a past danger to the person himself. Engel tells of numerous people who have walked away unhurt from train and car accidents only to collapse with fatal heart attacks within a few hours. The threat may weigh against status or self-esteem rather than physical safety. This could explain Wilhelm Reich's death of a coronary a few days prior to his release from prison.

Engel's eighth category covers the puzzling phenomenon of sudden death at a time of reunion with a loved one, success, or triumph. There is the case of a 55-year-old man, for instance, who died on meeting his father for the first time in 20 years — and whose father then dropped dead himself.

In core energetic terms, it is not hard to understand how a tragedy or acute danger can break the heart. The shock of the event produces such a severe blockage that the energy whips back on the organism with fatal violence. I discuss this causality at greater length in Chapter 6. But why would joy or pleasure emulate the lethal potential of grief or terror?

It is not the expansive emotion or the positive surge of energy that kills. It is a blockage, and a powerful one, against any feeling, even good feelings. That is, the joy or pleasure is not accepted. It meets with an immovable negation. This denial may arise from guilt, an overwhelming conviction that one does not deserve the joy. Who knows, for instance, what King Chilon of Sparta had done to his son in the past.

Evidence of the Case Studies

The inability to accept feelings, and specifically heart feelings, was a common denominator of the ten patients whom I was asked to evaluate by the two cardiologists at Montefiore Hospital, as well as of other cardiovascular sufferers among my cases. As I said at the beginning of this chapter, my task was to report what their auras testified about their conditions. After some interdisciplinary wrestling, the referring physicians circumscribed the scope of the sample so that a correlation could be established between the energetic symptomology and the physical pathology. I accepted the assignment. Here, in summary, is what I found.

The first trait I noticed in all ten patients was an atypical body structure: a passive, feminine aspect showing a masochistic lower half, energy-charged and holding, and a rigid-hysterical upper part. Some had immature chest configurations, denoting orality. All had a driving head, making a lot of contact with the eyes. Second, regarding their psychological pattern, the behavior of all ten men was passive-aggressive. Agression characterized their work; they were highly accomplished people. However, passivity marked their relationship with their wives.

The third level of observations encompassed the auras of the patients. Here again, as in body structure, there were marked similarities. All ten subjects had a very severe block at the root of the neck, where energy was flying out in a winglike protrusion. In that area, I saw a strong, reddish-brown color, which clinically denotes repressed hatred and held back anger. Almost everyone will manifest some of this tint at the root of the neck periodically; what distinguished these patients was its intensity and continuousness. A major block showed as well in the small of their back.

The most striking aural distortion came out of the front of the chest, just over the sternum. Here, in most of the coronary cases, I saw a very dark emanation shot through with some purple and yellow. It was cylindrical in shape, measuring 1½ to 2 inches wide at the base. This is shown, slightly enlarged, in Figure 18. On the other hand, patients whose attacks had occurred more recently—less than a year before observation—exhibited a spiral blockage shown in Figure 19. This was brownish-yellow in color and gradu-ated from 1/2 inch in width nearest the chest to two inches at its outer edge. It consisted of strings with grapelike formations in the middle. I do not yet know the meaning of this difference in configurations. The angina sufferers, like others I have treated, exhibited a shape resembling a honeycombed and many-pointed star.

These various formations all contained the backed-up and stagnated energy that was being prevented from flowing normally through the torso. And they demonstrated visibly how blockage damages the organism. The enormous excess energy within the chest bombards the heart, overcharges it, and bursts this most vital of man's vital organs.

As long as there has been human illness, human beings have tried to unearth its causes, aiming always at the ultimate and economical cure: prevention. We have come a long way since men ascribed disease to the egotism of quixotic gods. Medicine has defined a host of ailments in terms of organic failure or defeat, down to the nature of the crucial missing en-zyme or the invading virus. Epidemiology has charted the impact of culture on the organism. It has established, for example, the first-generation Americans from certain ethnic origins are far more susceptible to car-diovascular disease than their parents in the home country.

Yet researchers are at a loss to provide remedies, much less methods of prevention, for most of the deteriorating illnesses or sudden-failure syn-dromes. Cardiovascular diseases are not the only category that has so far eluded discovery of the true causes. The same is true of cancer. The answer will not come from further technical knowledge of the physical organism. They will come from understanding the meaning of each illness to the whole person.

The whole person, as Wilhelm Reich found, is an energetic unity. I have said many times and will stress again and again that there is no organic pathology without emotional disturbance; and there is no emotional illness without physiological consequences. The psychosomatic identity manifests itself unfailingly in every organism's energy field.

As one after the other of the heart patients under evaluation displayed the remarkable aural formation in front of the sternum, I thought: The time has come to broaden the investigation of the energy field, not only as a diagnostic but as a predictive instrument. The major purpose of the present chapter, therefore, as of the fuller study to follow, is to open a forum to prac-titioners in every specialty concerned with human health. For there is none among us, to take but one organic example, who would not rather keep the heart whole than try to mend it once it is broken.

Part VI:
The Work of Integration

Chapter 18
FROM DISTORTION TO SELF-TRUTH

An apple tree can't decide in practical terms to change the course of its history. A human being can. We can stay bound up in our distortions or move to dissolve them. We can muffle our exchanges with the outside world, or give them active welcome. As Martin Buber observes, we can relate to other existence as I-to-it or as I-to-thou. These sets of antitheses bracket a continuum in individual and collective experience. From the psychiatric standpoint, the first pole is illness — alienation, dissociation, disintegration. The second pole is health — alliance, association, integration.

Healing is the organism's process of moving along the continuum from the disunity of one pole to the unity of the other. Traditionally western schools of healing center on the sickness and aim to restore the functioning of the injured parts so that the whole may thrive. I share that goal, but from the perspective of the opposite pole of the continuum. Core energetics centers on the person's innate health and aims to restore the functioning of the whole so that the injured parts may also thrive.

The holistic orientation has radical implications for the process of healing, the suffering person, and the therapist. Core energetics builds on releasing the right energy of the core rather than correcting specific distortions or ailments. The sufferer marshals that energy and in actuality evolves the path of the work. The therapist casts a searchlight into the sufferer's core to illuminate that innermost truth, that higher self, which the path will reach.

The process of clearing the way for the higher self is called therapy because this is the closest term in the nomenclature of established disciplines to describe the process. But in fact, I consider the method rather as education in inner reality, as helping the person perceive from and act through the core. The course of learning leads the sufferer to open and invigorate the center of life, to stand aligned with it, and to take his or her existential perspective from it. I will say more about this later. The practice of core energetics, in keeping with this kind of process, calls on the therapist to serve as a teacher and guide rather than only a clinician. An educator knows that every person possesses unique gifts and will utilize the learning program in unique ways to further a unique life plan. The educator offers neither the gifts nor the plan — these are the student's. The same is true in core energetics.

We take our motif from the root word *therápōn*, the Greek for attendant, and we adhere to the Hippocratic doctrine that nature heals, not the physician. The sufferer's own vital force disperses the illness, not the practitioner's actions or antidotes. These are important but only supportive. The very essence of core energetic work disallows the conventional doctor-patient relationship: the status of "superior" to "subordinate", which Chapter 1 described as unworthy. This kind of relationship originates in the mask. We cannot touch the core of the sufferer unless we reach out from our own core. The mutuality between the sufferer and the therapist is such, in fact, that we have trouble finding a term to define our role. We tend to think of ourselves as guides or helpers, focusing on the fact that the person is conducting the search for his or her own truth, his or her unique path. I will return to this subject later in this chapter and in Chapter 19.

A further implication of the core energetic orientation needs to be communicated to the sufferer from the beginning of treatment in order to dissipate the self-condemnation that occurs in all forms of illness. The energies trapped in the mask are considered negative energies, it is true, because armoring is an instrument of denial. But the defenses are not treated as hostile forces to be eradicated, like a colony of toxic bacteria. The vital substance they contain is good substance, core substance, though it is stagnated. The character structure affects the person's capital of life by clustering it around the inner self and imposing warped imprints on it, which continue to suck more energy into themselves. But these distorted conditions begin as beautiful movements in the deepest part of the person, no matter how grotesque or destructive they may become as they emerge. If we search the face of a very fat man, for instance, we can see the wonderful and vibrant human being who is caged in this mass of flesh. The obesity is a peripheral expression of his attempt to preserve some of his dynamic equilibrium in some fashion. However misshapen his physical body, the energy formations that thicken it have innate excellence; his defenses simply misappropriate them.

Underlying these principles is the basic pattern of movement that is visible in every entity: the reciprocal energy cycle. Inner life flows together with outer life, since life force is universal; the out-there is the same as the in-here. Because of this, I am convinced that illness can take hold not only when an organism actively denies inner movement but also when it passively disregards outer movement. Full participation in objective reality calls for the exercise of meditation, intuition, and faith, which are the powers of the human soul. The people in my care showed me early in my career that spiritual growth has a primary place in treatment; omitting it came to seem like shearing off the top of a pyramid. The therapist therefore accompanies the person not only inward into his or her center but outward into the surrounding world. The healer and the sufferer travel with the core expressions as they evolve and orchestrate the person's life plan.

The process of core energetics can be divided conceptually, though not dynamically, into four planes and four stages. The planes are the body, the emotions, the mind and will, and the soul. As the work progresses, it bears on both the quantitative and qualitative aspects of the person's energy (its mass and its consciousness) and on both the centrifugal and centripetal pulsations of the energy system (the movements from and into the core). The stages start with the outer level of the mask, and advance by degrees of emphasis to the second level, the lower self, and on into the center of being, the higher self. The fourth stage moves to uncover the person's life plan. But each phase of the work involves the successively deeper energy aspects insofar as the person is able to open them, and each encompasses all the vibratory planes of being. The stages of the work will be described in Chapter 19.

The Four Planes of the Work

The mass of energy trapped in the physical body is a principal arena of work at the outset of treatment. All the defensive patterns impose chronic muscular tensions that not only restrict the organism's elasticity but drain its energy. The motility techniques we use derive mainly from the systems developed in the Reichian and bioenergetic systems, and my colleagues and I are designing others that bring out physiological expressions of core energy directly.

The motility work incorporates voluntary movements, stress positions, and externally applied pressures. The initial purpose is to loosen gross tissue blocks and to heighten breathing. Both of these effects increase the level of the energy in the organism, like any vigorous exercise. But the movements are devised to reach and stimulate the involuntary activity of the autonomic nervous system, which Reich saw as the foundation of psychosomatic identity. These spontaneous impulses resonate through the physical body to further enhance the flow of vital force, and the energy stream increasingly penetrates the subtler planes of the characterological pattern. So the body work, rather than verbal exploration, provides the opening wedge into the emotional and ideational distortions that make up the deeper tentacles of the illness.

The therapy does not take up the zones of armoring from the ocular to the pelvic in the order described by Reich, but allows the person's manifestations over time to show where each session should go. Opening the chest, however, starts immediately and continues throughout treatment, for breathing, the first semivoluntary function in a newborn's life, is disrupted by neurosis and impinges on all head and torso blocks.

The motility work generally follows the development of the human being from infancy to maturity. In the early sessions, the sufferer lies on his or her back, in the position of the newborn regarding the outside world. The person is encouraged to make the movements of a baby, particularly the ones that express negative feelings. These include vibrating the legs by sticking the heels out, flailing the mattress with the arms and the hands, and scissor-kicking with the feet flexed. The sufferer continues these movements in various combinations well beyond the ordinary fatigue point. The energy generated will force its way around and through the blocks in not only the limbs and joints but also in the torso. The resulting discomfort makes the person aware of where the gross physical blockages lie, while it activates the autonomic nervous system.

The person must not be pressed beyond the limits of strength and resilience at any given moment, because this would, of course, risk straining the tissues. We therefore intervene physically where we find drastic restriction. Many people, in fact, need externally imposed movement to sense even the big-muscle impactions. We may massage or knead the chest and root of the neck, or we may sidestep in sock feet up and down the back, avoiding the pelvic region if the sufferer is not ready for work on it. But the person's own efforts are infinitely more important than these induced movements for three reasons: they energize the organism straight away; they focus on the sufferer's perceptions of the self instead of those of the guide; and, over time, they foster an organismic commitment to healing.

As the energy flow improves, we introduce vocalizing. This vibrates the torso from midcolumn outward and gradually frees the voice from characterological distortions. One form of expression is a nonverbal "ahhh" through the open mouth and throat. The person begins at a middle key and medium volume, increasing the sound into a yell or scream to help bring up primal anger or fear. People also are given words to use: rejections like "No!" and "Go away!", and later attack terms like "Goddammit!" and "Shit!" and "Fuck you!". The attack phrases may let out more feeling if the sufferer lies face down and pounds with the fists at the same time. The energy that is freed by these movements and vocabulary often spills into cries of protest, such as "Why is this happening to me?" and "I want . . ?" And with the desire to receive, the core has been touched and opened, if only for a moment.

To intensify the experience of negative emotions, the person takes a standing position, the posture of youth and adulthood. Standing lets the arms move freely, to beat a chair or couch with fists oɪ bataka (a short bat covered with foam rubber) or wooden sword. The feet learn to kick and stamp, the lower torso to thrust aggressively, the jaw to jut, the voice to bellow, the eyes to glare. In this more vehement work, the guide may help the sufferer expand the emotions that are erupting, fairly spontaneously now, by acting as a counterfoil. We do this to handle transference productively as well as to add our own energy to that emerging from the person. I may shout or gesture violently or lock eyes with the person. I have found a tug-of-war with a towel between the teeth effective. So is punching. I hold a beanbag seat against my torso, and the person pummels me. It is a magnificent thing when the sufferer can integrate negative emotions with negative actions, even if the therapist sometimes has to duck fast. But is is worth mentioning at this point that in all the years I have used physical provocation and retort in therapy, I have never been hurt beyond a minor scrape or bruise.

The quantitative activity or energy increases consciousness and broadens access to it in the defense periphery. The work expands gradually from freeing the emotions to helping the person to really grasp them, to be aware of them, and to ride with them, to excavating the unconscious knots of feeling and volitional thinking that sabotage the qualitative potential of the energy system. This tendency is a more deeply embedded root of the character attitude than the conceptual and volitional imprints, for it grows from the stratum of the whole feeling tone he has developed since birth. His first task is to liberate the primary emotions that feed energy into the attitude. His next task is to understand how and why he misdirects the emotions. This work belongs to the faculties of self-awareness and self-direction, or the conscious mind and will.

The operations of thought and choice occupy more attention in the work as the sufferer can marshal the organism's energy flow and move away from just bailing out the boat. While the physical and emotional aspects of treatment have two aims, to explore unconscious content and expand awareness, the conceptual focus of core energetics has another purpose: to replace negative concepts and intentions with positive ones.

It is not enough to uncover hidden ideation and to work through its manifestations in the defensive periphery. We know how a new situation can trigger a misguided reaction based on a distortion we have thought out time and again. We behave as if we understood nothing about its roots. Prejudice is an example of mental distortion. We may be philosophically committed to evaluating every human being on personal merits and then find our opinion corrupted by discovering that somebody is a construction worker, a minority group member, or a welfare recipient. Thus, though understanding is a powerful corrective, it cannot by itself redirect the skewed consciousness. The roots of the misshapen perceptions run deep and grip like crabgrass.

The Work of Integration

Analytic techniques expose the roots of our problems to our reasoning capacity. However, intellectual understanding alone does not release the hold that the roots have in our deeper unconscious. If we deal with conceptual content, but leave the emotions and physical blockages untouched, the person will remain controlled by the childhood beliefs and feelings that crystallized in all planes of his being. Each kind of blockage must be dealt with on its own plane. The armoring of each plane must be addressed in its own terms. Whacking with a bataka, for instance, is no more than a physical exercise until the person reaches into the rage that the movement represents — such as the fury at having been rejected as an infant. Once the feeling is reached, the aura, which changes only a little with unemotional exertion, accelerates its pulsary rate and gains color and brilliance as the person releases the emotion.

Schematically, physical constrictions jell emotional disruptions; the emotional disruptions derail both physical sensation and volitional thinking; and the negative patterns in the mind and will organize the emotional deviations, somewhat like buoys gathering up sections of a net. The web of dysfunction penetrates all the planes of being — physical, mental, and emotional, but the emotional dysfunctions can be viewed as the foundation of the pattern of denial in the mask. Chapter 9 pointed out that the mask usually takes a destructive stance.

A man marries a woman, for example, who is tall and blond, like his mother. But he also marries the characteristics of his mother which helped concretize his destructive patterns. Whatever his wife does will affect him as if his mother were doing it. Where he perceives differences between the two women, he will try to "reform" his wife in his mother's image.

Perhaps his mother tried to control him by manipulating his emotions. His childhood defense was withdrawal from his mother. Conceptually, the man will see his wife's expression of need, as well as real efforts to control, as the same thing; and he will react in the same way to both. Emotionally, he may feel small and helpless and unable to deal directly with what he perceives as the woman's demands on him. On the physical plane, his energy will cut off where he froze it as a child. Perhaps his protest at the manipulation will be locked in his jaw, and his fury immobilized in his shoulders.

His mask may be compliance with his wife's wishes, but it covers the destructive hostility with which he meets the perceived demands. In addition to feeling the original rage and pain of the childhood trauma, he must be able to think through his relationship with his wife. He needs to develop the capacity to sort out her irrational demands from the expression of her real needs. In this way he can develop the capacity to respond to her appropriately as a human being, not as the image of his mother.

In working with this man, we would begin with the physical. Perhaps we would have him kick and pound while encouraging negative expressions toward his wife. As he breaks into the emotional material, his memories of the origins of his feelings will occur. He will begin to see that his rage originated in his relationship with his mother and is misdirected toward his wife. He must use his conscious mind and will to challenge his negative picture of his wife as a domineering bitch with a realistic picture of a woman who has real needs and real gifts to give him, a person who has both faults and virtues.

In the case we are discussing, the man may understand the origins of his problems conceptually, but he will react in the same defensive way if a woman should become his supervisor at work; or if he divorces and finds a new partner. Thus, though understanding is a powerful corrective, it cannot by itself redirect skewed consciousness.

We fall back into these old thought patterns because the will, our assertive principle, also participates in the armoring, both above and below the line of self-consciousness. Every illness contains a voluntary element. The suffering person elects to maintain the defensive structure, not because the primal emotions will spill out spontaneously as in childhood and bring punishment, but because of fear that they will. At bottom, every form of blockage expresses a refusal to perceive the flow of energy in the organism, that is, to feel emotion. On the plane of the mind, this habitual refusal constitutes the person's negative ideation. In the will, it can be defined as negative intentionality, which is the inclination to withdraw from the movement of life, to choose to remain in a restricted state because it is familiar. Taken together, the mental and volitional impediments sum up the systemic negative attitude.

The Role of the Will

Grace was an aggressive woman who could neither sustain a relationship with a man nor consistently earn a living. She relied on her father, a wealthy merchant, to bail her out time and again. In her work on herself, she repeatedly complained about the weakness of the men with whom she sought a relationship, but also that they did not take care of her properly. Grace had an exceedingly strong attachment to her negative picture of men, based on her childhood experience with her father, who had withdrawn his energy from her around age six. In spite of repeatedly seeing intellectually that her picture of men was distorted, Grace had a will to believe otherwise.

Willfulness such as this appears most visibly in the mask. It supports the facade of behavior that the person believes is most suitable. Grace, for example, believed that she had a perfect right to make excessive demands on men because she felt superior to them. However, willfulness permeates the whole third level of being, the defensive armoring, because of psychosomatic unity. From the character armoring, the various malformations of the will centers that show in the character types can throw the entire energy system out of kilter. (See Chapter 9.) The forceful, psychopathic businessman with his overdeveloped will cluster, for example, often equates his life with his successes as a company leader. He pushes his energy outward all the time, steers others to serve his ambitions, and may end up with a heart attack.

As the will can act to perpetuate a negative attitude, so it can act to remove blocks and to cultivate positive functioning in their place. This twofold operation consists first in what the literary arts call suspending disbelief and then in engaging belief.

Even when the mind can see distortions it has been maintaining, the defenses close repeatedly to reassert the long-held images. This is to be expected. Humans in good health can absorb only a small amount of new experience at a time, relative to the body of knowledge they already possess. A sick person faces a double job: unlearning misconceptions and learning reality. Both call on the will to let the mind lay aside established notions and to move out into the unknown.

Suspending disbelief, then, means choosing to receive the previously unknown and to perceive it realistically. To accomplish this, the sufferer usually needs to be primed for a while with new avenues of thinking. The person's awareness is limited not only by finite human powers (an existential factor) but by an individual history of denial (an experiential factor). On the one hand, we are used to certain concepts that are, in fact, radically incomplete. We strike a desk and feel its resistance. We therefore call it a solid object, when actually it is made up of a conglomeration of molecules that swirl around in a fluid dynamic structure. Though I am convinced that the core has a limitless potential for discovery and creation, most of us must be taught atomic theory. On the other hand, every one of us sees some portions of life awry. We reduce a spouse to a parent figure, or the essence of a person to an accident of birth or circumstance, or the myriad possibilities for growth to one career.

In Grace's case, for example, she needed to challenge repeatedly her belief that men were both inferior to her and owed her the honor of taking care of her. She had, in short, to suspend her disbelief in the reality of what a man is over and over again. At the same time, she needed to develop a picture of what a man is and can be. This did not mean replacing one idealized picture with another. She needed to learn that men have many positive, as well as negative characteristics, like all human beings. She had to understand what was appropriate for men to give her — love, understanding, companionship, an exchange of loving feelings; and what was inappropriate — making her feel good, taking care of her material needs, making her feel superior, subjugating themselves to her.

New conceptual grounding such as this aligns the will with a new flexibility to let the sufferer say, "I'm going to examine my fixed positions. I'm going to relinquish my categories or right and wrong, yes and no. I want to see what else might happen." As this process takes the brakes off the energy system, it readies the person for the ultimate movement of core energetics: learning reality.

Releasing the Core

The focus of the treatment can now shift to the farthest-reaching plane of the organism's operations, the spirit or the higher self — the core. The work with this power moves directly along two vectors at once, inward and outward, which correspond with the expansive and contractive phases of the reciprocal energy cycle. Inwardly, the treatment aims to merge the outer with the inner self, leading the person to identify with the higher self. Outwardly, it aims to enlarge the communion between the self and external reality. The task of the conscious mind here is to shape the positive concepts. The will's part is to develop positive intentionality, to engage in and to choose life rather than withdrawing from it.

The source for these reorientations is the universal life force that makes up the individual's core and the whole of existence. The free flow of reciprocal energy straightens and deepens the person's inner being along both vectors. To put this in another way, the process generates self-truth subjectively and realism objectively. The outer mind is systematically trained to heed the marvelous energy formations that surge from and into the core. The mind can then unleash the products of creative imagination, make intuitive connections, look for the vast opportunities in outside events, and assess all of these movements for their feasibility and value to the self and others. The will moves from suspending disbelief to engaging belief. It translates the qualitative potential of the person's living center into concrete actions. It puts its muscle behind plans so these can be carried to completion.

The most comprehensive aspect of the work with the soul concerns its embrace of what we think of as the unknowable. The more people learn about reality and the correspondence between inner and outer life, the clearer it becomes that only existential limitations restrict the choice of paths they are evolving in this life. Beyond that, the person expands the understanding that the yearning for unification with external reality thrusts forward all being in all time, toward infinity. This is the territory for the deepest human fulfillment, but commanding it calls for substantial integration of the organism's physical resources, emotional commitment, and positive volitional thinking. The integration process unrolls in four stages.

Chapter 19
THE FOUR STAGES OF THE WORK

My experience is that most people seek a therapist's help with their character defenses firmly in place. If they have some intuition of their center of energy, they cannot mobilize the movement, claim it, join it, and work with it. An unfathomable burden of obstructions has accumulated around the core, obstructions in the form of snarled knots of conflict and functional blocks.

The suffering human being begins to dissolve these blocks by enlisting the creative consciousness of the core, wherever it can be touched through the periphery. Every living person, including a full-blown psychotic, retains points of intersection between inner and outer realities. Psycholinguist Carole Offir reported recently, for example, on the marked successes being achieved in dealing with severely autistic children in a program that relies mainly on eye contact and sign language.

These openings to and from the core are points of relative strength. Core energetics brings them into the work from the outset. The person has an energy flow at these openings and therefore some feeling, mental perception, and, very importantly, some intention to sustain the movement. From these intact energy centers, the consciousness is extended simultaneously along two vectors. It is deepened in itself so that the person becomes increasingly aware of its functioning on all dimensions: the body, the emotions, the thinking and deciding mind, and the spirit. And it is expanded, through the patient's deliberate concentration on these four dimensions, to penetrate the areas of armoring. Thus, the work aims beyond the illness toward the unique and precious being whom nature intends to function from the core.

Stage 1: Penetrating the Mask

The first stage is relatively short, because it receives impetus by the desire to relieve pain that has prompted the person to enter treatment. The work confronts the mask for what it is: a counterfeit of inner reality. Self-observation with the help of the therapist / guide uncovers the obvious distortions discernible in the body structure and functioning. This work is fostered by the motility work described in the preceding sections, particularly the activation of the negative emotions through kicking, striking, and vocalizing. As described, the physical work increases the energy level that activates the tensions and blocks and makes their existence and location apparent. The therapist then proceeds slowly to understand the meaning of the blockages in terms of the dynamics of energy movements and their role in withholding and limiting the flow of feeling. He does this by observing what is expressed in the patient's body as he speaks, breathes, and moves voluntarily and involuntarily during the rigorous exercises.

Much voluntary physical movement may be needed before the sufferer can open the consciousness to the negative movements and allow them to flow spontaneously. It may take most of the course of the treatment before the movements are accepted as part of the gift of life. The mask returns again and again to remove the self from the negative movements.

The mass of energy trapped in the defensive perimeter is a major focus of core energetics from the outset. For every sufferer, the experience of new inner movement pinpoints the location of the gross physical blockages. For a few, this experience quickly throws light into the whole complex of the mask — the strictures on the psychic as well as the somatic planes. Most people, however, must go into considerable physical work as well as conceptual grounding of the consciousness to reach such insights.

First for the therapist and then for the sufferer, every expression of the body has a meaning. It tells a story of the past experiences of the individual and shows his way of handling, in the here and now, his difficulties in expressing emotions. Many such expressions are chronic and habitual and constitute the personality pattern. For instance, the way a person walks, whether he is constantly smiling, the look in his eyes, the tone of his voice, all are expressions of the chronic attitudes that have become structured in the body and that limit the rhythmic and unitary movements of the organism.

For example: A 54-year-old woman came to ask for help. Her walk was slow, her shoulders were stooped, and facial expression was tortured — as if she were defeated and in despair. The jaw was jutting forward and determined. Her eyes held a painful expression. She looked as if she had been crucified. When we started discussing the help she needed, she said, "I am enclosed in an iron cast. My body is like stone. Help me to feel it; I am so burdened."

These unconscious expressions are prime tools for the therapist. To begin with, we do not listen only to what the person says, the content of the words, for much mumbo jumbo is carried by the speech through the hardened mask. We try to perceive how the sufferer's hell operates by working inward from the way it comes out, using the entire range of physical and emotional expressions. This entails visualizing the blocks through the evidence taken from the bone structure, the stiffness or flexibility of the muscles, the tone and color of the skin, and particularly the pulsation of the aura. All of this evidence reveals directly the intensity of the patient's energetic function and indirectly where the energy flow is being obstructed, as with the "crucified" woman, whose aura showed severe blockages of energy in her back and shoulders.

Vocal tones, body postures and gestures, skin texture and resilience, hair quality, eye luster, and other evidence reveal the location of blocks, their intensity, their interrelationship, something of their origin, and their overall configuration — the type of character structure. The masochist, for example, may speak in a complaining whine. The piercing, attacking eyes reveal the psychopath, covering a deep fear and insecurity. Dull, flabby skin and muscles pinpoint pools of stagnating energy.

While each person is unique, patterns can be discerned in the mask of the ego, as we saw in Chapter 7. For instance, the oral character often has a thin frame, like a long balloon that has not been filled in. The structure signals an early history of emotional starvation and an ongoing sense of deprivation. The predominantly oral person is generally undercharged with energy and carries armoring particularly in the occipital area, the back of the neck, the shoulders (which pull strongly up and inward), and the pelvis. Less tenacious blocks will be found in the knees and ankles. The masochistic structure shows a thick, overcharged body that restrains the energy flow throughout, but has especially severe blockages in the shoulders, throat, buttocks, groin, and legs from the thighs to the calves. Therapists can uncover regions of subtler armoring by palpitation as well as by the appearance of the aura, if they can see this.

A crucial aspect of penetrating the mask is the sufferer's recognition that the outer will conspires in maintaining the mask and the substratum of character armoring. Once this insight is gained, the person can begin to take conscious responsibility for his or her problems. The recognition is the first reliable evidence in the therapy that the core has been touched and the ego turned to positive action.

The work on the defensive perimeter turns the person completely around to gaze inward rather than outward. The crisis that brought the sufferer into treatment in the first place is located within the self, not in the outside world. Hence the requirement in core energetics that the person look at his or her life situation, not in terms of accusations and blame of others (though these may be quite valid), but in terms of the self's negation of the inner being, the self's responsibility for the crisis, the self's power of decision to transform its negative energies into positive energies. In sum, this first stage of treatment evaluates the mask and prepares the person to replace denial of life with affirmation of life.

Indeed, the person who has the awareness to ask, "Does it have to be so? Do I have to struggle this much? Do I exaggerate? Why do I do that?" has already begun his treatment before ever consulting a therapist. The repetition of these questions throughout the treatment helps penetrate and dissolve the mask and to reach the person's inner core of wisdom where the real answers lie. Most often, the therapist needs to introduce such questions to the sufferer. I try to be explicit, asking the person at the outset and repeatedly throughout treatment questions aimed at getting him in touch with his body: "Do you know that your voice sounds frightened?" "Are you aware that you do not feel the ground under your feet?" With comments like these as springboards, the therapist helps the patient to move from the conscious into the unconscious, and ultimately to reach the core of his being.

Stage 2: Releasing the Lower Self

Penetrating the mask leads to disclosing the underlying attitude of negation which is the principal target of stage 2. This proceeds in a series of steps, or probings from different perspectives, that lead back and forth into each other but than can be outlined as follows:

○ First, as just described, the sufferer and therapist find the attitude of denial as it appears in the physical body, the energetic body, the aura, and the character structure which is revealed through the dynamic situations created in the sessions and in life proper.

○ Then, I ask myself, what does this attitude mean? What view of the world does this person have? Does he have faith in life and the universe?

○ I search next for the intent. Why does this person use this attitude of denial? How does he rationalize it?

○ The fourth step is to uncover the cause of the attitude of negation. This is a function of the exaggeration of the character defenses and the hardening of the mask that it produces. For instance, the masochist wears a nice smile, but it shutters a multitude of negative emotions. Fiendishness lurks behind it, and fury. And below these lies the terror of being hurt, destroyed, obliterated, an illusion hard to perceive.

○ The fifth and most important phase is to displace the consequences of the primal emotions into the therapeutic setting. That is, I interact with the person to draw out the negative and positive feelings and let him express them under safe conditions that support and encourage their expression, without criticism, punishment, or rejection. Everyone has secret negativities that he will not express. In the healthy organism, these are not blocked but are rather voluntarily restrained. In the sick person, they are stymied by the character defenses.

The second stage of treatment emphasizes evoking the primal negativities undistorted. The mask grits its teeth to keep these under cover. Every living thing has experiences that summon hatred, rage, or fright. If the self is so immured in the mask that it cannot let these feelings stream out of the organism, they have only one place to go: back against the organism. Adding his own findings to the mounting evidence on the baneful effects of this whiplash, Dr. Henri Laborit, research director at Boucicaut Hospital in Paris, made the unqualified statement recently that "All pathology starts with inhibiton".

The second stage of treatment directs the analytic power of the self-aware mind to dissect the composition of the destructive elements in the unconscious. The spitefulness presented by the mask is excavated to uncover the rage and hatred trapped in the armor. These are life-aligned forces, whether appropriate or not when they originally ricocheted back into the organism, because their purpose was to protect the core.

To help unearth these primal negativities, I might direct a man with oral character structure to make physical movements and vocalizations that express anger. In the early sessions, these actions in themselves would not ordinarily connect him with his anger. But the physical work heightens his overall organismic charge and accelerates the vibration of energy into his blocks. I can then stimulate his consciousness to admit the dormant negativity by leading him to recall and protest against the emotional deprivatons of his early life. The oral person's powerful memory, linked to the open energy center between the eyes, usually can be trapped readily. Over time, we work together to help him sustain the anger, for as I said, the oral character structure has particular trouble staying with any stream of force, positive or negative.

As his strength expands, so does his awareness of his energy movements, his capacity to precipitate them with or without physical activation, and his determination to explore his inner self more deeply. The oral sufferer is now increasingly able to discard the origins of the blocks, the "because of the imprints on the energy body, and to experience his feelings with purity and intensity. That is, he does not need to use memories to evoke his resentment or fear, for example. He can press these expressions along their continuums to their ultimate forms, rage and terror. Simultaneously, he has been opening his positive emotions.

With the oral character, the qualitative differentiation of the movements from the core can begin early in treatment. Unearthing the memories of childhood rejection will expose grief as well as protest. The physical work can, therefore, be guided to translate grief into weeping and then, as the man's retention of energies improves, into the convulsive, whole-organism sobbing of unfettered childhood. On this continuum, he can gradually filter out the element of rejection response in the grief to focus on the pure expressions intermingled with it: the myriad forms of expansion and reception that the core instinctively craves.

With other characterological patterns, the positive emotions as such may not be so quickly accessible to conscious definition. Therefore, this second stage of treatment must concentrate for some time on simply using rather than differentiating the mass of the life force. A masochistic woman, for example, will need to work a long time on the hatred congealed in her blocks before she can recognize and identify with the constructive movements from the core. She will long perceive positive incoming energy as a threat to her independence and positive outgoing energy as an invitation to that threat. The schizoid sufferer will evolve according to a similar timetable but with other stepping stones. The schizoid human being is a marvel of creation, encompassing numerous energetic entities inside, though these exist in a state of mutual contradiction. Despite the generally depressed pulsatory rate of the aura, this person is capable of immense and diverse creative episodes, and of equally various destructive rampages; witness Van Gogh, for example. In the schizoid, the ricocheting submersion of one self by another not only severs the higher being from the lower, but fragments the lower self laterally, so to speak. Thus, in stage 2, the schizoid needs considerable experience with radiating energy across the barriers between the selves as well as with expressing negativity outward.

Core energetic treatment unfolds according to the sufferer's needs and strengths. The aggressive character, for example, needs to concentrate initially on opening and balancing the energy flow between the upper and lower part of the body. The crucial work of reactivating the receptive centers usually moves very cautiously until the person has some experience of interior rhythmicity. The masochist, on the other hand, needs to activate the tremendous reservoirs of energy locked within the massive areas of blockage.

An overview ot the approach to an oral character structure will perhaps help illustrate some of the diagnostic concepts and orientations of core energetics. The organism exhibits a depressed energy pulsation, around 15 per minute. While the aura is a healthy blue between the blocked areas, it takes on a muddy, brownish hue at the blocks themselves. The low charge is particularly apparent in the bottom section of the figure 8, for the person has trouble connecting with the ground through armoring in the lower torso and legs. The available energy thus piles into the upper torso and head, depleting the lower body further. Characterologically, the blocks tend to dissolve fairly readily in the oral patient, partly because of the wide energy field that sweeps over the head. The oral person usually is quick to grasp and work with the understanding that emerges in the treatment. The energy centers reflect the same imbalance and strengths. The third eye and the will center in the back of the head are open. All the other funnels are more less inoperative, most of them taking the reverse funnel shape. In other words, the mouth of the funnel instead of the tip, is close to the body.

The therapy begins, as I said, by approaching the inner being through the accessible centers, in this case the relatively free movements of thought and ideational will, or conceptual choice. However, these aspects of consciousness are exaggerated and distract the person from holistic functioning. But they are powerful energy beams for charging and integrating the underdeveloped abilities to perceive emotion (the feeling centers), express it (the two lower will centers), and understand and fuse with external realities (the mental centers between the eyes and at the crown of the head).

In terms of technique, the treatment spans the four dimensions of the person's being. Motility work progresses from gentler to more vigorous voluntary movements and then toward increasing participation in the spontaneous emotions these expose. With the oral patient, I pay special attention to heightening the charge throughout the system, helping the person connect with the ground, and opening the heart and sexual centers.

The mask of the oral person is more permeable, because the blocks contain less resistance than most of the other character structures. But there also is a greater tendency toward apathy. This means that though the person can be *led* rather quickly into recognizing and expressing both negative and positive emotions, the initiative to *sustain* these movements develops rather slowly. The mask rises again and again to negate volitional commitment to the whole energy flow. In other character configurations, the patient is usually able to accept the destructive impulses before the constructive ones. The mask returns in a flash after the cries of rage that the voice has been mustering translate into sobs of grief and longing.

The mental and spiritual aspects of the therapy coextend with the physical work. Because of the particular capacity for conceptualization, the oral person needs continual help to activate the full realm of consciousness. With psychoanalytic procedures as a base, the perceiving self is guided to explore the content of past experiences and their causal links to the illness. But these discoveries are only a foundation of the work to extend the consciousness.

The excavation and working through of the primal negativities of the lower self is an essential component for the stage which follows: reaching for the core. As I work with a patient over several years, conflicts unravel and defenses lower. The patient transcends his peripheral level of being, moving slowly on a spiral path toward the center of creative energy. This movement often is painful and frightening. Most patients feel it first as a descent, a falling into chaos, into destruction. As they make initial progress toward the core, they begin to draw fresh energy outward from it, energy they may not have experienced since childhood. But this fresh strength almost invariably is corralled to reinforce the person's negative resistance. The therapist's task is to help him perceive this pattern and come to grips with the negation itself.

As the ego grows stronger from the release of the organism's energy, it can more readily explore the relationship between the primal negativities and the peripheral defenses. The person begins to understand that the early experiences congealed in the armoring were only the precipitants of the blockages, not their cause and substance. Their cause was and is the negative set of the conscious and unconscious components of the outer will against the flow of energy in the real self. Their substance was and is the overflow made up of primal negative emotions that have not been allowed to erupt freely from the organism but have been stopped in the periphery.

The character defenses are tenacious. Every unexpressed negativity acts like yeast. All it takes is one destructive impulse to activate the whole denial syndrome over again. The work on this dimension reaches the center of right energy, opens it into the primal emotions, and clears the blockages that have frozen the feelings behind the mask.

Transition: Reaching for the Core

The unraveling of the negative emotions and their divestiture from the mask opens ever wider channels into the core. As already explained, this is a lengthy process that requires the patient again and again to confront the mask and the raging negative emotions that undergird it. Time and again, through experience after experience, the patient must plunge beyond his character defenses into the stream of energy from the core. This back and forth process illustrates the interpenetration of the levels of the human entity in the work of reaching the pure creative energy of the core.

This spiral movement of the human being into and out of his core is a dynamic process which follows a continuum through the levels of reality. But for the sake of clarity, I sometimes treat the movement as though it were divisible into parts. To illustrate this, I put three chairs in a row, and explain to the patient that we use them because all people have common emotions and expressions that can be handled better if separated according to the levels of being where they belong. Chair 3 represents the distorted reality of the character defenses and the mask of the ego. Chair 2 holds the lower reality of the primal negative emotions. Chair 1 is the greatness of the human being, energy and consciousness, the primal positive emotions, those aspects which comprise love.

In the second and particularly the third chairs, the various character structures have different attributes, though some of the expressions are common to all. When the schizoid structure sits in chair 3, he says, "I don't care. It's all the same to me". When he sits in chair 2, he is full of fury, murder, and rage. The oral character in chair 3 says, "Please like me". In chair 1, his expression is, "You owe it to me. You must give it to me. You don't feed me enough. That's why I have troubles. Fill me up; I am an empty sack". There is accusation and bitterness here.

The masochist will sit in chair 3 and say, "I am so good. Poor me. I am an innocent victim." In chair 2, he will threaten, "I'll provoke you to prove how bad you are. I'll give it to you." The psychopath from chair 3 says, "I can do anything". But from chair 2, he menaces, "If you don't let me have my way, I'll destroy you". The rigid-hysteric structure declares in chair 3, "I am beautiful. I am efficient. I am organized". In chair 2, he says, "I hate you. I'll cut you up in pieces. I will never give my heart". Every sufferer will signal from chair 3 that he is good, that he is not responsible for his negative feelings. And in chair 2, everyone will show hatred and a desire to destroy.

Here, at the outset, the therapist introduces his own centripetal energy in the treatment. The practitioner introduces his or her own core movement through recognition of the sufferer's inner beauty and worth. Any sensitive healer does this to some extent, of course, if only by discarding moral judgments. In core energetics, the guide includes his or her inner person in the healing process throughout, reinforcing every mode of centrifugal movement from the sufferer save one, the mouthings of the mask.

In core energetics as in all psychiatric approaches, projection and transference arise, encouraged by the safety of the therapeutic setting. All skillful practitioners accept whatever material the suffering person can grapple with, and the patient's relief at being so fully welcome leads gradually to a testing of the welcome in terms of the developmental age when the neurosis first became fixed. Because transference is also an avoidance device, it must be dismantled. Core energetics utilizes some of the methods discovered by the psychoanalytic and bioenergetic schools to resolve these dependent impulses, but from a totally different perspective. I actively use myself as a proper if temporary object of the negativity in order to demonstrate that it will not annihilate the sufferer or me.

Force from the sufferer's core is the principal solvent of the pools of negative energy. Centripetal movement, my energy and consciousness, penetrate the person's source of life, call it out, accompany it, but do not act in its place. The therapist addresses the person's core through the energy funnels that diagnosis has revealed to be relatively functional. The target is the heart emotions, whichever channels of reception are open.

The interaction with the sufferer likewise engages the therapist's whole person, not only thinking communicated in words. Since we are working with dynamic movements, these have to be expressed. As the patient tries to bring up his feelings, he gradually focuses them on the therapist. This is, of course, transference based upon projection. People will insist on finding someone to whom they can attribute their complexes, be it a social acquaintance who resembles the mother or father, or a physician who represents authority.

Traditional treatment calls for the therapist to remain neutral to these expressions. In core energetics, on the contrary, we actively evoke the expressions and respond to them, utilizing our own energies and specifically our feelings to help penetrate the outer level of the sufferer's reality. This is a delicate process. For instance, the therapist may have the patient kick and yell while his body is in a stress position, shouting along with him to intensify the movement from simulated to actual anger. In itself, this interaction creates a fluid transition between doctor and patient, and the transferred feelings can turn into a physical attack on the doctor. The therapist mobilizes the energy of the anger and redirects it constructively. Thus, the work proceeds in a spiral movement that leads gradually to the patient's core.

We work so close to the brink of violence because projection and transference, particularly when they are negative, strongly sustain a person in a state of disconnection between inner and outer reality. From one standpoint, it is harder to reorient this sort of distortion than to awaken deadened feelings, which contain and hold great energies. At least, if a person is blaming others for his pain, he keeps functioning, with a machete, granted, but functioning nonetheless. This movement feels better to the organism than emotional apathy.

This active introduction of the therapist's centripetal energy into the work constitutes a second reason we call ourselves helpers or guides.

I have said several times that the uniqueness of the human being belongs not to the outer self, with its mask that is usually shown to the world, but to the essence ot the inner self, which is the core. The "superior" status of the practitioner, the professional knowledge and techniques, and other presumed distinctions are acquisitions of the outer self and have nothing to do with inner worth. As beings, the two people involved in the process of core energetic treatment are equals. Each one, like every other person who comes into existence, has an irreplaceable task to perform in life, which is just as important in the universal design as every other task.

Countless plants compose the earth's vegetation. It would be absurd for a tree to claim that it is better than a vine since it is bigger, or the vine to put itself above a cabbage because the cabbage can't climb, or the cabbage to scorn the carrot for growing underground. It is just as mistaken for the guide and the suffering person to place any weight on the superficial distinctions between them. Both are unique entities, both are accepting the mandate to develop from the core, and both are contributing to the unitary movement in the chain of existence by working out their tasks together.

This is why it is essential for the therapist to be as real and involved in the treatment as the patient. We all wear our masks much of our waking life; even we who are versed in core energetics can feel ourselves doing it. I have difficulty many times when I speak to an audience. I feel self-conscious and embarrassed, like a little boy, wondering, "Will they accept me? I want to please them so they won't criticize me". And then I say to myself, "If they criticize me it will be very painful. Well, of course, I can hide from them". What I am doing is trying to keep certain inner feelings from being exposed, feelings that have negativity behind them.

I know some of my negative emotions and understand their origins. I had a very serious and severe father whom I blamed for everything. But today it is not my father who hurts me, because he is not alive. And it is not any other person whom I might put in his place. I have the duty to work with my feelings in order not to project them onto others who have nothing to do with evoking them. Others are only the catalysts for those feelings.

So I have to sit in chair 1, the chair of the core, and tell myself, "It's uncomfortable to address an audience, but that's okay. Why should everybody agree with everybody else? There are all kinds of plants in the forest — short trees and tall trees, clinging vines and flowers. Each has the right to express its own life, even if this means opposition and struggle, as nature often decrees."

At the speaker's lectern, in my private sessions, or in the rest of my life, if I cleave to the mask of my ego, I do not allow the lives of others into my own. I subordinate everything to me, and I blind myself to the reality of others and their feelings. I count only who *I* am, how *I* look, whether *I* am accepted, liked, and accepted. And in doing this, I trap myself in selfishness, and lose contact with other human beings.

From the mask to the negative unconscious — from chair 3 to chair 2 — is always a painful transition. The suffering organism defends itself against new pain. The patient, therefore, resists the transition, and at the center of the resistance is the determination, "I won't let you discover how angry I am". Thus, patients barricade themselves into their hell which is created by their stifled negative emotions. They defend against the pain that is caused by the feelings that have been hidden throughout life, if only because this pain is familiar. This is then a defended pain.

The pain of transition is an undefended pain. It can be agonizing to transmute the energy trapped in negation from stillness into movement, from stagnation into flow. But the reward for accepting this pain is the gift of life.

Life, the gift of living, requires human beings to take responsibility for their feelings. In therapy, as patients sit in each chair, they have to accept this responsibility by acting their feelings out in movement and vocalizing them in words. They sit first in chair 3, where they face their mask and the crust of defenses behind it. Here they pierce the rationalizations that turn negative emotions from level 2 into defenses on level 3. They relinquish transference, the habit of attributing their suffering to causes outside themselves, and they prepare to accept the fact that they are angry because they are angry, they hate because they hate. They learn that there is no external reason for their negativity.

As the sufferer allows the mask to fall, he moves to chair 2. Here he declares the feelings for what they are. He accepts the flow of his energy through his negative unconscious. He perceives the distortions in his life. These distortions can be very subtle; they need not be evidenced in great conflicts and events. For instance, a person who claims, "You know, I love nature; I feel spiritual values in the whole of creation", can then walk down the street and say, "God, those Niggers. Look at that guy with a crooked nose". In chair 2, he sees the source of his contempt not in the passerby but in himself. And he begins to realize that what he feels for others he feels first for himself.

The sufferer is now ready to make the final transition, for as he removes his own rejection of otherness from people who are blameless, his energy, his love of life, flows into the vacuum and carries him to chair 1. From this chair, he can say at last, "I don't want to hurt you. I don't want to abuse anyone. I want to have contact with all human beings. He can open himself to the whole of reality within and without, as a leaf opens to its tree. Humanity is such a tree. All of us grow on the tree of life. Its millions of leaves each connect with a little stem, which connects with a small branch, which connects with the large branch, which connects with the trunk and down into the roots. And the roots are nourished by the universal energy that permeates the primordial earth: the energy of love.

Stage Three: Centering in the Higher Self

The third stage of treatment begins when the sufferer has regained a good measure of integral functioning. Now, the self knows the core, can allow energy to flow into and out of it, and can interpose the negative emotions and the periphery appropriately, against real dangers from the outside world, not against inner movements. But the magnificent creativity of the human center does not end with internal fusion, any more than the scope of a life ends with birth. For this reason, core energetics continues where other therapeutic approaches leave off, after the resolution of the dysfunctions. The skin of the apple of the bark to the tree are not the core. They are only the protective casings that preserve the being whole so they may proceed with the purpose of being, which is self-fulfillment. The third and fourth stages, then, are devoted to evolving the person's path toward unification with all of existence.

In the third stage of treatment, the creative ego, as opposed to the limited, self-will ego, begins to assess the potential of the core directly. The compass and direction of the person's task in life are generated by the core's capacity. People tend to think personal development is limited by lack of opportunities in their environment. It is not true. The opportunities surge around us in mind-boggling profusion. What prevents us from seeing them is negative intentionality.

Negative intentionality is a largely conscious tendency at this point in the treatment. The linked clusters of volitional negations that produced the illness can be summed up as negative intentionality. Even when the illness has been deeply relieved, and even when we know that the agency of healing is the life force from the core, some hangover of negative intentionality can restrain us from plunging into the life processes outside of us to bring our core's creativity to fruition. We hesitate still, we procrastinate still, we feel unsure still of what reception we will meet within outer reality.

The inner consciousness, the core of the human being, needs concentration and work to activate its full potential for moving in strength and harmony with outside reality. An emotionally ill person is like a sailboat dragging its anchor, the stagnant and deviant consciousness. When the anchor is raised, how well does the boat sail? Can it move freely, cut across the wind, respond skillfully to gusts? Can it plot a good course to its destination? In fact, does it know, having wallowed so long at the end of its anchor chain, what places it wants to reach?

The trajectory of a whole life, just like the functioning of a cell from minute to minute, embodies the principle of reception and assertion of energy. The difference lies not in the nature of the movement but in the two other parameters of existence on this earth, space and time. In keeping with the laws of motion, the greater the vibration of a human entity — that is, the greater the freedom of the center — the more energy can interpenetrate external realities in a given period. Our fulfillment depends on how clearly we perceive our inner world of innate and acquired capabilities, and how effectively we apply these of the infinitely varied outside world.

This is a truism, of course, but it is equally true that lasting self-realization is an elusive condition. I think this is because we don't grasp the fact that constant movement means constant change, qualitative as well as quantitative. Every intake of energy can expand our consciousness. Every outflow of energy can enrich our context. There is nothing arcane about the process of merging the inner and outer worlds, the assertive and receptive pulsation of a life path. The final stages of core energetic treatment employ numerous concrete methods of exploration and learning that bring the person to center in the higher self and to move through it. In the third stage, the fundamental practice is meditation, which helps reorient awareness and intentionality from negative to positive.

At this point in the treatment, I see the essential problem as less a revival of the old resistances or a renewed defense of the defenses than as an underdeveloped connection with external life. The person hesitates to move forward because of inadequate experience with the receptive phase of the concentric energy systems surrounding us all. In short, there is a lack of trust, a lack which mirrors many aspects of human society, as I will discuss in a moment, but not its central purpose. That purpose, once again, is creative evolution.

This third phase of the work, centering in the core, sets the stage for the ultimate aim of core energetics, which is unveiled in the final stage. Briefly, the aim of core energetics is to help human beings free their core. By opening this center, we can unify the dualities that appear to be conflicts, whether they appear mainly as habitual distortions, temporary circumstances, or only passive acceptance of received ideas. Our core can dissolve our state of alienation from creation, no matter how drastic.

Forces undeniably are split, as least in three-dimensional reality: for example, the pull between gravitational spheres, the antagonism between some parasites and their hosts, and most importantly for human beings, the distinction between internal and external life. When we let these seeming contrasts close us off from outer reality, we trigger pain and illness, because our inner and outer being is composed of the same essential force.

Yet western theories of healing have taken existential duality as the ultimate reality. They have based therapeutic methods on a selective view of its fundamental causes. Some thinkers have believed that the source of suffering is alienation from God or gods; hence, the spritism of the Middle Ages. Some have blamed it on material deprivation, which has provoked many kinds of physical conquest of the environment or of fellow humans. Some healers have faulted one or another of our innate powers. Therefore, the early Christian era as well as the Victorian age taught contempt for "bestial" emotion, if for different reasons. But each of these explanations pits force against force. On the contrary, because all energy is one force, the purpose of every healing approach must merge force with force, the inner with the outer. And that is the central premise of core energetics.

The Final Stage: Uncovering the Life Plan

In the fourth stage of core energetic treatment, much work is focused on expanding the person's sense of trust. Fundamentally, this consists in extrapolating the ground feeling developed during the therapy into other spaces and future times — in other words, shaping the onmoving life according to the higher consciousness. A world of possibilities extends outward from every human, because no one and nothing in existence is immutable. The sufferer's movement from crisis to integration testifies to the dynamism of right energy, as do changes that have already remolded his or her encounters with other people and outside circumstances. The healing shows that the reception of another's life force, in this case the therapist's, has promoted inner balance, but that it is the person's own life force, the core, which has unified the self. Reciprocally, the assertion of the therapist's life force has promoted the changes in others, but it is their cores which have caused their inner transformations.

The principle of reciprocity underlies the whole of existence. It makes the celestial universe cohere. It makes ecosystems sustain the lives of their members. And it makes each species of being interconnect as a family. Human beings are sisters and brothers, like the generations of fruit of an ancient apple tree. We belong to the tree and it belongs to us — and to the soil, the sun, the atmosphere between, and the stretches of space beyond, as well as the generations before and after us. If we open our core to these radiating energy spheres, not only do we illuminate our own truth, but we vitalize the universe.

One lifetime in one generation is a tiny particle in the sweep of all being through space and time. These prospects can be terrifying, and can tempt the self to shrink from the unification with the cosmos that the soul yearns for. But if the work has opened the organism to the core on the slower vibratory planes, it is my experience that the inner resources can sustain the person, even through such dark nights of the soul as described by John of the Cross.

The exploration process centers on who the person is at present and where he or she can move in the future. It begins with the hardened mask of the defenses and spirals into and through the layer of negation to the vibrant center of right energy. At each of the four stages, it is important for the suffering person to take responsibility for the truth of his being as he can perceive it in the moment. He may need to blame others for a time, but must learn to understand that he is blaming, and that the blame covers up a deeper level of negation, the level of pure rage and hate.

In this way, the person learns that the shape of his life depends on how he molds it. The creative thrust of the core spirals dynamically like a cone along a continuum of time and space, with its own apex in the here and now. The energy of that core is available at any and every stage of the treatment to help the patient through the difficult and painful stages of his growth. He learns that other people can't move his energy; he does. Other people don't force his emotions on him; these arise from his own perceptions. Other people, including the therapist, can't integrate him; that is his task.

The concept of self-responsibility pairs with the concept of innate beauty to form the theme of core energetics. In the work with the consciousness directly, the person undertakes a meditation process that has four distinguishable focuses, though they blend in the act of meditating. Two are inner-directed and two are directed outward.

The first focus attempts to build clear ideas of the inner truth. This is mainly the work of the perceiving self, who faces the crippling negation in the mask and objectively evaluates the person who is behind it. This perspective helps the patient see who he or she can be and accept the effort it will take to evolve. The next focus is deeper and wider. It aims at the core itself. The perceiving self allows the warmth and gentleness of the movement of love to stream through the mind and impress upon the core the ideas of the developed person, the fulfilled and integrated person, who was visualized in the first focus.

In this fourth stage, the meditation and work are informed and moved by the element of choice. Choice here does not mean fitting the will to some static or instinctual framework of behavior. It rather commits the consciousness to the operation of positive intentionality. Through choice, the person elects to accept rather than reject, to search out the constructive factors behind the destructive phenomena, to pursue the best among the alternative goods one can perceive. Choice is the key aspect of all four focuses of meditation.

Looking forward and outward, the third focus concentrates on where the person wants to go. "What is my task in being?" is a question I suggest for this exploration. It examines the marvel that the core is. For here, not in the personality, is where each human is unique. Here are the innate gifts that nature has granted with the fact of life, not only the primal positive emotions, but the talents of mind, will, and body. Here is where the policewoman learns she wants to be a singer, and where a businessman understands he needs to be a carpenter.

The fourth focus, which actually moves inward and outward, calls on the person to trust the environment — the whole universe — as the setting for his or her individual growth. I said before that the core reaches for infinity. This is not a metaphor. In terms of the mass of the person's energy, the repercussions of its outward movements have no end, according to the theory of the expanding universe, just as the energy surrounding it has no practical exhaustion point, according to the subdisciplines of physics. In terms of the consciousness of the person's energy, I believe the testimony of my own development, of people who have been and are in treatment with me, of soaring minds from every culture and age, that there is a unifying, creative principle toward which living things strive. Many venerate it as God. I venerate it as the god who is every human being.

Chapter 20
CORE TO CORE: GROUP THERAPY

"No man is an island complete unto himself", John Donne wrote. Human beings harvest their highest individual fulfillment in relationships with other human beings. The person evolves from within, radiating outward according to the principle of mutuality: interaction between all his parts and then with the parts and the whole of another. This mutual exchange replicates the principle of reciprocity, which allows energy to move outward to merge with others, and to penetrate inward from others.

Mutuality means that different aspects of people fuse into a comprehensive whole. They open toward each other, creating a new entity in the incorporation and contact. According to the principle of mutuality, an idea must be followed and focused on with the intention of executing that idea. This execution requires conscious and persistent effort. Creation and execution must synthesize for inspiration to bear fruit. Both must be present for creative living. The balance between these two factors is the mutual pool existing in the human relationship — the balance, for instance, in an exchange of love. Mutuality is a movement toward unification.

For mutuality to take place, there must be an expansive movement from one person toward another, two "yes" currents approaching one another. There must also be receptivity on both sides for the currents to fuse. The ability to sustain increasing pleasure and a richer life has to be obtained gradually through mutuality. The capacity to develop, to tolerate more pleasure, to become integrated as a whole person depends upon saying "yes" when "yes" is offered. Actually, many times we say "no" to the "yes" of another, forcing the other person to close up, so that when we open up, the person says "no" to our "yes". This puts us in a hellish cycle of negation.

There are reasons of culture and history behind every "no" to pleasure, expansion, and growth. Society, beginning with parents, imposes restraints on the person. Authorities such as organized groups and some religions forbid what they perceive as sin or wrongdoing so that people are often required to act against their needs. While at times restrictions may be legitimate, at other times they are imposed arbitrarily, causing the person to fluctuate between opening to pleasure and withdrawing from it.

Love is the impulse behind the principle of mutuality within a person as between people, and it rises from the core.

Most people rarely touch the nucleus, the core of their inner being. Why? Because a great number of emotions are blocked. The result is a deadening of feelings, which are the person's perceptions of his emotions. When feelings are not felt for many successive years, a paralysis develops in the person, a dullness, a "laziness". This is caused by fear, which is no longer the direct fear of the pain suffered by the child but fear of that fear. The fear of fear becomes a habit and then a pattern, miring the person in slowed, sticky energy.

The principle of mutuality can't operate where there is fear of fear. As many schools of psychiatric treatment have discovered, explaining the divisive emotions is often not enough to integrate the person, either within himself or with others. Core therapy works to tap energy as the ultimate healing agent. It sees the division between the person and the group as a necessary outcome of the division within the sufferer, because the person who is alienated from himself denies the possibility of expansion and therefore of mutuality. He therefore will remain separated and "safe" in his isolated state. When he does experience an impulse toward unification, he withdraws sooner or later in anxiety or panic. He throws up internal walls against perceiving the emotion and external walls against the person who has activated it.

We see this continually in individual therapy. The suffering one no sooner opens his core emotions than he goes into a frenzy and rids himself of the positive feelings as fast as he can. One of the most typical comments patients make is, "I'm in a hurry. I want to get out of here, I want to get going". And oddly enough, that feeling — though taken in a different way — was a principal reason for my decision to try to utilize the core process in group therapy.

Some Aspects of Group Dynamics

About a decade ago, I began to observe the auras of groups of people, particulary lecture audiences, who relate collectively to one person. At the beginning of a meeting, I find audience members seem a little detached or tired. The energy field over the head and shoulders of each person pulsates slowly and independently, though fields interpenetrate somewhat because the people are seated close together. Then as the speaker addresses them, remarkable things happen to the auras.

If the lecturer's voice is vibrant and has energy behind it, and the concepts he discusses affect the audience, a resonance phenomenon sets in. Each person's aura vibrates increasingly faster, rising from about 15 pulsations per minute to perhaps 35. At this rate all the fields coalesce and start moving up and down *in unison*. Conversely, if the speaker isn't getting his ideas across, the individual auras dull and slow down, showing that the energy level of each member has dropped. The same thing happens when an audience or a section of it is hostile to the speaker.

The feedback in either case is palpable as well as visible in the energy fields. I have found invariably that when I'm speaking to a receptive group, my words practically fly out of my mouth, because the tremendous unified energy of the audience reaches out to include me. But when I'm expressing myself badly, or the audience is feeling resistant, my words seem to be hitting a barrier, and it takes a lot of energy to get through to the people.

Anyone experienced with audiences senses these things. I was struck with the potential of the resonance phenomenon as a therapeutic instrument. If one person's self-expression could heighten the energy fields of an entire group in a lecture setting, what might happen if suffering human beings came together for the direct purpose of affecting each other energetically? Could group work, using the resonating energy generated by several people at once, break through to the core of each member more intensively and more persistently than could individual therapy? The possibility was tremendously exciting.

By 1972, core therapy had evolved into an approach distinct from its matrix of bioenergetics. The work with individual patients suggested many orientations that group treatment might take. I realized, of course, that a group of people would function on a different dimension, with different dynamics, from a single person. New applications and techniques had to be invented, and some of these will emerge in the following pages. What I couldn't foresee was how far core therapy can penetrate the whole fabric of each group member's outside world.

Group work, like individual therapy, has two main thrusts. One is to elevate the energy level, which is the quantitative aspect of the organism. The other is to increase each person's consciousness, which is the qualitative differentiation of the emotions, the energy current moving in the organism.

Both processes unfold simultaneously, from without inward and from within outward. Raising the energy level entails not only removing the blocks in the character structure but drawing core energy outward. In the beginning, group participants work a great deal with their bodies to expand and free their energies. Enlarging the consciousness relies heavily at first on analysis of the body structures, the feelings, the underlying emotions and blocks, and the interconnections these have as expressed in the character of each member.

As the group matures, these processes gradually merge, because consciousness is a fundamental attribute of energy. Thus consciousness increases as energy increases. Most of us have had some experience of this effect. If a person feels vibrant and rested, he can perceive many more things during the day and has greater variations and depths in his perceptions. When his energy level is low, he carries a minimal level of activity. So in the group, increasing the energy quantitatively also increases its qualitative aspects, the specificity and clarity of the emotions.

Generating New Energy

Let me at this point give a few very brief examples of movements used in group therapy to energize the participants. These parallel the successive steps used with individual patients, and the progression in both contexts mirrors the growth of the human being from birth to adulthood.

In the individual work, described more fully in Chapter 8, the patient begins by taking the prone position and making the movements of a baby. Negative movements are emphasized at first, such as kicking and hitting. The negative expression often changes organically into a desire to receive, if only temporarily, at first. The negative emotions may be intensified by having the person stand, as would a youth or adult. Gradually, the negative emotions can change into positive ones. The same approach is used in group therapy.

Very early in the core work with groups, I had the notion of asking participants to lie down in a circle with their feet in the center. The idea may have been prompted by the basic longitudinal movement of energy in the human body. Energy flows in a figure 8, or a kidney bean in Reich's description. It streams counterclockwise, from left to right, around the head and shoulders, and clockwise in the lower torso and legs. Reich defines two distinguishable currents meeting at an angle and sustaining the spinning circle that is visible in each sector. These individual movements fuse and flow in an overall movement of group energy, as I shall describe shortly.

I call this circular arrangement of people in a group the mandala position. It has proved to be a veritable cyclotron, and is vastly more energizing to a whole group than any other placement I have observed. I use three variations of the basic mandala placement.

In the first, a group of up to 14 people are arranged in a wheel position or mandala. Each member's feet face the center of the small circle, with their heads radiating outwardly. This position stimulates the working out of many problems. The therapist stands at the hub of the wheel to observe every group member who is starting to breathe deeply. Thus, the therapist can detect physical blocks and unstable energy movements in the body. The person joins or touches feet and hands with the person on each side of him or her. The wheel formed by this contact becomes an energy cyclotron that spins the energy movement around the circle in a counterclockwise fashion.

The deep breathing is regulated by the therapist and initiates a variety of vibrations in the feet. Stiffness in various part of each body can be observed. Energy movement creates an overcharge in the weak spots of each individual. The muscular blocks apply pressure which makes the person aware of physical inadequacies or blocked movements. On the other hand, the moving energy also builds up the energy level in weaker individuals — the schizoid personality, for example — and makes it possible for these people to express their feelings in a stronger way in the group than they could do in individual sessions.

Amazing phenomena occur when the group breathes in unison. Many people, who have been holding back, let go and sob. It is the first time that they have been able to cry or release anger. Of course, this reaction must be carefully followed and graduated so the participants do not panic. I have found the most effective breathing is a short inhalation, followed by a long exhalation which is vocalized as an expression of negativity, such as, *"No!"* This provides a cleansing expression of the group's acceptance of its negativity and destructive tendencies. Once this occurs, good feelings can flow. The mandala experience is similar to an orchestral ensemble with the group leader acting as the conductor. He determines the pitch, tone, and rapidity of the released emotions. He may also accelerate the process. It is important to note that by encouraging the release of the negative emotions, the therapist can then lead the group into an expression of tender feelings.

The second variation which is most helpful and safe, after the mandala arrangement has been formed and the leader is in the center of the circle, is to alternate men and women. Several intervals of deep breathing ranging from two to three minutes should then be initiated accompanied by deep sighing. The breathing accelerates. I instruct the members of the group to flex their ankles and push on their heels, which stimulates a vibratory movement that unifies all of them. Simultaneously, they are asked to move their heads from side to side and express the feeling of *"No!"* Several intervals transpire of stopping and working on individual blocks until the stage of the temper trantrum is reached. With fists clenched, the participants pound the floor with feet and fists together, moving the head and screaming, *"No!"* These episodes, of course, are not allowed to continue more than one or two minutes, but they are repeated successively. Naturally, the therapist must acutely observe each participant. Bodies should be exposed, or half nude, so that he can observe the blocks in the participant. For example, if one member has a block in the back of the neck, the therapist's helper on the outside must release it so that the group can progress to a deeper level of emotion. Amazing experiences occur during the mandala position: there is deep crying, sobbing, anger and temper tantrums, expressions of genuine rage pent up within the body and soul.

The third variation is also effective for group use. Their heads face toward the center with the feet in the peripheral direction. Again, I begin with the deep breathing. I ask the members to raise their hands toward the hub of the wheel and touch one another. Expressions of tender feelings are initiated, the smacking of the lips, crying mama, asking for her to come. Deep experiences emanate from this stimulus: deep sobbing occurs, cries for mother to help, heart breaking emotions which have not been expressed for years. And vibrations stream through the body. When it is over, the participants are asked to turn toward one another. They hold each other while lying in the wheel position and look into one another's eyes without making demands or eliciting expectations. They are simply to make contact. During this time the sobbing appears to become deeper in many of the couples.

The wheel ends when every member stands in a circle facing the center and follows the group leader's instructions. After the person has experienced these early childhood emotions in the temper tantrum position, the *"No",* and the crying, he can now stand on his feet, grounding himself with the life energy of the adult person. I ask the participants to stand with their feet approximately one and a half feet apart, heels out, hands on waist, breathing, and allowing the vibratory movements to flow through their bodies. The circle is maintained through the touching of their feet. Again, in this position, negative expressions are verbalized: *"No!" "I won't!"* Also in this position and at this stage, they vocalize the negativity with the long expiratory phases. This vocalization builds in resonance and feeling which communicates itself to the whole group. Ultimately, the resonance phenomenon evolves into a harmonious reality which assumes the form of singing. It is extremely difficult to explain this occurrence but it happens so often that the mandala position may stimulate the experience when it is worked through. From my own observations of the energy field, I have come to the conclusion that the energy field of each individual becomes greatly activated and fuses with the energizing movements of the person next to him. Thus, a dynamic, powerful movement is created, which ignites the entire group. The effulgent light and movement thus generated are formed by the energy current. It evokes an effect which makes the individual feel like one person; yet he is part of the group. The emphasis, therefore, in this group work, is on the individual experience of each participant. For it is only through this kind of experience that he can really particpate effectively in the group. He must develop his own personal feelings, body awareness, and sensation, which through the deep breathing he is able to share his energies with the others in the group. Therefore, the principle of mutuality, creative movements, fusion, and unification which transpires within each person, is extended to the whole group.

However, I wish to add a word of caution. These techniques can only be used safely when a person is equipped to read the structure of the participant and is aware of his own blocks. He must then release them by specific techniques developed in bioenergetics. These sessions are not parlor games; they should not be led by people who are unaware of their own bodies, their blocks, because it could result in panic reactions.

Fusion exists when the group is handled successfully and a sense of unity and consciousness is attained by the progressive development evolved from the experience. Only when the individual is not cut off or his experience denied, can this happen. Ultimately, the person is with himself — and with the group — connected, feeling, and whole.

As I indicated earlier, the energy cyclotron created in the mandala work fuses the individual energy movement into a group whole. Three basic energy formations appear.

One is the longitudinal stream in each person, which moves up and down each spoke, so to speak, in a systole-diastole pulsation. The rhythms differ from person to person. The independent energy systems of group members accelerate as they begin to work with their bodies, usually through breathing and vibrating and without using their voices at first. Above the rate of about 25 pulsations a minute, a second and third energy formation appear, one at the center of the mandala, where the feet are, and one on the periphery. The single energy currents have begun to fuse, and because of the differing rhythms, the new formations move in a continuous flow. The diastoles of each of the individual pulsations are filled in by the systoles of the others. The central energy stream move clockwise and the peripheral stream counterclockwise.

The cyclotron is a far more powerful exemplar of the resonance phenomenon than the unified energy of an audience, and it charges the group vitally. Group members report that when the energy has accumulated, they feel themselves brought together almost as a new entity, a mutuality not of separate beings but of the parts of a single being.

The cyclotron almost seems to take on a life of its own, independent of its immediate sources. For instance, when one or two group members are critically blocked, the new body of energy bridges over them, connecting the people on either side who are contributing to it. This resolution is like the sweep of a river: if there is a deep groove in the river bed, the water simply fills it and runs forward on its course. The person who is the groove feels pressured and miserable, to be sure, but there is value in this. The new energy streams starkly outline the contours of the blockage, and if they don't break through the person's resistances, they show the group who needs most to be focused on in that session.

These are only some of the energy movements in the mandala. The moods, points of contact, and body placement of the group members create variations so numerous that we are still discovering them. The effect of position warrants some further comment here. The feet-in mandala drives energy toward the legs and increases the awareness of the negative emotions. The body work used in this position, such as kicking and screaming, grounds the participants. When we want to bring out positive primal emotions, the group lies with heads at the hub of the mandala, and members may use verbal expressions of longing, such as "Mama, Mama", "Help me". A tremendously strong circuit is created if each person turns on his side and places one hand behind the neck and the other under the pelvis of his neighbor.

Only when a group has coalesced and matured to some degree, we introduce the standing position, the stance of the adult. Now the participants face each other, taking responsibility for themselves as persons vis-a-vis each other — their looks, their reactions to each other's expressions of feelings, their interrelationships. Arranged again in a circle, members work particularly with movements that vibrate the body and then may progress into big gestures with the arms, legs, and torsos. The voice is used frequently in this position, which makes the body's inner tube vibrate as well. Combining vocalization with leg vibrations resonates the whole organism and enormously amplifies the individual energy pulsation, which again mount in intensity until they join in a new energy formation. The rise in energy occurs faster if participants touch the outer edges of their feet and hold hands, as indicated earlier.

The new energy formation created by the standing circle spins counterclockwise, and like the cyclotron in the mandala position, it curves into a haystack shape. If the therapist is standing in the middle of the circle, the energy can quite literally be felt between the hands, as an elastic medium. Also like the cyclotron but more so, the unified aura shimmers with light, surrounding each person in a glow that brightens as the excitatory process radiates between the individual fields and the new formation accelerates.

The infusions of energy reach to the core of the group members, awakening each person's awareness of how it feels truly to live. But the work of core therapy has only just begun. If the core is to remain open, accessible to the person within and the world without, the suffering one must press through the blocks in the character structure again and again, examining how they sunder inner harmony and distort relationships with others. The heightened consciousness that is the heightened energy gives the mind something to work with.

Exploring the Inner Person

The analytic focus in core therapy is directed toward the person's self-perception and perception of others as unique and immeasurably wonderful beings. His horizon is not "What is my sickness? How do I stop my pain?" but rather "What is my task in life? Where do I want to go? How do I unify myself to go there?"

This vista calls on the group members to envision themselves at the core level rather than according to appearances. It helps overcome the common tendency — therapists have it too — to pigeonhole people as types, whether attractive to oneself or not. There are patterns of human behavior, of course. Psychiatry uses terms like "masochist", "schizoid", and "paranoid", and not without reason. People do manifest definable nexuses of illness as well as "personalities". But it does a person a great injustice to equate him with his problems or his mask. Groups come to perceive this rapidly through the energy exchange. Their understanding carries them across even barriers of dislike that some members might ordinarily have for each other.

Participants approach themselves and each other analytically from the surface as well as the center. Much of the early work concentrates on displacing the virtually universal belief that the negative emotions are "evil". They are not. On the contrary, they are expressions of the life force. In terms of the core process, they are alterations of energy caused by constrictions of the core as Chapter 14 describes more fully. For example, when a person is made to feel worthless, by rejection from without or self-contempt within, anger flares in the negative unconscious, like a spark on a shorted circuit.

Evil in fact derives not from the negative emotions but from denial or negation of emotions, both the positive and the negative. Every block, every sickness, every ungenuine feeling, is a denial. Group members begin their perceptual exploration by examining the denials embedded in their masks: the bland smile on the face that denies an interior rage, the smug superiority that veils a sense of inadequacy, the apologetic droop of the shoulders that hides a fear of doing murder. These indications show in the body, not only in the words of each person.

An appearance of laziness in some people covers a deep reaching inertia; this is the case, as I have described before, when the feelings have remained untouched for years. In fact, the deadness causes great suffering, which the person may misrepresent in an attitude of I-don't-care. Others may deny the completion of a movement of energy. An employee may sense anger rising against a boss and then skew it, sending out instead a complaint or a whine. A date may flirt seductively, but let the prospect of intercourse arise and he runs. A wife may make love and then turn on her husband in coldness, finding fault and picking a quarrel to cut off the flow of warmth between them.

All these and countless other ways demonstrate withdrawal behind the mask — the periphery of the human being. Group members scrutinize such mechanisms in their own makeup and exchange observations with each other. The purpose is "to see ourselves as others see us", never to criticize as such. Criticism is merely projection.

The subject of each person's exploration in the group is always himself: his own mask, his own negative emotions behind it, and ultimately his own positive affirmations of life. The assumption that "I am right and you are wrong" is not allowed to stand. If he attacks someone's character in this way, he is doing destructive things. He is rejecting his responsibility to discover his own negations lurking in his mask, because everyone has the capacity for the "wrongness" he attributes to the other person. And he is provoking the other into a counterdenial or counterattack. At worst, he is actively reaching out to inflict cruelty.

In the group, no one needs to keep up pretenses. Actually, no one is allowed to for long. The participant who paints himself as a Don Juan has to confront the fact that he really hates women underneath and wants to punish them. It is far better for him to admit this openly than to hide from it.

Projection and transference are among the commonest defensive tactics we use to avoid dealing openly with our true emotions. The sicker a person is, the more he will blame others for his suffering. A healthy person accepts others as they are. If they cause him pain, he tries to see it as an accident or an honest collision of interests. He tries to say, "That hurt me", rather than

"You did that to me deliberately!" Transference and acting out may take positive forms that give others pleasure, but they equally misconstrue each person's inner reality. These devices cast other people in images usually carried from early childhood. Therefore, as an adult a person encounters and interacts not with the human being who is really there but with a phantom. Group work utilizes transference and acting out to penetrate to the neurosis, but the substitution is always pointed out for what it is, a misguided target for the genuine feelings.

The keynote of group core therapy is responsibility for one's own emotions. Each participant concentrates on how he himself feels, where his own blocks shackle him, what his reactions to other members mean. Each learns to drop his mask and grapple directly with his primal movements. Each regresses to infancy, so to speak, supported by the profound mutuality that the group has created. Negativities, each participant learns, do not destroy others and do not goad them to throw him into an abyss. The terror he suffers, the fear of the fear, has given him the illusion that if he lets himself go, he will drown in the river of life. Fellow group members help him to experience again and again that this is not so, that they accept his negative as well as his positive expression. They work with each other engergetically and analytically, and they steadily gain and grant unhampered access to their cores.

Because a group constitutes a society for each participant, the therapeutic process does not stop at releasing the primal emotions. The participants are adults, no longer babies dependent on parents for their meaningful relationships. They have grown-up bodies, they can move as they wish, they can support themselves, marry, and have children of their own. All these strengths are tested in encounters with other human beings that call for response as a whole person. The responsibility demanded of each participant, the exchange of trust and faith, the intensive experience of mutuality, moves the group in its mature stage to reintegrate each person not only within himself but with the outside world.

Initiation and Development of the Group

The energizing processes and perceptual penetration just discussed manifest in every group with whom I have worked. It doesn't take special "types" of people to compose an effective therapeutic setting. Actually, I feel that it is good for participants to represent a broad sample in terms of character structures, ages, and backgrounds, and I try for an equal number of men and women. A heterogeneous group practically impels its members toward rapid interactions. Consider the confrontation, for example, of an oral person with a masochist. The first says, "Give it to me, do it for me". And the second retorts, "I won't". An older participant will gravitate toward a parent role, and if the group contains a young member, they may pair up. There are people who can be disruptive and who have to be removed from the group. These are usually psychopathic personalities who monopolize the group, sucking its energy, so that the work cannot be focused on anybody else.

The maximum number of people is fourteen and the minimum eight. A greater number would be crowded in the mandala, and a smaller number would find it hard to reach each other's hands. I have worked with as many as eighteen in workshops, but not in a continuing group. Sessions run two and a half to three hours, and members meet once a week. They usually alternate a session with me and a session with a body therapist. This specialist works with the participants to heighten the relationship between physical movement and emotions, though the characterological analysis of the interconnections is undertaken only in the meetings with the core therapist.

The nature of core works makes it necessary for group members to be in individual therapy at the same time. The emotions evoked in group work can be overwhelming and must be guided independently as well. Moreover, a person should enter individual treatment up to a year before joining a group, for his own sake as well as the other participants. My colleagues and I have found that an unprepared person cannot stand the impact and pace of the group movements. His resistances expand geometrically in the contact, so that the whole group is stymied.

The content of the individual sessions is intentionally linked to the material unearthed in the group. The patient may focus on repressed feelings that fellow members have pointed out. He may work through a negative reaction to another participant that he is not yet able to express directly in the group. Or I may bring up feelings I think he should carry into the next meeting.

There are few rules for group members, but these few are firm. Participants are asked to commit themselves to one year of work and to attend every session. If a person doesn't come twice in a row without a compelling reason, fellow members decide in their next meeting with him whether they feel he should drop out. We have found that people rapidly develop the attitude that the group work is centrally important to them, and members rarely leave it after the first weeks.

Confidentiality is as binding on group participants as on the therapist.

People cannot discuss with any outsider, not even their spouses, any revelations that have been communicated in the sessions. Group members are encouraged from the outset to try to trust each other and discard the supposition that any expression of feeling, from themselves or the others, derives from ill intent. The work requires much patience and permissiveness, far beyond the thresholds of toleration encountered in the outside world. Social conventions need to be laid aside in large part.

I caution people coming into a group to be careful about acting out, because most of us can use this *ad infinitum* as a pressure valve and to keep us from exploring the impulse. Once the group has made some headway, participants who feel an urge to hit or wrestle with each other may do so under supervision, as the following pages will describe. But they are not allowed, of course, to really hurt each other.

I also ask members to guard against being drawn into a close friendship with one or two other participants outside the sessions. This is not a hard and fast rule but rather a guideline to keep the group from subdividing into cliques. I discourage outside sexual relations between group participants on the same ground. Sexual partners particularly will find it hard to bring up their relationship in the meetings. Their efforts to hide their attraction to each other militate against the openness and honesty that must infuse all participants. It is my feeling too that a group member who takes up a sexual relationship with a fellow participant early in the work is most often acting out a negation, such as vengeance against the spouse or resentment because sexual feeling for the therapist hasn't been responded to.

The leader in core therapy does not stand apart from the group but becomes one with the participants in a very real sense, sharing their goals and their work. He must bring the members a profound sense of warmth for their uniqueness as persons, and he must also impose on himself the same rigorous openness and honesty they are called upon to sustain. His attitude has to be that the group members have come together to cure themselves, not to be cured by him.

Participating does not mean that the therapist abdicates his responsibilities as the group leader, for that way lies chaos. His *raison d'etre* is to give group members his insights and guide them in their work. But he must not force explanations on them or herd them in directions he wants them to take. Insofar as possible, the group should tell him how and where it wants to move in each session. If he is puzzled or unsure of what the members need to do at any point, he has to admit it. They will get him back on their track.

Above all, the group leader may never use the notion of truthfulness as an excuse to feed his own ego or let out his own unconscious drives. There have been groups where this has happened — where the therapist has attacked a member who has annoyed him or taken a patient to bed who attracted him. This is manipulation, not openness. Openness in the therapist means accessibility to his core. From the birth of a group and throughout its life, I interrelate with the members as a physician, yes, but I am first and foremost simply John, another human being.

The evolution of a group, as I mentioned earlier, is like the evolution of the human person. The group develops from infancy into adulthood as the core work advances. And it follows a rhythm of growth in terms of the material it comes to grips with during its successive stages.

In the early phases of the group's life, people concentrate on themselves, just as children do. Their attention is riveted on the "me" that each one is. For a few sessions the members will speak fairly freely of their sufferings and where they feel their major problems lie. Then there comes a point where they sit back and wait, looking to the therapist to take them in hand and produce solutions for their difficulties. The leader's task now is to help them begin moving toward unification as a group, for it is their coalescing energy and consciousness that will integrate them individually.

Gradually, the participants open their focus of concentration to include each other. Their attention broadens from the "me" to the "us", and transferences inevitably ripen as the people reveal their true character structures. Masks have dropped, and negative emotions emerge to the surface. Much work is done at this stage to intensify the positive feelings. As the members grow in mutual trust, they bring in dream material and fantasies for the group to explore with them. Their sense of responsibility for each other strengthens markedly in the process, and the group moves into its last stage of growth.

The mature group combines the "me" focus with the "us". Participants examine their human condition, assess their functioning relationships, and work toward integration with their outside worlds. They need increasingly less guidance from the therapist in this phase. Emergencies that arise are likely to be taken up with fellow members directly rather than with him. The group has fused within itself, and in the process, it has raised each person's gaze from the pain of life to the promise of life. The group has opened his river to the sea.

Let me trace now some specific applications of core therapy during the various stages of a group's growth. No single technique is reserved to one phase. Methods introduced early may be utilized throughout the life of a group. The work in each session does not follow a pre-established program but evolves as needed to deepen the members' font of energy and con sciousness. Nor are the stages mutually exclusive. Again like the human person, the group swings back and forth between negative and positive, between clearing the river and strengthening its flow. But broadly speaking, there are aspects of therapy that pertain to each phase, from infancy to adulthood.

Stages of Development: Infancy and Childhood

When a group assembles for its first meeting, its members are apt to feel a little shy and nervous. They are already calling me by my first name, and I use theirs to introduce them. This eases the tension; it also strips them of roles that society assigns a hierarchical value to — as a lawyer, a clerk, a janitor.

We ordinarily do not take up physical work in the first several sessions, for I feel it has a mechanical quality until there is some real sense of acquaintance among the members. We start with each person telling the group why he wants to join it and what he wants to accomplish through it. This is the short period of airing problems, and during it or in the following few sessions, the work of observation and analysis begins.

For this purpose, I ask each participant in turn to stand and move before a mirror while fellow group members watch him. All of us, himself included, speak of what we see in his physical body. The body, revealed in a leotard, can't lie, and group members are attuned to its messages from their individual treatment. "You look like a tall, thin cypress", one person may learn. "You seem to be cut in half at the waist, like a wasp", another hears.

The group draws inferences from each person's physique about where his blocks are, what they indicate of his character structure, and how his defenses relate to the problems he has described. I may point out to a woman, "There is a narrow structure to your hips and pelvis, like a boy's, as though you aren't recognizing this part of your body". Or a participant may comment to another, "Your neck looks stiff. Are you mad at the world?"

Commentaries like these provide the group with a good deal to work on, for they not only give the people knowledge of each other but stimulate reactions. The therapist asks each member how he feels about the others. Some people are embarrassed. Others are frightened. Still others are outraged. Everyone is encouraged immediately to try to perceive why he is experiencing his particular reaction.

The body work introduced in these early meetings depends on my perception of what the group as a whole is prepared for. If the people are already active and moving, I may ask them to take the mandala position and launch into some rather evocative gestures, such as kicking. If I feel them withdrawing into themselves, as is more often the case, I will proceed with gentler warming-up exercises, done usually in a standing circle. I work part of their bodies they feel are moving with their respiration, those parts they don't feel, and where they have pressure or pain. The group members observe and comment on these movements in each other. Observation of the body, incidentally, is an instrument the group uses periodically throughout all stages of its development.

Following these introductory sessions, the people will usually draw back into themselves. They have information about each other but as yet little sense of cohesion. A stillness sets in, a resistance that the therapist must break through to begin shifting the group's attitude from dependency on him to self-reliance. This is a complicated stage, and we use many techniques to advance it.

I may start with perceptual work on the group as a whole. I ask the people to sit in a circle and speak in rotation about their sense of several other participants — not rational judgments but good feelings. The group does the round, attempting to expose true if surface reactions. This activity can stir up a lot of emotions. Then, working with the people who have spoken most vehemently, we take up each emotional response and move it from the fact — the "I don't like you" or "You annoy the hell out of me" — to the why. We connect the projection with the person's inner self: his resentments, his patterns of response to authority figures, his predispositions toward men and women in general.

It may seem better on the other hand to involve the group first in physical movement. I will ask the members to lie down in the mandala formation with their feet toward the center. They begin with breathing and then add leg vibrations, continuing with a long series of movements that may last half an hour or more, to open the energy transmission of the group. Resistance can't be allowed to persist because it creates an atmosphere of futility.

Work like this through a number of sessions generates some awareness of unification in the group, and participants arrive at subsequent meetings more ready to move. Collective withholding does recur, of course, and there are times when I let the stillness and waiting develop until discomfort provokes one or more people to break through. This is a useful tool for bringing out resentments between members. But generally, from this time forward, the group increasingly shows the leader where it wants to go, and the participants need less and less stimulus from him to get to working.

The leader continues to guide each meeting, particularly in deciding how to start it. I take my cue from what I find on evaluating the members as the session opens. Several things enter into this evaluation. The auras of the members are the surest index of their energy level, but there are many other kinds of evidence. Most therapists learn to sense the "mood" of patients the way you can feel what the temperature of a hot stove is at some distance from it. Facial and body expressions tell a lot. A participant may be making conversation but his face may be blank and colorless. This person is holding in. Another may enter the room and lie on his back; he doesn't want to participate. Neither does the member who sits down and hunches forward, arms around the knees. Many positions denote anxiety: a rigid back, tightly clasped hands plunged into the lap, hunched shoulders, shallow or held breath. People who show such tension states need to be focused on specially during the session.

I will ask the person who seems to be suffering the most to come lie down on a mattress with the rest of the group sitting around him in a circle. By this stage, the other participants can usually see right away that this person is in a tremendous bind, caught in the blocked emotion, the denial of the need to let go. It takes a little physical work to open him up. He is asked first to kick his legs and let his breathing expand; he may use his voice as well, perhaps beginning with a vibratory "Ahh" and then using a negative term.

When his movements are flowing, he is urged to shout out his destructive and irrational feelings at each member of the group. He isn't permitted to express judgments or opinions but is turned toward his own feelings, the movements he perceives in his own organism. For instance, he can say to the others, "I hate you, I want to kill you", but not "I hate you because you're hostile". The "because" isn't necessary; it's a copout of his responsibility for these emotions. The group members for their part are guided to accept his negativities, to let him scream at them without cutting him off.

When he has worked through his hatred and rage, it often happens that he experiences a welling up of positive emotion, and he begins to ask the group for help. He extends his hands to the others, and they gather closely and tightly around him, touching him. A heartbreaking surge of despair and suffering courses through his organism, an agony that we all carry within us but that we deny and sidetrack. It bursts out of him like a torrent, convulsing him with sobbing. And this emotion is so deeply enriching and moving that it can draw his comforters to weep with him, each perceiving his own deadness and despair, each confronting his own conflicts. So it is that one member, cleansing himself of his negations, can open the hearts of the whole group. This is the resonance phenomenon at work creating an enormous amount of energy. The experience gives the participants a profound sense of unity among themselves and a feeling of belonging to the human race. It humanizes them.

If no one participant at the beginning of a session urgently needs a focus, I may place the whole group in the mandala position to work into the primal feelings together. The people lie on their backs, their feet toward the center, and start kicking their legs as would a small child in a temper tantrum. I may ask them to bring up negativities without a target, or I may suggest that they visualize an early authority figure and pinpoint rage against that person.

Sometimes a participant will become so energized that he spontaneously gets to his feet in order to have more freedom of movement. He may then take a bataka and beat a mattress, yelling at a parent image: "You goddam monster, you fucked me up, you hurt me, you hurt me!" He may rev up so much hatred and anger in other participants that everybody grabs batakas with which to beat their parents.

When these explosion have worn off, the people often will sit close to each other in a circle and explore their problems in a way that is cleared of rationalization and the need to protest. Without any prompting from the leader, they will discard the accusations against the parents and take up the negative emotions and their implications in their present-day lives. When this happens, it is clear that the group is maturing rapidly.

Stage of Development: Youth and Adulthood

Though the emphasis in the early stage of a group's development is still on the negativities, we are aiming for the positive emotions. Sometimes in a session, the people work for a while in the feet-in mandala position but do not build up the momentum to open their positive movements. So, then I reverse them to the head-in mandala to channel the new energy formations upward in their bodies and evoke the heart feelings. They vocalize their distress, their pain, and especially their fear of fear: "I am suffering", "I'm going to fall apart", "I don't want to die!", and "Help me, help me!" Many people will weep, and the deep empathy around the entire circle makes the participants realize that they are not alone in their misery. Most importantly, it makes each one experience total expression and total acceptance — a total mutuality — of the positive emotions.

The group is by this time deeply cohesive; it has become a family, and the members are ready to assume not only more of the direction of the work but a greater share in carrying it out with each other. I am still guiding them, but only intermittently, and after an initial suggestion from me, they will move through perhaps the entire session on their own. For example, a meeting may begin with a member lying down, his fellow participants sitting in a circle around hin. As the person in the center expresses his negative feelings, the others react to these in kind. Suppose he is saying, "I hate you". They answer, *"I hate you!"*, accentuating his movement while at the same time feeding it back into themselves. It he regresses to denial and tries to blame any of the others for this hatred, they are quick at this stage to refocus him (as well as themselves) on the inner sources of the negativity.

In this stage too, the group is using the adult standing position increasingly, bringing big movements into play to stimulate the self-contained energy flow in each organism. These are particularly helpful if I feel that the group is becoming undercharged. I may line the men up on one side of the room and the women on the other. With each subgroup facing the wall, I have each line hold hands and I set them to vibrating, and little by little their jaws go out. Then someone begins to say, for instance, "Damn you". These messages spread along each wall, so that all the women are soon shouting things like "You're a bunch of sadists!" and the men are giving as good as they're getting with "You bitches, you tricky mothers!" In a while, one or more people will turn around and make threatening gestures at the subgroup opposite. Two people may lock eyes in a glare of rage. If I feel they can handle themselves well, I'll let them zero in on each other with batakas.

Participants are not allowed to act out hostility on each other physically until the group as a whole has developed considerable maturity. This is not because they will do each other bodily damage. By this time, the core emotions are moving freely enough to prompt bystanding members themselves to intervene before an interaction turns into a fistfight. It is because physical attack is so provocative that it can emotionally disintegrate a person who has not learned to accept negativity. Consider, for example, what might happen to the man and the woman in the following event if either were in an unstable condition.

A man who is very fearful of women comes to a session one day in a crisis. He has had a fight with his wife, or rather she has given him a tongue-lashing that he hasn't been able to stand up to, and it is driving him to despair. "The bitch, she's smashing me, and I can't say boo to her. I'm stuck with the feeling and I can't move". He has worked a great deal on this problem already and he has faced the denial of negativities that sustains it, but he hasn't been able to break through this block in his life situation.

The group listens to his story, and then a woman member says, "Let's try to bring this thing out. I'll be your mother, okay?" Then she starts imitating an overbearing mother, babying him, treating him like a helpless creature and putting him down. The man begins to get mad, and she continues to needle him until he catches fire. At this point, I ask her to get under the mattress, and I give the man a bataka. She sticks her head out and keeps on provoking the daylights out of him: "My bitsy boy, didn't I tell you not to hit other little boys?" She taunts and he whacks until he is pouring out rage.

The response throughout the group can be cataclysmic. As the man flails away, people who identify with his problem scream at the woman under the mattress, venting their own rage at their mother or at all womankind. The man's breakthrough is a tremendous victory for them. Others — men and women — empathize with the person under the mattress and grieve with her as she cries out, "Don't hurt me, don't hurt me! I love you, don't desert me!" The sense of loss and separation can sweep through both camps like a wind through a wheat field.

Much of the technique in the youth period is devised to sharpen the assertiveness of the group as a whole and the capacity of the individual members to express it. If I feel that they don't want to work against each other, I may put myself in the middle of the standing circle and call myself their father, goading them to attack me. The movements in this situation begin with vibrations and progress quickly into aggressive first-shaking and yelling. The therapist, of course, serves as a fine authority figure for transference purposes, and more than once I've just missed getting a bloody nose. Group members have always stepped in to restrain any free-swinging coparticipants who looked seriously bent on murder.

Most of the sessions during these phases of the group's development need no stimulus at all from the leader. For weeks at a time, my contribution will be supervision and analysis only, not piloting. The group moves itself, and there will be more than ample material.

It can still happen that the group as a whole doesn't get off the ground. The weather may be heavy, or several people may have just come back from vacations and may not want to move. Perhaps the group will be caught in a verbal streak and the atmosphere becomes very chaotic with no focus, no integration, no real work being done. At times like these, I will give the participants five or ten minutes to take flight themselves. If they don't, I will put them in one of the circular positions — usually the mandala first — to work until they are moving on their own. A mature group can take the full force of the mandala, so that the participants may choose to stay in it for an entire session.

The mature group will often sense for itself at the beginning of a session who needs its concentrated attention most. Then the members, not the therapist, lead the person into working through his suffering. They may form a circle around him and guide his physical movements, all of them pushing him ahead, goading him, helping him open up. This may seem bullying, but it isn't, for they are simultaneously working out their own feelings parallel and conjoined to his.

Participants now have little patience with evasions or deviousnees. They will cut through whining or rationalizing with a speed that verges on brutality. They are a good deal more abrupt with each other than the therapist would be with any of them. Yet rarely does this give offense, for they know themselves well. They know each other's character structures and blocks, conflicts and resources, values and hearts. Together they have built a reservoir of common trust.

Banking on that trust, they spend much time at this stage discussing their most troubling problems, their deepest emotions, their greatest shames. They compare and explore the meaning of their fantasies, existing relationships, and expectations in life. They assess their success in applying the strengths developed in the group work to the outside world. They give each other courage and motivation and love — energy from the core.

The organismic movement of the mature group reintegrates the participants beyond the measure that I feel individual treatment can accomplish. This is not to devalue the central importance of independent therapy, but to recognize that group work translates core therapy onto new dimensions.

There is, first of all, the significant differential of energy. The new formations generated by the group vastly surpass the energy mass available to the single patient. An immediate implication of this is that the core contact, which is the foundation of the entire therapeutic process, can be established virtually at once among group members but may require a tremendous infusion from the therapist in the one-to-one relationship. Until that contact arises, there will be no vitality in the treatment, which not only leaves the patient suffering but denies the therapist full perceptual enlightenment.

The effects of transference are tremendously magnified in a group setting. The therapist will accept and utilize the identities the individual patient clothes him in — as the patient's mother, father, sibling. But these cloaks can't all be worn at once. By virtue of its numbers and composition, a group enables a person to reincarnate his entire family in one sweep. Because each of at least eight people is transferring to the others simultaneously and reciprocally, the permutations are myriad. Then too, one group member may really resemble a person's boss, another his spouse, and a third his testy next-door neighbor.

Individual core therapy also uses the mirroring effect to help the patient intensify emotions and feelings. But the therapist is constrained by professional ethics not to give rein to his negative unconscious. A patient's fellow group members have the opposite obligation — to vent their negativities as fully and as irrationally as they can, short of physical mayhem. The cumulative acceleration and intensification of the energy flow feeding back into each person can shatter blocks that it might take months for individual therapy to chip.

The quality of personal responsibility that evolves in group therapy surpasses anything to be found not only in individual treatment but in life relationships. The single patient is obligated to account for his feelings to his therapist, but not vice versa. Lovers may urgently need open communication of emotions, but cultural inhibitons as well as passion foreclose the negativities. As for the human mask, the filter we all maintain between our inner selves and others, I have numerous times seen group members reveal vile actions to their coparticipants that they have not so much as hinted at in their individual sessions.

Granted the need for a society to place restraints on its members. Granted the right of any person to say "no" to another's "yes". Granted the internal struggle latent in humankind by the fact that we have primal negative and primal positive emotions. Granted all this, I nevertheless ask myself: What might we accomplish, we people of the earth, if we could replicate the mutuality of the core therapeutic group throughout our societies?

Chapter 21
THE FORCES OF LOVE, EROS, AND SEXUALITY

The forces that connect humanity are like rays of the sun. They reach from the center of the universe to build creation in the universe, the earth, and individual creatures. Energy and consciousness are the two great dimensions that dominate or represent the essence of cosmic and individual reality. Energy comprises the quantitative aspect of life, consciousness the qualitative aspect. Energy and consciousness are different sides of the same coin of reality. Very many forces operate along these dimensions in the reality of mankind, on earth, and of the spacetime continuum.

The three greatest of these forces are the erotic force, the love force, and the sex force. They need to be examined separately to understand them, but they actually comprise one force. They appear to be separate and have separate characteristics as they penetrate the personality and ego functions of human beings.

These powerful forces operate on all levels of existence, not just the sexual and not only in interactions between women and men. Their operation and fusion are the source of creativity and growth. The work we do is to uncover the blockages to the flow of these forces, to liberate them, and to release them. Love, Eros, and sexuality are part and parcel of the inner level of human reality, the core. They flow inexorably in and through each human being. Illness arises when these forces are dammed or diverted from their natural, organic movement. Because they are so powerful, the individual fears their free and open movement more than anything else.

The Spark of Eros

Eros is the most important force in existence, with tremendous momentum and impact. It is the bridge between sex and love. The erotic force acts like the first stage of a rocket that is fired toward space to try to overcome the earth's gravitational field. Once it burns out, Eros may be trapped in the gravitational field where it spins around until it plunges back into the atmosphere and disintegrates. If the rocket has a second stage, it escapes the gravitational field, moves into space, and establishes an independent course in the universe. As the first stage of the rocket, Eros is short-lived. It dissolves if the person does not know, or learns, how to love. But it leads the soul out of stagnation, if only temporarily. It enables human beings to surpass themselves, not matter how undeveloped they are. The selfish person becomes altruistic, the gangster tender, the delinquent good. The lazy person escapes inertia.

Eros is like a laser beam that breaks up stagnant energy into activity and excitement. In a sense, the erotic force provides people with a foretaste of unity, shows them their longing for life, and leads to unification. Often, the erotic force is confused with love. In our culture, all the love songs spring from the force of Eros, not of love.

Eros has a random quality. It hits with force, breaks the walls of separation between human beings, and blends the inner forces and unites them. Human beings enjoy the erotic force for its own sake. However, the person who avoids the emotions will do anything to avoid Eros. For Eros releases energy and movement in human beings, and the person who avoids emotion also seeks to avoid energy and movement.

The different personality or character types deal with Eros in different ways. But every way is an avoidance of the powerful unified force of love, Eros, and sex. People who are afraid of emotions resist Eros because they do not want to feel the emotions associated with isolation, sorrow, and loneliness. They fight off erotic force because they do not want to give. People who are over-emotional, on the other hand, seek the beauty of men and women. For them, Eros becomes the eternal quest and the great temptation. It seems like getting something from the outside, the excitement of life. Over-emotional people, however, want only the free excitement of Eros, but not the hard work of crossing its bridge into love. They believe they need Eros to go from emotional high to emotional high, without ever plunging into their depth where pain resides, but also the power of love. People who are rigid, self-composed, and proud will never allow the force of Eros to penetrate them. They are like a tight wall.

Yet your personality or how you feel does not matter. Cupid strikes with the arrow and the dignified man finds himself involved with a little girl. He feels silly and is ashamed. The erotic force is so beautiful, so exciting, so new that it makes the heart and body alive. They vibrate as with an electric current as Eros permeates the whole being with excitement.

But sought or accepted for its own sake only, Eros does not last. It fizzles out when the human being is not willing to invest more energy in the erotic relationship. It does so because it requires the commitment of the whole human being to reach the second stage. To become transformed and give its energy the love force, Eros must have the person's willingness to move toward love.

The Force and the Power of Love

Reich described the spiral of the nebulae and the galaxies as superimposed masses, fusing, connecting, vibrating, and creating new energies.[1] It is the same with love. The love force is a powerful, masterful, complete expression of life in the universe. It is both the substance and the movement of everything. In the human being it combines feelings, intelligence, physical being, and the spirit. Love moves in a spiral from the core of each human being, fusing, connecting, and vibrating energy and consciousness. As an emotion, love must be mediated and moved by reason and will. Love cannot be expressed by a human being without action. Love also is pure reason and intelligence, but again it cannot move, open, or develop unless the person commits himself to love through his will. Asked to describe evil and hate, Socrates replied, "It is ignorance".

When love is lacking, we feel a deep separation in us, a depression, a darkness. We feel that we are victimized and therefore we have a lot of resentment and blame. We experience the emptiness and hollowness of our lives, no matter how much we know as therapists, patients, helpers, workers, bosses, employees, or mates. The knowledge of men who develop an atomic bomb and throw it on millions of people to destroy them is knowledge without love.

A human being cannot really love without the intention to love. This seems very paradoxical. On the one hand, we know that love is a feeling. On the other, it appears that the intention is indispensible in committing to the act of love. But we have to wish for love and express our deep desire for love. Otherwise, our reason says, "If I love, I am going to lose, to be weak". The man says, "I'm going to submit to the woman and she's going to have power over me". The woman says, "The man is going to take over". Both say, "I'm going to be impoverished. You're going to take advantage of me". So you must really commit the will and reason to the act of love, to the plant of love, to give it the water it needs to grow.

The force of love is a sensation on every level. It is so powerful that a person who loves remains in a state of health, excitement, vibration. The muscles are in a state of tonus and the breathing opens up. The cheeks are pink, the heart pulsates. All of these biological reactions are obviously different from the face of hate. The face of the person who hates is pallid, drawn, de-energized, gray, yellow.

It is important at this point to differentiate among people's conceptions about love. It is possible for a person to love the trees, the universe, the woods, or great ideas and yet not love himself or herself. If you do not love yourself, it is very hard to love others. And if you hate yourself, you also hate others. A link exists between the individual reaction and the general reaction. Any feelings, positive or negative, loving or hating, must bring out all other feelings.

However, a person can, perhaps, love himself too much, at least in appearance. Such self-love is not in harmony with love of others. The person indulges himself in a sense that says, "After all, I must eat a lot because I'm so deprived. I must clothe myself with very unusual clothes because I'm deprived, a victim". This indulgence of our feelings fails to recognize that we are being very negative and hateful in other areas of our lives. The indulgence helps us avoid our feelings of deprivation and victimization.

Love's force and movement is characteristically balanced. It is firm and tender, honest and sincere, self-disciplined. In imbalance, firmness becomes in many ways self-hate. Tenderness becomes weakness and indulgence. Men and women who hate themselves are in prison. Hate equals illness; love equals health and truth.

To experience love, one must first experience, understand and dissolve the illness. To reach a state of love, one must first probe for the truth of the love force in its distortion of hate and separation. One must find where he rebels against life. By discovering and accepting all that is in oneself, one creates the possibility for love to express itself naturally and organically.

Once the preliminary work is done, love reveals itself, and one must then give it his intention, commitment, and will to action. The heart opens and dissolves the blocks to love, which yields the pleasure of creation. Many people fear that they cannot endure love. A voice in them says, "I don't deserve it". Out of the fear, the heart closes, for opening up to love also opens one to reality, including fear of death, or fear of losing what one holds most dear. Since we fear to take responsibility for our own lives, we blame others for our hate, fear, or lack of love and fulfillment. Therefore, we must hate those others.

One can explore this hate and fear of loving by being honest with oneself. We can only reach our core of love by going into and through our level of hatred and negativity. In the meditation we discussed in Chapter 19, we can ask, "Where and how do I hate myself? What characteristics in me seems to be worthy of my self-hate? How do I project this self-hate on others? What is the source of this hate? And how does this self-hate contain love?'' Then you can explore the ways that you love yourself — your mind, body, emotions, and spirit. For, as we have learned, there is only one force in the universe that we have divided with our consciousness. Once we deeply understand where, how, and why we hate, we can uncover the love force we have split off from the main stream, so to speak.

So love is a pulsating force. Biologically and energetically, it is like a potbelly stove that emits rays and heat more and more. Love does not ask anything, it just emits and penetrates. We love our brother or sister, not because we need them or because they are going to give something back to us, but just because we love them. In its essence, love is a state of being, physically, mentally, emotionally, and spiritually.

The person who can emit this tremendous love force becomes very intelligent. The person can be patient, wait, and choose. The loving person is not rebellious, but accepts the heart. The heart is two curves coming together, sinking into each other and fusing. The heart is not two counter forces that stop each other. The heart is a flaming jewel of life that has beautiful colors, emanates waves, and inundates the human being with messages. It is in effect a state of creation.

The Spiritual Symbolism of Sexuality

The sexual force is a very unique expression of consciousness in human beings that is reaching for fusion. People who are attracted sexually are like positive and negative poles of a magnet. They are pulled together. They want to enter each other, to connect with each other, to appose their orifices, to fuse their energies, and to connect and unify. Sexuality is a tremendous force for bringing the individual to a state of unification with another human being. Its pull is virtually irresistable and exists in all domains and at all levels of development. Sexuality exists where there is creative consciousness, as in human beings. Humans are the only beings that can create with their consciousness. They can mold the plastic substance of life or they can destroy it.

In lower stages of development, the sexual force can be seen as the separation of the gametes, the fusion of the infusoria and protozoa, the copulation of the amphibia and vertebrates. In all creatures that do not have the developed consciousness of man, the sex force unifies and connects them. It is interesting that the time interval is minute when primitive biological organisms fuse with the sexual force. As they develop and become larger, the time interval of copulation lengthens. It becomes longest and most fulfilled in human beings.

When chimpanzees and baboons mate, the male penetrates the female for half a second, copulates, and then moves out again. This is repeated many times. Animals approach each other from behind and form like two kidney beans a biological design which Reich calls the organum. Animals penetrate from the back and superimpose on each other. The back of one organism is superimposed through the belly of another.

In human beings, however, sexual fusion usually occurs face-to-face. The partners are conscious of each other and look at each other, fusing and unifying the consciousness. In consciousness, the human sexual experience represents all aspects and levels, the body, the mind, the emotions, and the spirit. If these levels are unified and do not oppose each other, a connection and unification occurs. If they oppose each other, disunity results. The most important thing is that when there is unification of all the levels, a new reality arises, the spiritual level.

In total sexual fusion, human beings experience the expansion of their consciousness and shine like stars. Unified sexuality transcends anything that the person experiences in the physical world. The person becomes the creative movement, the cosmos and the universe within that connects with the universe outside.

The physical level represents the yearning of two people to know each other, to reveal themselves to each other, and to find each other. Through such physical discovery, they can let themselves be known and find the truth of the other person. The desire for fusion is energized by an involuntary force that creates the electrifying, blissful feeling and longing. If the attraction exists only on the physical level, the sexual experience will be disappointing and fizzle out. Without feeling, consciousness, and spirit, the attraction for another person is not for the actual person, but rather for an image or an illustration of what one wants. When the illusion is exposed, the person seeks someone else. The illusion is born out of the physical longing of the infant. The infant is receptive and craves tremendous love through the physical level, through nourishment, physical contact, being cared for. In this, the infant is entirely passive, while the mother is the one who gives.

In the adult relationship, there is no giver and no receiver, but a mutual giving and receiving by both parties. Both participants must actively reach, give, dispense, sustain, nurture, receive, take in, and give out. This mutual nurturance expresses itself in an organic, involuntary, pulsatory rhythm. One voluntarily assents to the experience while at the same time allowing the involuntary forces to take over.

Blocks to the flow of energy in the organism stifle the movement of the sex force. These blocks exist because the infant within the adult personality still demands fulfillment according to the passive dictates of the infant. Mutual sexual experience cannot occur when either partner seeks only to receive passively and not to give actively. Thus, the person lives with perpetual frustration which seems to justify caution, withholding, and negativity. The movement toward fusion is split off, creating a counter movement which causes a short circuit in the energy system. This short circuit is experienced as an involuntary block, inhibition, and deadness.

Still another domain of sexuality is the emotional. Feelings are soul movements, like the waves of the sea that the wind creates. The waves move and flow and discharge their energy on the beach. In the human being, feelings flow toward a state of fusion. If the fusion is to take place, the movement must be expressed in an exchange of feelings. In sexual love, one perceives the reality of the other person. One must be open to the reality of the other person and ready to give and receive freely. To do this requires making your mind empty. You can have no illusions or expectations about who the other person is, because the illusions screen out the other's reality. You must be willing to experience what is before you, not the idea of what you want, but what actually exists, the truth of the moment.

When one opens to what actually exists, trials and tribulations are likely to follow. To open yourself to love and sexual relations, you must be able to stand frustration and pain at times, without feeling, "I've been cheated. I never should have opened, because it is too painful". One should not interpret the pain or the other person's actions and motives. Let the other person be who they truly are. Give your partner room, space, and acceptance. How is this possible? We are hindered by our images and life experience. Perhaps we had a mother who deprived us. We built a case around being hungry and wanting something but not getting it. This feeds the greed and all the other negative variations that have been described in orgone therapy, bioenergetics, and core energetics.

To achieve the necessary openess in the face of our preprogrammed expectations, it is important to use our mind and will to visualize the other person. We have to give the other person the benefit of the doubt, the love, respect, and dignity that the other person expresses. Visualize that person with tenderness, warmth, goodness, and trust. Visualize the whole person, not just the negative aspects. When the mind is filled with negative ideas and images, you cannot see the other person as a real human being. But if you recognize both the positive and negative in the other person, and do not make a big issue of the negative, the other person becomes a reality for you.

Somehow, we have to visualize loving the other person with the flaming jewel that is in the middle of our body, that emits waves, and colors and floods the area around us and our loved ones.

This visualization cannot occur if we maintain a mask of goodness. We must be able to express the truth, even if it contains cruelty. But the cruelty should never be acted out. For example, when people have sex, they must be honest about their cruelty. They may say, ''I don't want to hurt you, but I have these cruel feelings toward you''. It is important to reveal the secret fantasies everybody has. When both partners risk revealing and confronting, and speak of their cruelty, they can take responsibility for their own feelings and not project them on the other person. Where such revelation of the emotional level occurs, Eros is re-ignited and becomes a bridge to love.

On the mental level, two people must be compatible in order to have deep sexual relations and an exchange of love. They have to understand one another and have some common interests in life, though they by no means need to be identical intellectually. This mental compatibility fosters understanding of the other and humility about one's self. It enables each person to let the other person be who they fully are.

Mental sharing is necessary, even if the sexual relations are satisfactory. In some way, partners need to be similar to one another. Often, people have good sexual relations but are separate and do not communicate with each other. Such relationships eventually fade out. Sexual incompatibility frequently is not due to the inability to have an orgasm, but because of mental incompatibility that arises from mental blocks.

For example, the woman may think, ''I will never give it to you. I will never have an orgasm with you inside of me, violating me''. This attitude may arise from an image she has that the man wants to dominate and subjugate her. There may even be truth in the image, but it is not the whole truth. She thinks, ''But I want you to give me the orgasm by stimulation, by holding, but I will not submit to you''. Her mental picture of how satisfaction comes makes it impossible for her to attain through mutuality, through letting in the man as he is. The mental blocks prevent fusion and must be re-examined.

We now come to the spiritual level. The most important aspect of sexuality is reaching for the fusion which is beyond the physical, emotional, and mental levels that have been discussed. We reach for the spiritual self, for the person whose consciousness wants to expand and fill the inner and outer universe. The primary aim in life is to find ourselves fully, to find these deep connections that we long for. This fusion is the experience of oneness with the consciousness and being of another person.

The sexual experience represents whatever is in the human psyche. The shape of the psyche is revealed in the sexual experience. The psychopathic man will act out his drive to dominate in the sexual relationship as in all other areas of his life. It he enters a relationship with a passive woman, she will welcome this domination, at least on the unconscious level. If she is passive in life generally, she also will be passive in her sexual relationship. Indeed, more often than not, two such people are drawn into a relationship as filings are drawn to a magnet.

Thus, the sexual experience is an exact indicator of the personality and character structure of each human being. Whatever problems, attitudes, and ego trends exist in the person will come out in the sexual relationship. By the same token any sexual problems will be reflected in other areas of a person's life. If a person, for example, is withholding and stingy in work, he will withhold his sexuality as well. An employer who is cruel to employees will be cruel with his sexual partner. A woman who is catty toward her acquaintances will also scorn the sexual capacity of her partner. That these trends are often unconscious does not diminish their power and effect. Where the personality is disunified, all these problems will express in sexuality, as well as all other realms of life. It is important to recognize, however, that it is not only the negative sexuality that reflects the truth of a person. Sexuality can also express the beauty that exists in each human being and which comes from the deepest core. Tenderness, gentleness, and caring that are expressed sexually will also be expressed in work, in play, and in other human relations.

When people have sexual desires and do not connect them with the feelings, the relationship disintegrates and sex becomes flat. Such separation of sexual desires from feelings produces guilt, which may be denied. But it affects the sexual relationship. Any negative thoughts or feelings will lead to specific outcomes in the sexual relationship. These negative causes in each person will have a negative effect in the sexual experience. Indeed, the negative attitudes and emotions create the negative relationship in sexuality, as in any other area of human life.

A man, for instance, who has through his early experiences adopted a posture of cruelty toward the woman, will act out this cruelty sexually. He may be impotent otherwise, and believe he needs cruelty and brutality to arouse him. He will express the cruelty through emotional manipulation or artificial stimulation of the woman. Unless he puts the woman down and uses her, he cannot get or maintain his erection. The cruelty provides him the negative excitement that he cannot create positively. But if he could work with the woman to build the relationship on a positive foundation, his excitement would not come from his head, but from his whole being. It would arise from his heart, his love, from a feeling that his partner is open and wants to fuse. In an open and sharing relationship, the excitement, the Eros, arises from the love, the exchange of feelings, the vibrancy, the music that is between the two partners.

For a free and open exchange to exist between two sexual partners, each must examine what is negative in them, without projecting the negativity on the other or blaming the other for lack of fulfillment. This is the work of core energetics, and particularly of meditation described in Chapter 8. As the person becomes fully aware of the specific negative elements — cruelty, fear, distrust, superiority — it is essential to reveal such currents to the other partner. Only in this way can the involuntary processes take over. People very much fear the involuntary because they fear that it will bring out the negative trends. But if sexual partners are willing to reveal their secret fantasies, without acting them out in the relationship, the vital energy is freed to create a beautiful mutuality. Instead of acting out the cruelty under the guise of loving, the partners can say, "I want to hurt you; I want to put you down". If each partner recognizes that this negative fantasy is only part of the other person, the relationship can open up and develop. It is even possible to act out the negative if it is done playfully, tenderly, without actually hurting the other person. The energy thus liberated can carry the sexual experience to new heights of pleasure.

Ultimately, the result will be total fusion of two beings, two souls, on all the levels — physical, emotional, mental, and spiritual. The honesty of saying, "I want to hurt you", or "I'm not going to give it to you", for example, allows each person to dissolve the mask and abandon the defenses of the ego. The partners can accept and surrender to the involuntary process and reach for total fusion. They can give up their distortions of masculinity and femininity and allow themselves to be wholly themselves in the sexual experience.

The Ideal Partnership of Love

Instead of the fusion just described, what most often happens in sexual relationship is a split of the forces of love, Eros, and sexuality. It is likely that only one or two of the three forces are present in the relationship — Eros and sex, Eros and love, or sex and love. Most people do only one thing at one time and something else at another. So it is with sexuality. Sometimes a relationship expresses a lot of sexuality but no feelings. Or the relationship can contain a lot of feelings but no sexuality. Or some people tend to be romantic, to cling to Eros, but they do not want to go any farther. Such relationships tend to be Platonic. Often, the relationship starts with a lot of feeling, but the feeling departs and there is friendship and sex, but no true excitement. The partners no longer look at each other to learn more. They think they know all there is and do not want anything more. The relationship loses its excitement and energy, and one or both partners look elsewhere for the excitement.

The key to Eros is a sense of adventure and discovery. You must search for the knowledge of the totality of the other person. Many people maintain Eros for a while because they continue to discover and reveal the angelic, positive aspects of the soul. But they most often balk when it comes to revealing or exploring negative aspects. Then the fear comes in and the energy begins to wane and die. Often, people stop the discovery long before this point is reached, out of fear of what may be found or revealed.

Eros requires a continuous curiosity on the part of both partners if it is to live and thrive. The instant you think your have found all there is to know about your partner, Eros leaves and sexuality collapses. You may continue to live together as partners, but life becomes placid and uneventful, unexciting. To maintain the spark of Eros and to keep love alive requires the inner will to continue the process of revelation. And this revelation must be voluntary, not something extorted from the soul of the other person through manipulation or inducing guilt. But if you stay open and keep exploring, the force of Eros stays with you. In the ideal partnership, both love and sex will be present, and Eros servers as the bridge, instead of becoming the whole thing, as in romantic love. Eros keeps the relationship alive and vibrant.

How can people build and maintain the bridge of Eros? The main elements in maintaining Eros are a spirit of adventure, curiosity, and revelation of the self. In this spirit, one not only constantly learns about the other person, but also about the self. A deep exploration of two human beings is involved, an exploration that is fed by the curiosity and excitement of both partners for the quest.

The partners find adventure in the search for knowledge of the other soul. The desire is present in every human being, though it is often buried beneath the mask and the defensive structure. A continuous act of will is required to persist in the adventure. For one finds, not only the exquisite uplands of pleasure and love, but also dark jungles of hostility and deserts of emptiness. But even the threatening landscapes veil beauties and treasures that can be discovered by persisting in the search.

Intentional curiosity carries the person into this adventure. This curiosity constantly seeks to find what is new in the other person. What tremendous landscape lies beyond this seemingly dangerous precipice? What vista lies around the next bend of the personality? As long as one believes that there is always something new, and seeks for it, Eros will live. Thus the bridge of Eros is maintained. But the moment you think you have found all there is in the other person, Eros disappears.

But the forces of Eros will stay with you, if you have an open mind and keep exploring. Eros is like an angel that comes to you when you have the right energy. Love, Eros, and sex are angelic in the same sense that negativities are demonic. The dualism that exists in the earth's sphere, the space-time continuum, splits the emotions into positive and negative, but one force. They are split, though, by our life experience, and the task is to reunite them, in marriage and in all other aspects of life.

To reveal the soul to another person is a marvelous journey. On this journey, Eros is not replaced, but nurtured and transformed constantly into love. A deeply mutual marriage requires that each partner voluntarily reveal the depths of this or her own soul. The courage for this revelation comes from the will to love. This act of will does not replace Eros, but incorporates it into love.

In the ideal love relationship, you look at your lover's eyes and wonder, "Where do you come from? Who are you? How wonderful your eyes are, the breath, the warm breasts, the beautiful, sweet touch, the electricity and vibration". You do not know the other person. And next time, the person is quite different. If you want to look for the negative, you can close your eyes and say, "I know her. I know her. He wants sex". Curiosity dies and Eros flees. But where there is a mutuality, you can safeguard the relationship by saying Yes to a No. You say, in effect, "It doesn't matter how you hurt me. I'm open and not judging you. I know you love me."

The other person may be temporarily angry, but you remember that the other person loves you. That creates mutuality. For example, I often had arguments with my wife, Eva, when she criticized me about something. I would become furious at first, but then would say, "But she loves me". and in her next statement she would show that she didn't have anything against me. It was her nature to express herself, and to tell what she believed to be true. It is important to remember that the other person loves us, no matter how much pain they create, and to love the higher self of the other person. There is no limit to the soul of any person. It is endless and eternal, and you could use a whole lifetime and still not encompass and understand the soul. The soul is alive, not static, and it changes constantly. The idea in the ideal love partnership is to constantly reveal the soul, to constantly search.

Distortions in our perceptions of the forces of love, Eros, and sexuality lead to infidelity and polygamy. One constantly seeks the excitement of Eros. When it fades, one moves on to another adventure. But there is an aspect of the torturer and victim, when one abandons one partner for another, whether in divorce and separation or in infidelity. When there is compromising and selling out, rather than mutual sharing and exploring, stagnation results. One sells out to avoid pain, to avoid rocking the boat of the relationship. Truth is abandoned in favor of a false security. To punish the other person and to rekindle Eros, one seeks another partner. Until the distortions are dissolved, one will move from partner to partner in search of love, never realizing that love is an act of will. The constant quest for Eros reveals immaturity in the soul, an unwillingness to face the truth that is disclosed in the whole being of the other person.

When marriage partners settle into a comfortable familiarity into friendship only, the marriage is in trouble, for both have abandoned the quest for the other, and both have settled for peace without excitement. The courage and willingness to explore the other and reveals the self are created by the willingness to fully know the self, to discover and purify the negativities that exist. Marriage is sought and kept alive by a deep yearning to know another and to be known by another. The soul seeks the complete mutuality with another person. Nobody, at the deepest level, wants to be alone. The desire to be alone discloses an unwillingness to share life in its deepest sense.

The divorce and separation rate in our nation, the unhappy marriages that do not result in physical separation, reveal an unwillingness to go through the barriers with another person. Going through these barriers enables you to both bestow love on another and to find yourself. It is difficult to love humanity when you cannot love one other person. World events demonstrate the humanity is far from this ideal of sharing and knowing. The unwillingness is born of fear and ignorance.

Therefore, the ideal of marriage is one of mutual revelation. It is carried by a sense of adventure, curiosity, and revelation. Eros provides the spark and the bridge between sexuality and love. But by itself it is not enough. True love demands more. True love demands the intentions and the will to face the reality of the other person in all of its magnificent wholeness and to keep exploring.

Conclusion

The ideal love relationship is a model for life in general. Both the longing for true mutuality with another person and the work of achieving it reflect the steps necessary for fulfillment in all of life. For fulfillment comes not from conquest and subjugation of others, but from accepting one's own inner reality and the reality in the outer world. The longing of unification with one person is a first step toward unification with all of humanity, with the universe, and with God, however one wants to define God.

Crisis in one's personal life and crisis in the world are identical, in terms of human dynamics, to crisis in marriage. They arise from the negative triumvirate of fear, and self-will. We fear the other and project our own negative feelings on the others that confront us most immediately, be they mates, bosses, political parties, ideologies, or nations. We refuse to recognize the legitimate aspirations of others for fear that they will deprive us of our own fulfillment. We have trapped our positive energies in the negative excitement of our characterological defenses.

Therefore, peace in ourselves, in our relationships, in our society, and the world will come, not from rules, laws, treaties, and defensive armaments, but from a willingness to make a vibrant peace in ourselves. The outer restrictions may be temporarily necessary, but they are only temporary expedients that cannot work in the long run unless we have the intention for peace at all levels and in all domains. The essential work before us, the work that is mediated by core energetics, is to open to the realities and infinite possibilities that confront us. By first understanding, accepting, and then transforming the negative aspects of our personalities, we create the magnificent possibility of a world where mutual understanding and cooperation are a realizable goal.

Part VII:
Synthesis and Unity

Chapter 22
THE BIRTH OF A NEW AGE

In the early 1960s, an idea crystallized in American society and politics, which was examplified first in the civil rights movement. If each person refused to obey unjust laws, took personal responsibility for his or her own life and for others, and worked to change those laws, then positive change would result. This idea caught the imagination of millions of people. They worked to end a cruel system of segregation, which held that some people were inferior by law and nature to others. This ethic of personal commitment has wrought vast changes in our society for minority group members, although much remain to be completed.

The idea spread to other groups and issues — women's rights, educational reform, protection of the environment, and protest against what was perceived as an unjust war. In each of these areas, improvements in attitude and behavior have been registered, and important gains have been made. This is not to say that each of these movements has not contained distortions of its own. It would be surprising of we were otherwise, for the ideas and strategies of this movement in American society emerged from the existing culture.

However, all of these actions and approaches herald, I believe, the formation of a new age. This spreading consciousness honors personal responsibility and signals a declining reliance on established conventions, institutions, and authorities. The challenge to government authority and policy parallels a questioning of patterns of family life, the behavior of big business, methods of education, and the ethics of public office-holders. At the same time, millions of people have mounted a varied search for effective ways to reach and actualize their inner potential. In sum, people are sensing a crisis of values in their own lives. At the same time, they are struggling against the distortions they perceive in the social order and marshalling their inner truths to correct them. These individual and collective movements grow out of and reinforce one another.

More or less consciously, many people therefore sense and seek to activate the three principles that underlie this book. They perceive and want to correct the fragmented unity of energy, consciousness, and experience within themselves. They want to heal the rifts between themselves and their social and physical environments. And their increased willingness to assume responsibiliy for their own lives implies an understanding that the source of healing for their own and society's inperfections lies within themselves, not with some outside agency or power.

This re-emergence of consciousness of the wholeness and unity of life reflects a renewed understanding of creation and the trust in evolution.

The Evolution of Consciousness

Biologically, life evolves from the amoeba into mammalian development. The earlier organisms form groups as a means of fulfilling their function. Each living thing performs its specific tasks, whether we are speaking of cells, organs, or systems. Larger organisms develop individual patterns of movement, but retain their identity as single independent structures within the unifying structure of group cohesion. Each part lives with and cooperates with the others for the practical purpose of survival. In short, the parts serve the whole, which, in turn, serves each of the parts.

The same evolutionary movement can be observed in humanity where tribal culture formed around a leader, who represented the group's interest. Obviously, civilization itself is a progression from pristine group living to the emergence of the individual. The great religions emphasize individual development. They adhere to the principle that each person is inherently responsible for personal actions, thoughts, and decisions. Each human being is accountable for the perfection of his or her own soul.

Primitive society with its tribal ethos evolved toward cultural individuation which culminated in the brilliant Athenian civilization. This high culture crystallized in the philosophy of democracy. All citizens possessed inalienable rights to express their ideas freely. They were able to assume equal responsibility for conducting the political, religious, and personal affairs of the city-state. To be sure, Athenian civilization had its flaws. Slaves and women were denied the rights of citizenship. But human development obviously had come a long way from the time when priest and king, often the same person, determined what was good for both the society and the individual.

As the Athenian ideal faded, Judeo-Christian ethics became a powerful force. These ethics, with their moral and spiritual focus, emphasized the development of humanity's inner being. The onset of the Dark Ages, however, plunged the individual into domination by mystical religious influences and superstitions. People were subjected to the tyranny of a feudalistic society from which humanity emerged as it surrendered the misconceptions of the religious ideals expressed in the Crusades.

The concept of personal excellence through learning and intellectual achievement in the arts and sciences emerged during the Renaissance. This period of history produced remarkable artistic, philosophical, and scientific expression. This "rebirth" resulted, during the following five centuries of the industrial revolution with its influence in the development of the mass individual.

The United States has used its technical precocity and industrial knowhow during the last century to achive mass production virtousity. With other western nations, our society has thus created the mass individual who cannot participate in group living, nor, conversely, fully as a human being. As noted in Alexander Lowen's lecture, *"The Individual and Society,"* people have been cut off from their roots. They have succumbed to the society imposed upon them.

The Movement to Reunification

Uprooted from their connectedness with their emotional, intellectual, and spiritual heritage, individuals have begun to seek the recovery of their lost relatedness with themselves through the human potential movement in the United States. The movement operates in limited group settings. By stimulating group contact, the movement opens up areas of fresh experience and feeling in the individuals. Rather than imposing ideas, this form of group living allows individuals a chance to discover their own inner and outer experience — by themselves, within themselves, and for themselves.

Wilhelm Reich, who first formulated the concepts of psychosomatic unity and antithesis, first expressed these ideas and explored the relationship that exists between the body and the mind. These ideas developed into an understanding of natural self-regulation and the whole area of biological functions. Reich integrated these ideas of energetic movements which occur within the human organism. He contended that such movements must be left alone during childhood: "Let the living substance express itself in the way that is natural to life."

The sentence expresses Reich's principle that all natural drives should be self-regulating. During the formative years, children are best left alone to develop in the direction of their natural rhythms. This development occurs organically if children are given breast feeding, freedom of movement, and acceptance and love. Reich believed that these principles would ultimately build a healthy social structure based upon the kind of group living that stimulates the preservation of the individual personality.

Lowen developed Reich's work further. He emphasized the importance of the individual in opposition to mass living, mass production, and mass philosophy. When a group of people gather, either accidently or deliberately, they tend to be drawn into close contact. Each person's energy field affects the field of the entire group, and is affected by the group's energy.

The Mutuality of Life

All of us are independent. The living and breathing space of each person is also that of others. But, according to the principle of reciprocity, the individual's development evolves from within toward outer reality that includes others. As people open up toward others, they cooperate and create a new unity, a flow of rhythmic feeling, a new expression.

The spontaneity inherent in the mutality concept must be followed and fused with an attitude of execution, of action. Mutuality implies a two-fold experience. The creativity is synthesized. Then execution occurs to nurture the inspiration and realize it fully. For example, a scientist, drawing from his own work and that of others, may synthesize his knowledge into a new hypothesis. But he must follow through, execute, with experimentation to establish the hypothesis. Execution naturally requires intense effort and laborious work. Both the spontaneous feeling (the creativity) and the execution must occur to achieve the fullness and joyousness of living.

The balance between creation and execution is particularly striking in human relations, which were described in Chapter 21. The attraction between two people is sparked spontaneously. But once the erotic attraction fades, they must work to create a true and enduring mutuality. Their expansive movements meet and fuse. But the movements are certain to strike obstacles in each person, which then must be explored and understood if they are to achieve continued mutuality and love.

The reciprocity principle operates between the two people and within each other of them. Each partner's energy reaches out toward that of the other, and at the same time reaches inward to unearth the unconscious negativity, which unexamined, makes mutuality impossible. It is essential for the person to have awareness, not only of negative currents, but of the principles involved. Without such awareness, the person feels tossed about by currents not of his own making, blames others for personal unpleasantness, and finds himself unable to sustain a mutual relationship.

By rejecting the negativity within, one cuts off awareness and stunts the pulsation of energy. This rejection of the negative aspects of the inner self traps enormous amounts of energy which becomes frozen. To attain wholeness, one must make contact with the stagnant energy and release it, as we have seen. Only when it is released can this energy be made whole and utilized. Only then can the rhythmic cycle of expansion and contraction create a harmonious relationship with other people.

This reciprocity principle pervades all of creation. It operates within individuals, between and among them, in society, and in civilization as a whole. We have noted the pendulum swings of history between individual and group consciousness. This pendulum motion may be triggered by a concerted decision to pursue intuited new knowledge, to counter a danger to the commonweal, or to reaffirm truthful ideas. The first is an expression of direct core energy in creativity. The second and third are protective impulses. They are based on unifying capacities of the core, to defend the integrity of society or to modify change.

The collective movement is positive when it actualizes in a balanced way our potential in the four domains of human existence: the body, the mind, the emotions, and the spirit. But when a movement reaches such proportions that it impedes one or more of the four aspects of holistic functioning, it degenerates into an energy-greedy ism: materialism or spiritualism, rationalism or emotionalism or radicalism, individualism or collectivism. The movement then sets the group or society at odds within itself and with its surroundings.

The Price of Disunity

The impact of a fragmenting value network on individual group members is invidious. Psychological if not physical welfare depends on at least outward compliance with dominant thinking, as studies in sociology, cultural anthropology, and psychiatry have shown. When public values are asked, the truth of the inner person is denied. Therefore, energy is channeled into maintaining an internal constriction and an external defensiveness — the mask or idealized self-image.

For the group, the loss to creativity is severe. The unitary pulsation of life is stifled and the synergistic impetus fails. I noted earlier that people generate new energy forms when they are in strong, open communication.

Conversely, their individual auras dim and decelerate when they feel disconnected, afraid, or hostile. I would hypothesize that cultural gaps like the alleged undercreativity of some minorities are caused by energy barriers between them and the majorities with whom they live. The responsibility here is twofold, as in any unbalanced dyad. The more powerful group imposes its will on the less powerful, which then withdraws from the established order, thus perpetuating the denial of its share of both receiving from and contributing to society's well-being.

Aside from human beings, nature counters expressions of positive energy only as a prelude to evolution. Humans alone seem capable of disrupting the trend of nature and, in fact disrupting it. We have strewn testimony down the ages — and continue to do so — that our mask selves take us to suffocating extremes when we lose our perspective on the necessary mutuality within and between energy systems. In all such instances, we stockpile our commitment to a given set of values. This attempt to fix the current situation closes off our receptivity to other planes of life until a crisis of reaction spurs a new turn. Let me give a few examples.

Humankind cultivated North Africa and the American Middle West into granaries of the ancient and modern worlds respectively. Then, through exhaustive overfarming, humans turned these gardenspots into a desert and a dustbowl. Excessive acquisitiveness combined with pride in political forms turned Caesar's Rome, like Stalin's Russia, into a military empire builder. The same forces magnified the United States, like Great Britain before it, into an economic octopus.

Hinduism exaggerated spiritual life to such a degree that it sanctified suttee and the ideals of love and justice in their religion with crusades against "infidels," with self-flagellation, persecution of scientific inquirers, and burnings and bans of people and books. Science and technology, encouraged by ongoing industrial rewards, reduced the concept of the human being to a biological machine. No wonder that social conformity suppressed personal politics in Mao's China. Mental and physical values still dominate us in this last quarter of our century. However, the pendulum is swinging again to bring a balance among seemingly conflicting values. We continue to gauge human worth primarily by material or intellectual "success," by the acquisition of wealth or outer knowledge or control, to the neglect of inner life: the human mind and spirit.

The Pyramid of Growth

However, each age builds on the advances of the ones past. Each has emphasized one avenue or another of discovery. Out of the spiritism of the

Middle Ages developed the Renaissance, which rescued the contributions of classical antiquity from oblivion. It also launched the epoch of great empires, when men followed a powerful urge to explore other lands, to learn, but also to conquer and subjugate. The Age of Reason, the Enlightenment, emphasized the thinking mind — at the cost of suppressing feelings — to produce giants in pure and applied sciences. The industrial revolution stressed material progress and acquisition, made possible by those sciences, but plunged ultimately into a hopeless stalemate and the disintegration of two world wars.

Through these vast cyclical swings, humanity has shaped the vast treasure which succeeding generations enjoy. The average human lifespan has trebled in four centuries, despite the ravages of disease and wars. International associations move forward into myriad specialized fields ranging from microsurgery to metaphysics, despite hostilities among the home countries and cultures in other domains. Cognitive research has developed methods of teaching many people isolated by accidents of fate — the brain-damaged child and the stroke victim, for instance — despite continuing social prejudices against such handicaps. Propulsion technology has sent spacecraft to Mars, despite the unresolved discrepancies between Newtonian and Einsteinian physics. The catalogue of human accomplishments demonstrates again and again that the monumentum of right energy, unthwarted energy outrides even our witting service to a stultifying status quo.

Evidence of a New Age

I am convinced that we have reached a stage of development as a species where we can introduce a lasting equilibrium in human affairs. We need no longer be the victim of the swing of the pendulum. We now have the means to redesign our collective movements so that they change focus before they degenerate into inflexible formalism. If we do this, we can progressively transfer energy from restorative into creative activity. This is why I deeply believe that we are verging on a new age. My position rests on four bases.

The Information Base

First, we have accumulated a wealth of information about our inner development and our relationships with each other and with our environment. In these myriad energy systems, we can see that what blocks our life is not negative force but the negation of the creative self — the higher self. That is, stagnation sets in, not from rejecting a specific pulsation of energy, but from denying the recognition of positive energies. Every advance in human affairs has come from our movement, whether we direct force against force or force with force. We have not progressed by standing still. We can see the enormous strides we have taken when we intentionally joined forces to explore reality integrally, as in golden ages like Percliean Greece and Renaissance and Enlightenment Europe.

The Base of Our Intentions

We have an incalculable advantage today over those fruitful periods in the past. It comes, not only from immensely greater knowledge, but from the intention of vastly greater populations to think and act positively. This is my second reason for foreseeing a new age. Crippling social disabilities — legal, political, economic, and political — still afflicted the developed nations until virtually our own time. These inequities have helped trigger revolutions since the end of the Enlightenment and two world wars in the Twentieth Century. We surely have not cured such ills, but we are digesting a dual lesson from our collapses into collective violence. In negative terms, we are learning that human progress and societal disenfranchisment are mutually exclusive conditions. In affirmative terms, we are learning that our intention to act positively can change us individually and collectively affect the world.

This lesson has promoted widening efforts to equalize the social rights of persons and groups and represents a restorative tide from the core. But more direct proccesses to activate positive intentionality are at work. In food production, for example modern China and Israel have wrought miracles of agricultural engineering in their lands. China has assembled farm communes and harnessed the Yangtze River; Israel has established kibbutzim and reclaimed the desert. These extraordinary achievements rival the model of Japan which has sustained the largest population on the smallest arable territory in the history of humanity.

Underlying the very phrase "agricultural engineering" is a phenomenon that explains much of the geometric expansion of knowledge over the last half-century — interdisciplinary research and development. The sciences exhibit a growing receptivity to guidance from other fields, which once were viewed as irrelevant and even antagonistic to their concerns. Witness, for example, the bodies of inquiry into how we should present ourselves to extraterrestrial life if we encounter it. Those contributing to the enterprise would include ethicians, physicians, social scientists, lawyers, theoretical mathematicians, educators, and artists, to name only some.

In the growing mutuality among values and modes of thought have grown as contributions from numerous realms of understanding have approached each other and in many places overlapped. At the same time, Western thought systems have sustained the imbalances of materialism and formalism at the expense of inner human needs and the need for humans to fit organically in the universe. This seeming dichotomy challenges humanity on the one hand, to make sense of the immense accumulation of data. On the other, it indicates a crucial need for a reintegration of the person within himself and with the cosmic forces surrounding him. Fundamentally, these two tasks represent simply two aspects of the problem of synthesis.

Every contributor to human wisdom incorporates earlier thinking to some degree. But the farther a body of theory crosses fields of knowledge and explores the unknown, the greater its potential for synthesis becomes. In his massive *Study of History*, Arnold J. Toynbee argues that the course of human events is directed by overarching psychic forces. His insight reflects Carl Jungs's perception of the collective unconscious, which itself expands on Leibnitz' undeveloped notion of a universal symbolism of thought.

The Foundation of Personal Responsibility

The third support for my faith in the arrival of a new age is closely related to my second reason: personal responsibility increasingly is being incorporated into our network of public values. We are generally skeptical today of saviors who propose one true religious belief for all, one sure-fire economic stabilizer, one fairest political program — one best anything. Many of us, I believe, have become resolved to follow our own destinies and to shake loose from the rigid structures of ideas and practices in our individual and collective lives. I offer an illustration of this trend and its implications drawn from some elementary management texts.

Suppose we are all citizens of a small town whose main industry is an apparently prosperous manufacturing plant. But our community remains poor. We call a town meeting to find out why this is so. Our storekeepers report the rent they are paying the company to use the buildings it owns. An accountant figures out that the rent payments are the reason the vendors are making so little profit. A doctor describes the accident rate among the plant workers, and an insurance agent explains that this is the main reason that health-plan premiums are so high. Two grocers complain about the quality of the produce they are getting from local truck farmers, who protest that air pollutants from the plant are hurting their crops. And so forth.

We begin to ask ourselves, "What can we do? It's the system." But several people disagree. "Maybe we can change things." One suggests electing a committee to study the poor conditions traceable to the plant and to take these up with the company's owners. Several citizens volunteer to serve. A plant worker offers to relay this plan to his bosses and to ask them to prepare a cost accounting of their operations for comparison purposes. One of the farmers will seek advice from the agricultural extension service on ways to counter the pollution problem. By the end of the meeting, everybody in town is taking on the tasks of trying to change some aspects of the "system."

The system, in this case, is an inflexible structure that expresses an insidious use of "reasonable factors" to dominate a society and to continue a negative status quo. It causes self-doubt, disheartenment, and apathy in everyone caught in "the way things are," even those who are ostensibly profiting. The problem is difficult to expose, much less to dissolve. But unresponsive systems are only stagnant energy formations, like the character formations of an armored person. The social body can breach these walls of obstructionism and negation by working from its center of movement. Today, across the human family, more and more people, wakened to their constituency as as social body, are assuming individual and group responsibility for its vitality.

The Core: The Ultimate Foundation

The fourth cornerstone of my expectation of a new age is the creative, generating power of the human center when it is open. I have experienced it in my own life and in my work with armored and defensive people through core energetics. But there are many proven ways to free the human heart, and many others — developed privately — that we can only infer from the lives of their discoverers. Every approach that guides the person to his or her core is to be valued, because it leads to the seedbed of creative evolution.

The past fifty years have given clear evidence that humanity's current evolutionary cycle is moving to correct the disproportionate emphasis laid on our outer mind and our material assets. Values based on intellect and materialism are crumbling before the reassertion of the inner domains of emotion and intuition. The last decade and a half, however, have witnessed more than a restorative impetus. A new dimension is entering our understanding of the life process as a whole. We are learning that opening the heart and spirit also opens inner reason and will to the outer mind. This opening joins our personal truth with all truth, for our core knows only distinctions, not separations, in the energy it emits and absorbs.

Moving from the core, from the higher self, therefore, means moving toward fulfillment of our greatest potential. This movement enables us to respond flexibly to new obstacles and new opportunities in our particular or collective existence. It directs us to acknowledge ignorance or unintentional mistakes, and to correct them. It gives us the trust to admit deliberate wrongs, and to redress them.

This movement urges me to say to you — who seek my help, who criticize me, or whom I have not yet met: between you and me, there is a process of humanizing ourselves, which consists in contributing what each of us can to the other. I have a lower self and I have a mask, and I sometimes use you or put you down, or withdraw from you and reject your gifts. But that is not why we are here, in the same universe and in our specific relationship. Your assertion of your core is my reception into my core, so that, literally, you are substance for my life and I for yours — if we call out and welcome each other's vital force with our own.

Chapter 23
TOWARD A HOLISTIC SYNTHESIS: THE FUSION OF ENERGY AND CONSCIOUSNESS

Human evolution is coming full circle. It is approaching the fusion of energy and consciousness in the sense of the three themes which guide this book, and which were stated at the beginning of Chapter 1. The movement toward fusion has guided human evolution from its beginnings to the present. The movement will continue to be the principle driving force of humanity into the future.

The fragmentation of energy and consciousness in the human entity began in the earliest stage of human development. Throughout the ages, human beings have not seen themselves as psychosomatic identities, or more likely, did not consider the question at all. Energy and consciousness were divided in human perception, and therefore the division became the reality that human beings experienced. Healing, whether of the individual, tribe, nation, or world, has been seen as the province of an outside agency — spirits, shamans, God, government, physicians, ministers, or therapists. Human beings believed and acted, by and large, as if creation was fragmented. They saw themselves as distinct from everything else, which they then sought to appease, understand, manipulate, or control.

Today, we see a process of fusion underway. Numerous individuals and groups seek to unite energy and consciousness in various kinds of therapeutic and spiritual practices. Many human being are trying to find the sources of healing their ailments and discontents within themselves, though many use helpers to assist them. These helpers are not seen as gurus, saviors, or physicians, but as guides, teachers, and fellow seekers.

Finally, as exemplified most dramatically in the environmental movement, there is a growing perception that each person is at one with everything else, including other human beings. The force of events parallels and is part of the changes in human consciousness. International communications and economic interactions reinforce the understanding that we live on one earth and are part of one humanity. On the negative side, the threat and possibility of thermonuclear extinction makes us realize that we must all work together or we will all die together.

The Spiritual Fusion

We have seen in Chapter 11 and 23 human consciousness in its evolution swung between energy and consciousness, emphasizing one or the other of the four domains of human functioning — the body, the mind, the emotions, and the spirit. In modern times, the fusion has been furthered by Freud's work with the unconscious, Reich's synthesis of the body and the mind, and bioenergetics' incorporation of the will into the work of human integration.

After many years of bioenergetics work, I came to feel that something was lacking. Though bioenergetics provided a beautiful clinical approach to resolving blocks, difficulties, and neurotic symptoms, it lacked a fundamental philosophy because it did not incorporate the spiritual nature of human beings.

At this point, I met my former wife, the late Eva Broch Pierrakos, who was doing very specific work called the Pathwork. This work based on 258 lectures, which were transmitted through Eva by a spiritual Guide. The lectures present a cosmic view of psychology, medicine, and religion. In themselves, the lectures provide a conceptual fusion of energy and consciousness. They incorporate and unify all aspects of life's energy and consciousness at the greatest depth possible for human beings at this stage of our evolution.

The lectures led me to years of further work to unify, not only energy and consciousness, but psychological and spiritual practices as well. Out of this fusion I have developed the concept of core energetics. In fact, this book was written through the insights acquired through the study of the lectures, as well as the knowledge I had acquired through my medical training, my work with Reich, and my total life experience. Here, briefly, is the process of work presented by the lectures.

A community of people formed around the lectures to try to live the principles of the Pathwork in their daily occupations and in their preoccupations with each other. The main focus of the word, as I explained in Chapter 18 and 19, is to overcome the motivation of the little ego to dominate and distort the truth, to create a negative intentionality, and to foster a split in one's perception and experience of life.

Even one trained or expert in a specific branch of science, art, or politics probably has personality aspects that are divided and incomplete. Each of us has some hidden corners in which we harbor selfishness or immaturity. These tendencies create hidden motivations that seek to fulfill the selfish aims of the negative ego.

Every person contains these characteristics to a greater or lesser extent. Psychoanalysis speaks of them as the unconscious mind and the impulses of the id. As this book seeks to explain, the principles of the Pathwork and core energetics are implemented in a consciousness search within the person and between the person and others to discover the negative intent as it is expressed in small, individual actions or in the more important decisions of life. A slight to another person, a negative judgement, or a harmful thought can be as fruitful for exploration as an action that visibly harms others or oneself.

This holistic approach focuses on both the unconscious involuntary processes and the conscious, voluntary aspects. The involuntary processes are expressed in life through the pulsations of movement of energy streaming through the body. These pulsations are perceived as sensations, warmth, or perhaps as pins and needles. When these streamings are allowed to continue, the person experiences a vibration and resonance in the whole organism, which helps to integrate the consciousness with the unconscious. The inner movement of energy reaches all levels of the human organism.

We explore the human psyche not only through what is said but how it is said. The exploration seeks to discover the emotional and physical blocks as expressed in the person's outer expressions. For example, the expression of the face, the set of the jaw, may indicate anger or suppressed feelings. The color and tone of the skin, the stiffness of the joints, and the flexibility of the muscles all provide the experienced eye with the clues to the person's inner state. Most important, the observation and diagnosis of the pulsation of the aura's energy indicates the type and vitality of the personality's energy movements. The ability to see these pulsations requires special training.

The Evidence of the Intentions

In a second major avenue of the work, we seek and find the person's intentions. These negative and positive choices are made in real life situations and in terms of the stance the person takes in the face of reality. Here, I recapitulate the levels of reality in which human beings operate. The diagram presented in Chapter 2 shows four levels of reality, which envelop each other in concentric layers.

At the center, level one, the core expresses the primal positive feelings — love, the creative force of life. This level of energy is immense and is identical to cosmic consciousness. The core represents the vital life energy, the highest intelligence of the indiviudal and the place where the human being has the deepest connection with the universe within. The core is, in effect, the sun of life, which expresses a unitary perception of reality. It can find the right solution to problems and deal very effectively with the distortions of the mask by unifying opposites. In short, the core is both the aim of the healing process and its most effective tool.

Level two, which surrounds the core, expresses the primal negative feelings — the negative unconscious of psychoanalytical theory or the lower self of spiritual teachings. These primal feelings include hatred, anger, rage, terror, and cruelty.

The third level contains the character defenses. For example, the defenses may be expressed as hostility, superiority, withdrawal, or aggression. The mixture and predominance of these major defensive postures creates the character types which were described in Chapter 9.

At the periphery, surrounding the rest of the energy structure, is the mask of the ego. This mask contains the rationalizations and intellectualizations of the personality. It seeks to appropriate the expression of the core to cover the negativity of the second level and the character defenses. Expressions of the mask, however, are not always positive. They can include arrogance, the will to control, and feigned weakness and helplessness, as well as an appearance of goodness, cooperation, and other positive characteristics.

The Direction of the Work

In working with these energy levels, the main focus is not to ask, in effect: "What is my sickness?" It is rather, "What is my task in life? Where do I want to go? How do I unify myself to get there?" From this perspective, all emotional and physical dysfunctions are symptoms of a deep alienation from the core. As the repository of the person's highest ability and intelligence, the core synthesizes all aspects and provides intuitive solutions.

Energy in the human organism travels from the core to the periphery and expresses itself in the pulsatory movements of the aura. Energy also moves from the periphery to the core via the energy centers or chakras, which Chapter 7 discussed. Contact with the core is prevented in human beings by such feelings as fear, panic, and life-denying attitudes such as negative judgments and criticisms.

However, it is crucial to remember that both positive and negative emotions flow in the same energy current. They differ only in the way that the current is slowed down or speeded up — its energy charge. Negative feelings usually flow more slowly with a certain degree of thickness, inertia, or stagnation. The positive emotions, conversely, flow in an alive, dynamically charged current. The person experiences the positive emotions in the body as expansion and feelings of pleasure. It is important to recognize that these emotions are expressed and experienced in the present.

To reach the dynamics of the emotions, the work begins at the periphery of the structure and moves through it layer by layer to reach the center. This procedure entails dealing with the distortions in thinking and feeling and with the body blocks which appear as the stifling or lack of energy. The work reaches for the core, the deepest level, which anchors the whole being. The person who loses contact with the core has lost touch with reality and feels handicapped.

Interactions between or among individuals create a mutual exchange of emotions, energies, and experiences. This interaction expresses mutuality, which is a movement that unifies different parts into a whole. It leads to the ability to sustain pleasure and to produce greater movement of energy in the body. Core energetics emphasizes the importance of taking full responsibility for one's own physical reality, especially to grasp one's lack of connection with the flow of energy in the body, or the lack of flow, which shows itself in the energy blocks.

The holistic work seeks a fusion of emotional reality and conceptual thinking, because misconceptions and mental distortions of reality must be dealt with in a very detailed way. It does no good, for example, to free the flow of energy if a woman who cannot establish a mature relationship does not understand that she believes that men are by nature hostile and domineering. The final goal of the holistic approach is the expression and experience of pleasure, which comes from the total pulsation of the energy flow.

The Energy Movement

Every organism exists through the great pulsatory movements of expansion and contraction. These movements represent the common function of pulsation, which is the quality of all living things. Most individuals experience expansion as pleasure and contraction as discomfort. To a great degree, contraction is experienced as pain. However, contraction is a natural movement. The pain is produced by the organism's struggle to fight off the contraction to sustain the pleasurable expansion. But continuous expansion would ultimately lead to fragmentation, for the organism needs contraction to consolidate the gains and learnings of the expansion.

After one connects the movements of the emotions through the body, inner reality can be reestablished. The release of the emotions which are perceived as negative — anger, rage, hostility — results in crying and pain. The pain particularly must be released to restore the pulsatory movement of the life force. As long as there is pain, the person is in a chronic contraction. In the end, crying and the release of pain lead to expansion.

To be in reality, one must possess and explore the inner state of one's being and establish a realistic view of life as consisting of the core of each individual in relation to others. People can learn to see their own depth as well as the nature of their ideas and relationships with others. Life's reality must be expressed through the total unification of the inner and outer life of each individual, which leads to pleasure. So in many ways, the holistic approach promotes the unification that leads to pleasure.

The Work of Fusion

The human being possesses an unlimited capacity for expansion of consciousness, which is the main characteristic of being human. The real and natural condition of life is joy and fulfillment. To the degree that we fail to reach fulfillment, we have to understand that we have blocked the flow of positive energy and consciousness, which is the essence of the core.

In effect, the core both expresses and is the spirituality of human beings. Each person has the ability to mobilize this powerful creative force by becoming aware of the psychological and emotional forces that create blocks which inhibit the life movement. As we increase our awareness of these inner forces, we also increase our capacity to understand life and to be in control of our inner forces.

In this way, we begin to change the quality of our lives and to fill them with the happiness and loving feelings that we yearn for. It is essential, therefore, to establish a method, a way, a discipline, that can take a person beyond the goals of therapy. The method must help the person adjust to both inner and outer reality, to the perception of the new reality of the core. What we have is no longer therapy but a unified and holistic process that connects the mind, the emotions, the body, and the spiritual self into a unified whole which expresses the total reality of the person.

This means that the work lasts a lifetime. One does not always need to work with a guide, but the work always will uncover new resistancec, blockages, and areas of negativity. Therefore, each person has the responsibility to continue the exploration, now with assistance, now alone. The work never ends because the task we have undertaken in life has very many gradations and positive and negative expressions.

Given the universal nature of human beings, carrying on or failing in the task we have undertaken becomes extremely important, not only for the individual but for all of creation. I believe that the problems and crises that afflict the world — poverty, hunger, war, political repression, environment despoiliation — arise from the fragmentation of the essential unity of creation, from the split between energy and consciousness. Therefore, the work of each individual does take on universal importance and represents the only way that the problems which torment the whole can finally be resolved.

The unity of life makes many things depend on making the right choices, on understanding how the negative is chosen intentionally (if unconsciously), and perceiving how we block the created self and lose our way. This negative spiral, if unchecked, propels us into despair and deep crisis, whether as individuals or collectively.

Connecting with our own inner truth is the only way toward the creation of a unified life, pleasure, and abundance for all. The connection that needs to be made is with the loving consciousness of Christ that directs people toward a path of truth and enlightenment. But there are no shortcuts and one cannot skip steps. It is illusory to believe that one can by an act of will operate directly from the core without first penetrating the mask and character defenses to redirect the negative energies. When purified, these energies contain much beauty, truth, and creativity.

My own 30 years of experience in working deeply with human beings convinces me that the old format of doctor / patient no longer meets the needs of the emerging new consciousness. My own personal development has led me on a journey that has enabled me to resolve deep-seated problems which previously could not be resolved. In recent years, I have begun to use new approaches that have yielded similar results in people who committed themselves to search deeply within themselves.

The Spiritual Dimension

In working with the Pathwork lectures, I realized that these new methods can be communicated to other therapists — psychiatrists, psychologists, and all who help other human beings. I realized that work that incorporates but transcends psychotherapy opens the possibility of finding the highest potential in each human being, not just "curing neuroses" or helping people to resolve their problems.

The Pathwork represents, I believe, a most powerful discipline for reaching the human core, and it occurs at Pathwork Centers in the United States and Europe. This work is not a theory and philosophy only, but a dynamic, living process which enables any human being willing to do the hard work to explore the deepest self, first by focusing on the individual's evolutionary process and how it is blocked. If people persist in doing this work diligently, they will be able to open within themselves a new consciousness, and also to help others in the same direction.

The marriage between psychological and spiritual practices can also be used in therapy as core energetics. As I have said, core energetics reveals new levels of inner reality which psychotherapy ordinarily does not address. Core energetics is not therapy in the sense that it deals with neurotic processes as a side issue. These processes constitute the obstructions, confusions, misunderstandings, defenses, and negative emotions — the ultimate focus of therapy. In therapy, the neuroses are viewed as stages to go through, and the going through becomes the ultimate goal of psychotherapy.

In core energetics the "going through" is only a preliminary stage to the ultimate goal of the work. That goal is learning how to activate the core, the spiritual self, of each human being. Therefore, working with the defenses takes on a different meaning.

Only when the spiritual self is cultivated and mobilized does core energetics deal with the defensive reactions. Again, the core is the target and the principal tool of the holistic approach. Much, of course, depends on the personalities of the individuals we seek to guide. What are their dispositions and defenses? However, as people deeply activate their spiritual selves, they become more able to deal with their obstructions and negativities. Core energetics, therefore, differs from psychotherapy particularly in this respect.

All human beings sense a deep longing to reach their innermost, deepest selves. They feel that a more fulfilling state of consciousness exists and that a larger capacity for experiencing life lives within them. We often become confused by the doubt which says such a state is unrealistic and that to be realistic we must abandon this deep longing. On the other side of this doubt lies a demand that life be perfect and without frustration. This demand constitutes a defense which hides angers and spitefullness and implies that deep joy and fulfillment is unrealistic. However, the voice of our longing constantly says there is much more in life than we now experience. This longing can be fulfilled when a person is in touch with his or her core.

A misunderstanding arises that the longing is not real because it usually is placed defensively in magic and fantasy, and fulfillment is sought that avoids the realities of life. Therefore, when we meet the truth we become enraged and defensive. To reach the source of our longing, we must face the pain and make deeper connections. We need to learn not to be afraid that the pain will last forever. We also must constantly remind ourselves that through the holistic approach we can release powerful creative energies and open to the deepest possible contact with reality, our own and that of others. And we need to examine how we attract the pain through our negative beliefs.

We do not need to abandon the longing *per se* but examine why we want to avoid it. If there are too many outside problems, they probably will not disappear through the deep core energetic process, in and of itself. But the work opens a flow which leads to the release of the core consciousness with which we can solve problems, not all at once, but over time.

In effect, a crisis is a sword of life. The real problem is not the degree and severity of the crisis, but that our body and soul cannot sustain pleasure in the mental, emotional, and spiritual domains. Spiritual pleasure cannot be separated from the other domains, because it results from working through problems in the body, mind, and emotions. We have to learn to endure the state of bliss after we have worked through the state of pain and the negative emotions of suffering, guilt, fear, and terror. This is what the life process is all about.

So the feeling of longing is a very important message to us that we need to embark on a new road of development. If we really want the truth, the process becomes harmonious. It neither exaggerates the positive nor emphasizes the negative side of our problems. We have to remember that the negative and the positive are one, as I have said. When the negative is worked through, it leads to and becomes the positive. Hate becomes love, fear becomes courage, weakness becomes strength, and so on.

One of the main difficulties is that the personality has a stake in avoiding certain aspects of the self that constitute the defenses. However, if one makes a deep commitment to live and perceive oneself truthfully, the resistances are easier to handle and difficult situations and crises become exciting and challenging.

Truthfulness with the self is paramount in the holistic approach to self-development and growth. The present reality is very important if we are to eliminate the outer defenses and the masking attitudes and pretenses to experience our vulnerability. We can begin to arrive at the truth about ourselves by asking: "How do I feel about life? How rich and meaningful is it? How do I feel about myself and others? Am I secure? Do I have joy in giving and receiving? Am I worried with resentments and tensions? Do I need overactivity to neutralize my anxiety? Am I exhilarated and enthusiastic?"

A negative answer to any one of these questions means that there is a longing somewhere, perhaps hidden away from conscious awareness. In addition, dissatisfaction with any aspect of life reveals a fragmentation within us of energy and consciousness. Blaming the dissatisfaction on forces outside of ourselves merely perpetuates the problem. Only by accepting full responsibility for our lives can we explore the inner territory to find the high ground of the core, from which we can view life in a perspective that yields lasting solutions.

This approach is true spirituality, grounded in every-day reality. For true spirituality does not contradict the practical aspects of life. Nor does it imply self-deprivation. It is the opposite. Sacrifice and deprivation are diametrically opposed to spiritual reality.

The universe is abundant with joy.

GLOSSARY

Aggressive Character. The person whose defensive strategy is over-aggression, intimidation, manipulation. Also known as the psychopathic structure. This structure originated in the seduction and rejection of the child by the parent of the opposite sex.

Armoring. The condition of incorporating the emotional blockages and mental distortions in the physical structure, particularly the muscles.

Aura. The energy field which pulsates around the body of a human being and which can be seen with the aid of special filters or, with appropriate training, the naked eye. The distortions of the aura are an important diagnostic indicator for core energetic treatment.

Bioenergetic Analysis. The method of treatment developed by John Pierrakos and Alexander Lowen that combines conceptual, emotional, and physical work, including the element of the will.

Character Structure. The configuration of physical, emotional, and mental distortions that comprise a person's defense against a reality that is perceived as painful or dangerous.

Common Functioning Principle. The term Wilhelm Reich applied to the underlying unity behind seemingly diverse and unrelated phenomena.

Core. The innermost reality of human beings, the source of positive energy which, if undistorted, serves as the source of harmonious functioning.

Defenses. The system of conscious and unconscious strategies that human beings devise, usually in early childhood, to fend off situations that threaten to be painful or dangerous. In adult life, these defenses are the sources of human dysfunction and illness, for they do not accord with reality, but are reflexive.

Ego. The human faculty that mediates the flow of energy out of and into the core of the human being. It is the faculty which chooses, discriminates, analyzes, and regulates the flow of energy and experience.

Energy Body. The configuration of energy that vibrates at a higher rate of pulsation than the physical body and which replicates the human body in exact detail. There are a series of energy bodies which are believed to contain the faculties for feeling, thought, and spiritual experience.

Energy Field. The configuration of energy that pulsates around the human body and all other living and inert entities. Each entity has its own characteristic energy vibration under given conditions. See aura.

Higher Self. The level of human reality that knows the truth, that operates harmoniously, and that directs the human entity according to reality. See core.

Life Force. The movement of energy in the universe and in human beings which, if undistorted, provides for the unity and harmony of all things.

Lower Self. The source of the primal negative emotions, or the negative unconscious described by Sigmund Freud. The lower self contains the emotions that react if the organism is hurt or in danger.

Mask. The outer husk of the human defensive structure which presents a false face, an idealized self-image to the world. The mask seeks to conceal the lower self by misappropriating the energy of the higher self.

Masochistic Structure. The person who has developed a massive and tightly bound physical and emotional structure that is designed to fend off the movement of energy, either inward or outward, which is perceived as a threat to the person's integrity.

Oral Structure. The person whose defensive strategy is to pretend weakness and need. This elongated structure cannot long sustain any natural movement of energy.

Psychopathic Structure. Also known as the aggressive structure.

Orgone. Wilhelm Reich's name for the universal energy, the life force.

Reciprocity Principle. The principle that described the interchange of energy between an organism and its environment. Every organism and entity experiences a reciprocal or mutual interchange of energy between its inside and outside.

Rigid Structure. The character structure characterized by the ability to organize and control its environment, and to appear successful, but which is cut off from the heart feelings.

Schizoid Structure. The defensive structure that is fragmented, usually due to hostility from the parents in infancy, or even in the womb.

Appendix A
THE EFFECTS OF FILTERS
ON THE VISIBLE LIGHT SPECTRUM

Dr. S. A. Silbey, Physics Department, Princeton University, tested the effects of filters I had developed and prepared the graph shown in Figure 1. The figure plots wavelengths in nanometers versus percentage of transmission of light (logo scale).

As the curves indicate, filter 1 and 2 suppress sections of visible light from green to orange. Blue-green to red are screened out by numbers 3 and 4. Filter 5, which is cobalt blue in color, has the widest blocking effect, suppressing the wavelength from about 480 to 680 nanometers, from the blue well into the red portion of the spectrum.

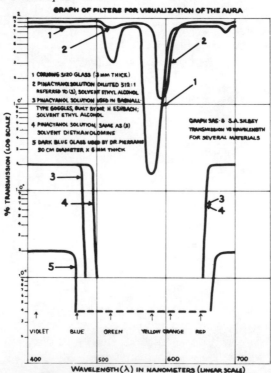

Figure A 1. Light-blocking capacities of five filters used for perceiving energy fields. (Courtesy

Appendix B
INTEGRATION OF ENERGY FIELDS
OF AIR, LAND, AND WATER

The graph on page 64 summarizes the progression of the energy movements over the 24 hours from sundown to sundown, on an average high-energy day according to comparisons with other measurements during the two-year study. The observations plotted in the figure were made every two hours for 3 to 5 minutes.

For simplicity's sake, I characterize the pulsations as P_a (air), P_l (land), and P_w (water). The harmony of rhythm among the three fields makes the curves on the graph qualitatively similar. The pulsation rate of all three decreased from 8 P. M. to the following 4 A. M. During these hours, P_a and P_l lengthened and slowed to 2 to 4 seconds, and their lumination weakened correspondingly. P_w contracted on a parallel line, with the waves reaching a height of only 2 to 4 feet and fizzling out on the seashore.

The three fields began to amplify again at 4 in the morning, and P_a and P_l rose very steeply, peaking at 42 pulsations a minute around noon. As the frequency increased, the individual energy surges strengthened and luminated intensely. At their maximum rate, the interval between the pulsations compressed to less than 1 second, which made it hard to distinguish phase I of the energy cycle from phase II. Phase III was extremely brief. P_w expanded in a similar but shallower profile in this period, which was low tide. By noon, the waves were reaching 5 to 6 feet in height and were hitting the beach with a much stronger discharge of energy at a rate of about 11 per minute.

From noon to 8 P. M., P_a and P_l underwent a gradual overall decline that included a sharp drop between 1 and 2 P. M. This indicates to me that after an energy entity reaches its maximum pulsations, it cannot sustain this pace. The temporary rise in the sunset period that was noted earlier brought the pulsations up from 16 to 18 per minute. Then the rate continued to drop throughout the night, except for the gentle expansion around 10 P. M. The phase I movements immediately after sunset were slow and prolonged, lasting 2 to 5 seconds. They came in clusters of three and four, and were

separated by intervals of 3 to 4 seconds. Once again, P_w described a syn-
chronous curve, quieting down after midday into a progressively slower
rhythm that carried it through the night except for the two short intervals of
reactivation. It is as though the earth's envelope, tired after its day of interplay with the sun-flooded atmosphere, went to sleep.

The integration within the earth's three-zone field is observably replicated
by its integration with its two contiguous energy masses, the globe itself and
the atmosphere beyond. Emanations pulsating from the core of the planet
and from outer space affect its shape variously in different longitudes and
latitudes as well as in different seasons and diurnal periods, but the pattern
of the rhythm, the dynamics of the movements, and the directions of flow
in phases I and II retain their essential characteristics.

The vectors of the interacting forces explain the great concavity I mentioned that appears in both zones A and C everywhere I have studied P_a.
Figure 1 shows how this bowl is formed. To an observer standing at K, the
earth field is swinging from X to Y in the line of the arrows lettered **a** — that
is, from west to east, as I said earlier. Energy from the earth's core streams
out in vertical pulsations, illustrated by the **b** arrows. These vectors intersect
with the **a** flow at countless places, exemplified by points 1, 2, 3 and 4 in the
figure, and the commingled movements swerve upward in the energy streams
marked C_1, C_2, C_3 and C_4. Because of the west-east direction of the earth's
envelope in phase I, surges of P_a light up successively from X to Y like an
array of rockets igniting rapid-fire one after the other across the horizon.
The tidelike illumination due to the direction of the movement produces the
concavity in the west-northwest that is illustrated in Figures 2 and 3. In phase
II, when the energy movement reverses, the concavity appears in the east-
southeast.

The speed of illumination from X to Y, incidentally, could be taken as a
base for measuring the relative velocity of the earth's energy envelope over
the observation region. Adding the earth's rotation speed to this figure
would give the absolute velocity of the field.

I believe, too, viewing my findings in the light of Reich's meteorological
investigations, that the energy field phenomena could be used for weather
projections if observations of them were systematized. There is definitely a
strict correlation between field formations and weather conditions. When
the day is beautiful and the humidity low, as in the Mediterranean basin in
the warm months, the energy envelope is bright and clear, and the pulsatory
rate is very high. On oppressively humid days, the frequency can drop to half
the standard count. Falling barometric pressure and an approaching storm
likewise depress the field. The phenomenon of Foehn, in Switzerland,

follows this pattern. The condition is accompanied by the formation of energy concentrations with a low pulsatory rate. They appear as yellow-red patches over the mountains and landscapes, and the population senses them palpably. The influence of the weather on other energetic entities, in fact, is one of the most universally noticed manifestations of the cosmic dimensions of the reciprocal energy cycle.

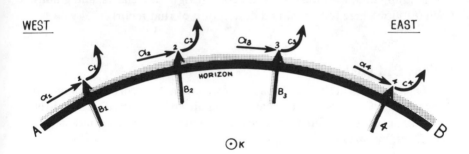

Figure B 1. The shaping of the Earth's energy field.

Appendix C
ANALYSIS OF CHART RECORDINGS
OF AURA OF CHRYSANTHEMUM
By Dr. Serge Silbey

Dr. Pierrakos gave me a strip-chart recording of a chrysanthemum's aura. He asked me to analyze it as well as I could. The resulting technical monograph described the results in detail, with tables, charts, and graphs. What follows here is a simplified description of that report.

What Did He See?

He looked first at the leaf, then the flower, then the stem of the plant. He saw a colored aura, each plant part having different colors. The aura itself was made up of different components, which looked like radial rays, curlicues, and zigzags.

How Did He Record It?

If the aura was an electrical phenomenon, we could merely attach a voltmeter and follow the fluctuations of the pointer. However, such a transducer does not exist, so Dr. Pierrakos himself was the "voltmeter". That is to say, he prepared a 5-foot-long piece of paper, arranged an apparatus to move the paper past him at a constant speed of 100 inches per minute, and took a position such that he could simultaneously record his impressions on this chart with a felt-tipped marking pen while he looked at the plant.

What Did He Record?

For each plant part, Dr. Pierrakos summed up the intensity of all the components and all the colors of the aura, and recorded the changes in the amplitude of this sum, that he saw. Thus, when the flower "breathed", the intensity of its aura increased, and the pen would then trace an ascending line as the chart paper flowed by. Similarly, a decreasing aura would result in a descending line. Samples of what Dr. Pierrakos saw are shown in Figures C1, C2 and C3. It is important to understand that these are only *samples* for several reasons:

1. The rate of "breathing" is not constant; thus the pulse gets wider and narrower as a function of time.
2. The wave shape is not constant, but changes slightly from pulsation to pulsation. These differences in waveshape are small, however, compared to the differences in waveshape between the various plant parts.
3. Each test run was only 1 minute long. A 5- or 10-minute run would give better statistical results.

What Were the Results?

Firstly, the fact that each plant part had its own "signature" or pulsation waveform, as indicated in Figures C1, C2 and C3. The pulsation rate for the leaf and flower are similar, that of the stem considerably slower. For the latter it is about 9 per minute, while for the former two, it is about 12 1/2 per minute.

Secondly, the fact that the pulsations were not constant, but increased and decreased in their rate. This is analogous to a heartbeat with might be 70 beats per minute, increase to 100 beats per minute, and then return to 70. Again, the change in pulsation rate for the leaf and flower are similar, that is, from about 12 to about 16. The change in pulsation rate for the stem is from about 9 to about 12 pulsations per minute. Note that the changes in pulsation rate for all the plant parts are almost the same, 30 percent. This analogous to saying that any changes in the heartbeat rate can be measured anywhere over the human body.

Thirdly, the fact that the "signature" of each plant has its unique shape, which permits us to get additional information concerning the pulse rate *capability* of each plant part. This is somewhat analogous to interpreting an ECG of the heart to learn about the heart's health and pumping *capability*.

In order to understand the techniques involved, let us review a little bit of easy-to-follow science. The electricity in our homes is, as is well known, a *sine wave* which pulsates at 60 pulsations per second. One of the main reasons that a sine wave was chosen, and not a square wave, or a triangular wave (or a waveshape similar to the chrysanthemum's aura), is that the

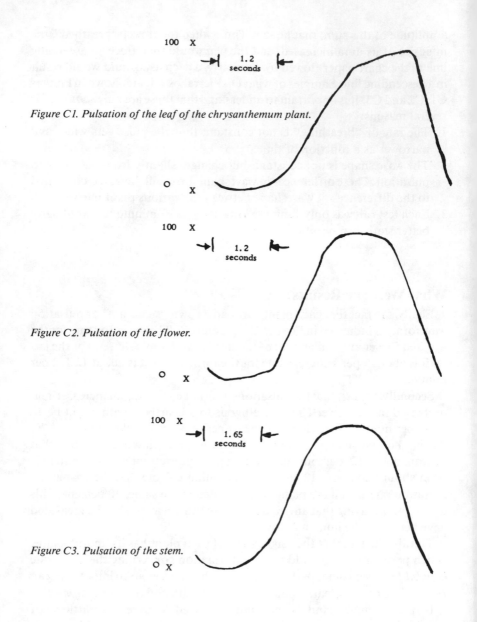

Figure C1. Pulsation of the leaf of the chrysanthemum plant.

Figure C2. Pulsation of the flower.

Figure C3. Pulsation of the stem.

sinusoidal waveform contains only one fundamental frequency, which, in the case of household electricity in the USA, is 60 pulsations, or cycles, per second. Any other waveshape can be shown to possess other frequencies mixed in with this primary or fundamental frequency, and would constitute a less efficient transmission of electrical power.

An example of a harmonic in the field of electricity is easily found — high fidelity amplifier hum. After rectifying the incoming electricity in the power supply, the resultant waveform sometimes has a ripple or noise component at 120 cycles, which causes an irritating buzzing in the loudspeaker.

Now, to get back to the signature of the plant parts: if the signature were a sine wave, then we would know that the radiated aura has only one frequency, that frequency mentioned previously in earlier paragraphs. However, this is not the case. All three signatures are different, they are non-sinusoidal, and hence they must contain harmonics. Once the waveshape has been determined, that is, once Dr. Pierrakos has finished making the chart and the various pulsations have been averaged in a meaningful manner, there exists a straightforward technique to evaluate these harmonics. This has been done for the leaf, flower, and stem.

What Were the Highest Harmonics?

In the case of the leaf, there were significant traces of second, third, and fourth harmonics — the latter being about 48 pulsations per minute. Note that it is the summing of these three harmonics with the fundamental (about 12 pulsations / minute) frequency which precisely accounts for the observed signature. That is to say, the leaf's waveshape is *made up* of the fundamental and various amounts of the next three harmonics.

In the case of the flower, there were significant traces of third and fifth harmonics — the latter being about 62 pulsations per minute. This is a rather spectacular result — that a plant part can radiate over one pulsation per second!

In the case of the stem, there were significant traces of third harmonic, the latter being about 27 pulsations per minute.

What Didn't He Record?

1. The amplitudes, which in each case range from 0 to 100 on an arbitrary scale, are not relative; i. e., the way the charts were drawn, all three auras went from 0 to 100, indicating an equal range of intensities. This, however, was not

the case. Some plant parts had a smaller range of amplitudes than others. Knowing the relative magnitudes of the auras would indicate the relative energy component of each plant part.

2. The amplitudes were not absolute, that is, 0 on the chart did not represent a complete absence of aura, but merely a minimum of aura. Knowing the absolute magnitudes of the aura would indicate the absolute energy, or power, contained in the various rays.

3. As explained at the beginning, the chart trace is a summation of two or three different colors and two or three different components (curlicues, rays, etc.). To extract the full information about the chrysanthemum's aura, one would have to make a separate chart for each of these variables. This preferably should be done simultaneously to correlate the interactions.

Naturally, all of this information is impossible to record with the present technique — there is just too much for one gifted person to do at once. However, they indicate avenues for further exploration. Certain improvements are immediately possible, using a commercially available recording apparatus with sufficient chart speed and pen speed. But until a transducer is developed which is directly sensitive to the aura, we shall have to wait . . .

Selected Bibliography

Alexander, Franz G., and Selesnick, Sheldton T., *The History of Psychiatry: An Evaluation of Psychiatric Thought and Practice from Prehistoric Times to the Present,* New York: Harper & Row, 1966.

Bayly, M. B., *et. al., The Mystery of Healing,* Wheaton, Illinois; Theosophical Publishing House, 1958.

Behanan, Kovoor T., *Yoga: A Scientific Evaluation,* London: Martin Secker & Warburg, 1937.

Boadella, David, *Wilhelm Reich: The Evolution of His Work,* London; Vision Press, 1973.

Burr, H. S., *Electrometrics of Atypical Growth*, Yale Journal of Biology and Medicine, Vol. XXV (1952-1953), pp. 67-75.

—, and Northrop, F. S. C., *Evidence for the Existence of an Electrodynamic Field in Living Organisms*, Proceedings of the National Academy of Science, Vol. XXV, No. 8 (April 1939) pp. 284-288.

Cannon, Walter B., *The Wisdom of the Body,* New York: Norton, 1932.

Cayce, Edgar, *Auras,* Virgina Beach, Virginia: ARE Press, 1945.

Corte, Leonard P., *Radionics, Fact or Fiction?,* Delawarre Laboratories News Letter, Oxford, England: (Spring 1974), pp. 14-22.

Day, Langston, and de la Warr, George, *New Worlds Beyond the Atom,* London: Vincent Stuart, 1956.

Drew, Rue Faris, *The Truth of Your Art is in your Imagination*, article on Stella Adler, The New York Times, August 15, 1976, sec. 2, pp. 1, 17.

Eeman, L. E., *Cooperative Healing: The Curative Properties of Human Radiations,* London: Frederick Muller, 1947.

Energy and Character, David Boadella, Editor, (Abbotsbury, Dorset, England) 1970 —.

Engel, George L., *Sudden and Rapid Death During Psychological Stress*, Annals of Internal Medicine, Vol. 74, No. 5 (May 1971), pp. 771-782.

Filliozat, J., *The Classical Doctrine of Indian Medicine,* Dev Raj Chanana, Translator, Delhi, India: Munshi Ram Manohar Lal, 1964.

Freud, Sigmund, *A General Introduction to Psychoanalysis,* New York: Liveright, 1935.

Friedman, Meyer, and Rosenman, Ray H., *Type A Behavior and Your Heart,* New York; Alfred A. Knopf, Inc., 1974.

Garrett, Eileen, Editor, *Proceedings of Four Conferences of Parapsychological Studies,* New York: Parapsychology Foundation, 1957.

Hartmann, Franz, *The Life and Doctrines of Philippus Theophrastus, Bombast of Hohenheim, Known by the Name of Paracelsus,* reissue, Mokelumne Hill, California: Health Research, 1963.

Herron, Caroline Rand, *The Cosmos: From Where to Where?,* The New York Times, September 12, 1976, p. E6.

Jung, Carl G., *Symbols of Transformation,* New York: Harper & Row, Torchbook, 1962.

Hippocrates, *Ancient Medicine and Other Treatises,* Francis Adams, Translator, Chicago: Henry Regnery (for Great Books Foundation), 1949.

Karagulla, Shafica, *Breakthrough to Creativity,* Los Angeles: De Vorss, 1967.

Kilner, Walter J., *The Human Aura,* New Hyde Park, New York: University Books, 1965.

Krishna, Gopi, *The Biological Base of Religion and Genius,* New York: NC Press (for Kundalini Research Foundation, New York, and Research Institute for Kundalini, Kashmir), 1971.

Laborit, Henri, *The Roots of Frustration, Atlas World Press Review,* Vol. XXIII, No. 10 (October 1976), pp. 24-26.

Legge, James, Editor and Translator, and Suzuki, D. T., Editor, *The Texts of Taoism,* New York: Julian Press, 1959.

Leibnitz, Gottfried, *Monadology and Other Philosophical Essays,* Paul Schreckler and Anne Schreckler, Translators, Indianapolis: Bobbs-Merrill, 1965.

Lowen, Alexander, *The Betrayal of the Body,* New York: Macmillan, Collier Books, 1967.

—, Pleasure: *A Creative Approach to Life,* New York: Coward-McCann, 1970

—, *Love and Orgasm,* New York: Macmillan, Collier Books, 1975.

—, and Pierrakos, John C., *A Case of Broncho-genic Cancer,* Energy and Character, Vol. I, No. 2 (May 1970), pp. 26-33.

Mann, W. Edward, *Orgone, Reich and Eros,* New York: Simon and Schuster, 1973.

Marquès-Rivière, J., *Tantrik Yoga: Hindu and Tibetan,* H. E. Kennedy, Translator, reissue, New York: Samuel Weiser, 1973.

Mesmer, F. A., *Mesmerism,* V. R. Myers, Translator, London: Macdonald, 1948.

Metzner, Ralph, *Maps of Consciousness,* New York: Macmillan, Collier Books, 1971.

Motoyama, Hiroshi, *Do Meridians ('Keiraku') Exist, and What Are They?,* Research for Religion and Parapsychology, (International Association for Religion and Parapsychology, Tokyo), Vol. I, No. 1 (February 1975), pp. 1-48.

Neuman, Erich, *The Origins and History of Consciousness,* Princeton; Princeton University Press, 1954.

Offir, Carole Wade, *Visual Speech: Their Fingers Do the Talking,* Psychology Today, Vol. X, No. 1 (June 1976), pp. 72-78.

Ostrander, Sheila, and Schroeder, Lynn, *Psychic Discoveries Behind The Iron Curtain,* Englewood Cliffs, New Jersey: Prentice-Hall, 1970.

Pachter, Henry M., *Paracelsus: Magic into Science,* New York: Henry Schuman, 1951.

Palós, Stephen, *The Chinese Art of Healing,* Translagency, Inc., Translator, New Yorks Herder and Herder, 1971.

Pierrakos, Eva Broch, *Guide Lectures for Self-Transformation,* New York: Center for the Living Force, 1984

—, *The Pathwork Lectures,* 258 lectures, New York: Center for the Living Force, Inc., 1957-1979.

Pierrakos, John C., *The Aggressive Functions in the Upper Half of the Body,* New York: Institute for the New Age of Man, 1975. (Monograph)

—, *Anatomy of Evil,* New York: Institute for the New Age of Man, 1974. (Monograph)

—, *The Core-Energetic Process in Group Therapy,* New York: Institute for the New Age of Man, 1975. (Monograph)

—, *The Core of Man,* New York: Institute for the New Age of Man, 1974. (Monograph)

—, *The Energy Field in Man and Nature,* New York: Institute for The New Age of Man, 1973. (Monograph)

—, *Human Energy Systems Theory,* New York: Institute for the New Age of Man, 1976. (Monograph)

—, *Life Functions of the Energy Centers of Man,* New York: Institute for the New Age of Man, 1975. (Monograph)

—, *Observations of Group Phenomena and Group Therapy,* New York: Institute for the New Age of Man, 1975. (Monograph)

—, *Rhythm and Pulsation, The Rhythm of Life,* New York: Institute for Bioenergetic Analysis, 1966. (Monograph)

—, *The Voice and Feeling, Self-Expression,* New York: Institute for Bioenergetic Analysis, 1968.

Pringle-Pattison, Andrew S., and Allman, George J., *Pythagoras*, in *The Encyclopaedia Britannica*, 11th ed., New York: 1911, Vol. XXII, pp. 698-703.

Rahn, Otto, *Invisible Radiations of Organisms*, Berlin: Gebrüder Born-traeger, 1936.

The Rationalists: Five Basic Works on Rationalism, Garden City, New York: Doubleday, Anchor Books, 1975.

Ravitz, Leonard J., *Application of the Electrodynamic Field Theory in Biology, Psychiatry, Medicine and Hypnosis*, American Journal of Clinical Hypnosis, Vol. I, No. 4 (April 1959), pp. 135-150.

—, *History, Measurement, and Applicability of Periodic Changes in the Electromagnetic Field in Health and Illness*, in William Wolf, Editor, *Rhythmic Functions in the Living System*, Annals of the New York Academy of Sciences, Vol. XCVIII, Art. 4 (October 30, 1962), pp. 1144-1201.

Reich, Wilhelm, *The Discovery of the Orgone*, Vol. I, *The Function of the Orgasm*, Theodore P. Wolfe, Translator, New York: Orgone Institute Press, 1942: 2nd ed., New York: Farrar, Straus & Giroux, 1961.

—, *The Discovery of the Orgone*, Vol. II, *The Cancer Biopathy*, Theodore P. Wolfe, Translator, New York: Orgone Institute Press, 1948.

—, *Character-Analysis: Principles and Techniques*, Theodore P. Wolfe, Translator, 3rd. ed., New York: Orgone Institute Press, 1949.

—, *Cosmic Orgone Energy and Ether*, Orgone Energy Bulletin, Vol. I, No. 4 (1949)

Reichenbach, Karl von, *Abstract on Researches on Magnetism and Certain Allied Subjects, Including a Supposed New Imponderable*, William Gregory, Editor and Translator, London: Taylor & Walton, 1846.

Rosenman, Ray H., and Friedman, Meyer, *Neurotic Factors in Partho-genesis of Coronary Heart Disease*, San Francisco, 1972. (Unpublished Monograph)

Spinoza, Benedict de (Baruch), *The Chief Works of Benedict de Spinoza*, R. H. Elwes, Translator, New York: Dover, 1975, 2 vols.

Tielhard de Chardin, Pierre, S. J., *The Phenomenon of Man*, Bernard Wall, Translator, New York: Harper & Row, Torchbooks, 1961.

White, George Starr, *The Story of the Human Aura*, Los Angeles: by the author (Phillips Printing Co.), 1928.

Wilson, Margaret D., Editor, *The Essential Descartes*, New York: New American Library, 1969.

Worrall, Ambrose, and Worrall, Olga, *Explore Your Psychic World*, New York: Harper & Row, 1970.

John C. Pierrakos, M.D. is a former student and colleague of Wilhelm Reich and co-founder, with Alexander Lowen, M.D., of Bioenergetic Therapy. He went on to develop Core Energetics and found the Institute of Core Energetics in New York City. Dr. Pierrakos conducts a private practice in New York, lectures, teaches and gives workshops in the USA and Europe.

If you want more information concerning workshops, conferences, trainings and research, please write to:

Institute of Core Energetics   or   Institute of Core Energetics West
115 East 23rd Street   P.O. Box 806
New York, NY 10010   Mendocino, CA 95460
USA   USA

LifeRhythm Publications

Ron Kurtz BODY-CENTERED PSYCHOTHERAPY: THE HAKOMI METHOD

The Integrated Use of Mindfulness, Nonviolence & the Body

220 pages, illustrations, $15.95

Hakomi is a Hopi Indian word which means "How do you stand in relation to these many realms?" A more modern translation is "Who are you?" Hakomi was developed by Ron Kurtz, co-author of *The Body Reveals*. Some of the origins of Hakomi stem from Buddhism and Taoism, especially concepts like gentleness, compassion, mindfulness and going with the grain. Other influences come from general systems theory, which incorporates the idea of respect for the wisdom of each individual as a living organic system that spontaneously organizes matter and energy and selects from the environment what it needs in a way that maintains its goals, programs and identity. Hakomi also draws from modern body-centered psychotherapies such as Reichian work, Bioenergtics, Gestalt, Psychomotor, Feldenkrais, Structural Bodywork, Ericksonian Hypnosis, Focusing and Neurolinguistic Programing. Hakomi is really a synthesis of philosophies, techniques and approaches that has its own unique artistry, form and organic process.

Malcolm Brown, Ph.D. THE HEALING TOUCH

An Introduction to Organismic Psychotherapy

320 pages, 38 illustrations, $16.95

A moving and meticulous account of Malcolm Brown's journey from Rogerian-style verbal psychotherapist to gifted body psychotherapist. Influenced by C.G. Jung, Abraham Maslow, Erich Neumann, Carl Rogers, D.H. Lawrence, and Wilhelm Reich, Dr. Brown developed his own art and science of body psychotherapy with the purpose of re-activating the natural mental/spiritual polarities of the embodied soul and transcendental psyche. Using powerful case histories as examples, Brown describes in theory and practice the development of his work; the techniques to awaken the energy flow and its integration with the main Being centers: Eros, Logos, the Spritual Warrior and the Hara. Because he includes spiritual and subtle imaginative psychic dimensions of the embodied soul in his work, his unique approach sets a new guideline in the field of therapy.

Bodo J. Baginski and Shalila Sharamon REIKI; Universal Life Energy

200 pages, illustrations, $12.95

The roots of Reiki reach far back into the ancient origins of natural healing but the method here has been rediscovered in modern times and is now a widely practiced form of folk medicine used by practitioners, therapists and healers. Reiki is described as the energy which forms the basis of all life. With the help of specific methods, anyone can learn to awaken and activate this universal life energy so that healing and harmonizing energy flows through the hands. Reiki is healing energy in the truest sense of the word, leading to greater individual harmony and attunement to the basic forces of the universe. This book features a unique compilation and interpretation, from the author's experience, of over 200 psychosomatic symptoms and diseases.

Cousto **THE COSMIC OCTAVE** Origin of Harmony
128 pages, 45 illustrations, numerous tables, 24 page scientific appendix, $12.95
"...it was the result of a way of seeing things which moved me to combine the old teachings of harmonics with new findings in physics and other sciences. The result is an all-encompassing system of measurement with which it is possible to transpose the movements of the planets into audible rhythms and sounds, and into color."   Hans Cousto

Cousto demonstrates the direct relationship of astronomical data, such as the frequency of planetary orbits to ancient and modern measuring systems, the human body, music and medicine. Cousto's scientific work is to be seen in the tradition of Johannes Kepler, whose life work *Harmonices Mundi* he has been able to considerably enlarge upon and improve. This book is compelling reading for musicians, astrologers, physicians, healers, and all those who wonder if a universal law of harmonydoes exist behind the apparent chaos of life.

THE COSMIC OCTAVE TUNING FORK *Tuning Forks tuned to the*
Sun, Earth, Moon and our planets Mercury, Venus, Mars, Jupiter, Saturn, Uranus, Neptune and Pluto, each $16.95
Handcalibrated in the tone of the stars and exactly corresponding to color and sound. By tuning into chakras and internal processes, you can revitalize and enhance your whole energy system. Meditate and chant the sound of the planets, activate acupuncture points. Tuning forks are available only from LifeRhythm directly.

In Preparation:
Reinhard Flatischler **THE FORGOTTEN POWER OF RHYTHM**

Rhythm is an elementary expression of all that lives. It unifies all parts of our lives. Out of shamanistic traditions Reinhard Flatischler has developed a system of experiences and exercises which let each of us experience the energies of different rhythms. We come to know the rhythm-worlds of Africa, Indian, Korea, Brazil, Cuba and Ghana, each rich with its own cultural offering. Reinhard Flatischler developed this path to rhythm consciousness after many years of apprenticeship with master drummers all over the world.

John C. Pierrakos, M.D. **THE DYNAMICS OF JOY: LOVE, EROS AND SEXUALITY**
John Pierrakos, founder of Core Energetics, writes of new pathways toward developing, sustaining and integrating these dynamic core qualities into the personality. He discusses the nature and main elements of love, eros and sexuality, showing their relationship to personality and character structure; their influence in shaping love, marriage and cultural relations; the integration of these forces with egoconcepts and energy centers and the intention and will to love as a key creative element in this process.

Anna Halprin, Ph.D. **CIRCLE THE EARTH**
Circle the Earth is a dance ritual created with a purpose: to make peace. Day in and out our consciousness is infused with the mythology of conflict and war, the illlustion of separation and the potential for total destruction. This mythology is strong and deeply rooted. Circle the Earth gives us a time, a space and a way to develop and ritualize a new mythology, equally strong and rooted in the truth of interconnection with all life and the possibilities of peace. Anna Halprin is a pioneer and innovator in "new theatre", a leader in the evolution of performances combining improvisation, audience participation, environmental and street theatre, and collective creativity. Today she is deeply involved in making a contribution as an artist to world peace. She is director of the Tamalpa Institute in California.

LIFE RHYTHM

Connects you with your Core and entire being — guided by Science, Intuition and Love.

We provide the tools for growth, therapy, holistic health and higher education through publications, seminars/workshops and research.

If you are interested in our forthcoming projects and want to be on our mailing list, please, send your address to:

LifeRhythm · P.O. Box 806 · Mendocino · CA 95460 · USA
Tel. (707) 937-1825